German
phrase book

**Berlitz Publishing / APA Publications GmbH & Co.
Verlag KG, Singapore Branch, Singapore**

Contacting the Editors
Every effort has been made to provide accurate information in this publication, but changes are inevitable. The publisher cannot be responsible for any resulting loss, inconvenience or injury. We would appreciate it if readers would call our attention to any errors or outdated information by contacting Berlitz Publishing, 193 Morris Ave., Springfield, NJ 07081, USA. Fax: 1-908-206-1103, e-mail: comments@berlitzbooks.com

Satisfaction guaranteed—If you are dissatisfied with this product for any reason, send the complete package, your dated sales receipt showing price and store name, and a brief note describing your dissatisfaction to: Berlitz Publishing, Langenscheidt Publishing Group, Dept. L, 36-36 33rd St., Long Island City, NY 11106. You'll receive a full refund.

Layout: Media Content Marketing, Inc.
Cover photo: ©Larry Dale Gordon/Getty Images

TABLE OF CONTENTS

TRAVEL

SIGHTSEEING

LEISURE

MAKING FRIENDS

PRONUNCIATION

This section will make you familiar with the sounds of German using our simplified phonetic transcription. You'll find the pronunciation of the letters and sounds explained below, together with their "imitated" equivalents. This system is used throughout the phrase book: just read the pronunciation as if it were English, noting any special rules below.

THE GERMAN LANGUAGE

German is the national language of Germany and Austria and is one of the four official languages of Switzerland. It is also spoken by groups of Germans in other countries. These are the countries where you can expect to hear German spoken:

Germany Deutschland

German spoken properly, i.e. without a noticeable accent, is called Hochdeutsch. Native speakers often have accents or speak dialects that vary from region to region.

Austria Österreich

German is the national language for over 7.8 million people.

Switzerland Schweiz

German is spoken by 70% of the population, mainly in the north and east. Other languages: French (20% of the population) in the west; Italian in the south; and the much rarer Romansh.

German is also one of the languages spoken in eastern France (Alsace-Lorraine), northern Italy (Alto Adige), eastern Belgium, Luxembourg and Liechtenstein. There are also about 1.5 million German speakers in the U.S., 500,000 in Canada and sizeable groups in South America, Namibia and Kazakhstan.

The German alphabet is the same as English, with the addition of the letter ß. It also uses the Umlaut (diaeresis) on the vowels ä, ü, ö (see below for pronunciation).

English has its origins in German and words, such as Hand, Butter and Name, mean exactly the same as in English. You'll be able to guess the meaning of many other words that have slight spelling variations such as Silber (silver), Fisch (fish) and blau (blue).

CONSONANTS

Letter	Approximate pronunciation	Symbol	Example	Pronunciation
b	1) at the end of a word or between a vowel and a consonant, like **p** in u**p**	p	**ab**	*ap*
	2) elsewhere as in English	b	**bis**	*biss*
c	1) before **e, i, ö** and **ä**, like **ts** in hi**ts**	ts	**Celsius**	*tselziuss*
	2) elsewhere like **c** in **c**at	k	**Café**	*kafay*
ch	1) after back vowels (e.g. **ah, o, oo**) like **ch** in Scottish lo**ch**, otherwise more like **h** in **h**uge	kh	**doch**	*dokh*
	2) sometimes, especially before **s**, like **k** in **k**it	k	**Wachs**	*vaks*
d	1) at the end of a word or between a vowel and a consonant, like **t** in ea**t**	t	**Rad**	*raat*
	2) elsewhere like **d** in **d**o	d	**durstig**	*doorstikh*
g	1) always hard as in **g**o, but at the end of a word more often like **ck** in ta**ck**	g	**gehen**	*gayen*
		k	**weg**	*vek*
j	like **y** in **y**es	y	**ja**	*yaa*
qu	like **k** followed by **v** as in **v**at	kv	**Quark**	*kvark*
r	generally rolled in the back of the mouth	r	**warum**	*varum*
w	usually like **v** in **v**oice	v	**Wagon**	*vagon*
s	1) before or between vowels like **z** in **z**oo	z	**sie**	*zee*
	2) before **p** and **t** at the beginning of a syllable like **sh** in **sh**ut	sh	**spät**	*shpait*
	3) elsewhere, like **s** in **s**it	s/ss	**es ist**	*ess ist*
ß	always like **s** in **s**it	s/ss	**heiß**	*hiess*
sch	like **sh** in **sh**ut	sh	**schnell**	*shnel*
tsch	like **ch** in **ch**ip	ch	**deutsch**	*doych*
tz	like **ts** in hi**ts**	ts	**Platz**	*plats*

v	1) like **f** in **f**or	f	**vier**	*feer*
	2) in most words of foreign origin, like **v** in **v**ice	v	**Vase**	*vaazer*
w	like **v** in **v**ice	v	**wie**	*vee*
z	like **ts** in hi**ts**	ts	**zeigen**	*tsiegen*

Letters **f, h, k, l, m, n, p, t, x** are pronounced as in English.

VOWELS

a	1) short like **u** in c**u**t	a	**lassen**	*lassen*
	2) long like **a** in c**a**r	aa	**Abend**	*aabent*
ä	1) short like **e** in l**e**t	e/eh	**Lärm**	*lehrm*
	2) long like **ai** in h**ai**r	ai	**spät**	*shpait*
e	1) short like **e** in l**e**t	e	**sprechen**	*shprekhen*
	2) long like **a** in l**a**te, but pronounced without moving tongue or lips	ay/eh	**geben**	*gayben*
	3) at the end of a word, generally like **er** in oth**er**	er	**bitte**	*bitteh*
i	1) short like **i** in h**i**t	i	**billig**	*billikh*
	2) long like **ee** in m**ee**t	ee	**ihm**	*eem*
ie	like **ee** in b**ee**	ee	**hier**	*heer*
o	1) short like **o** in g**o**t	o	**voll**	*fol*
	2) long like **o** in n**o**te, but pronounced without moving tongue or lips	oa	**ohne**	*oaneh*
ö	like **ur** in f**ur** (long or short)	ur	**können**	*kurnen*
u	1) short like **oo** in f**oo**t	u	**Nuss**	*nuss*
	2) long like **oo** in m**oo**n	oo	**gut**	*goot*
ü	like **ew** in n**ew**; round your lips	ew	**über**	*ewber*
y	like German **ü**	ew	**typisch**	*tewpish*

DIPHTHONGS

ai, ay, ei, ey	like **ie** in t**ie**	ie	**einen**	*ienen*
au	like **ow** in n**ow**	ow	**auf**	*owf*
äu, eu	like **oy** in b**oy**	oy	**neu**	*noy*

STRESS

Generally, as in English, the first syllable is stressed in German, except when short prefixes are added to the beginning of the word. Then the second syllable is stressed (e.g. **bewegen** *to move*, **ges<u>e</u>hen** *seen*). As most English speakers will naturally put the stress on the correct syllable, we have not included stress on individual words.

PRONUNCIATION OF THE GERMAN ALPHABET

We have used a friendly system to achieve a close proximation of the pronunciation, although this means some simplification of the more subtle aspects of German pronunciation.

In addition, there is the **ß** letter, used in lower case only, a combination of **s** and **z**. It is pronounced exactly like **ss**.

A	*aa*	**J**	*yot*	**S**	*ess*
Ä	*ai*	**K**	*kaa*	**T**	*tay*
B	*bay*	**L**	*el*	**U**	*oo*
C	*tsay*	**M**	*em*	**Ü**	*ew*
D	*day*	**N**	*en*	**V**	*fow*
E	*ay*	**O**	*oa*	**W**	*vay*
F	*ef*	**Ö**	*ur*	**X**	*eeks*
G	*gay*	**P**	*pay*	**Y**	*ewpsillon*
H	*haa*	**Q**	*koo*	**Z**	*tset*
I	*ee*	**R**	*ehr*		

BASIC EXPRESSIONS
GREETINGS/APOLOGIES

ESSENTIAL	
Yes.	**Ja.** *yah*
No.	**Nein.** *nine*
Okay.	**Einverstanden.** *aynfehrshtanden*
Please.	**Bitte.** *bitteh*
Thank you.	**Danke.** *dankeh*
Thank you very much.	**Vielen Dank.** *feelen dahnk*

Hello./Hi!	**Hallo!** *hahloh*
Good morning.	**Guten Morgen.** *gooten morgen*
Good afternoon.	**Guten Tag.** *gooten taag*
Good evening.	**Guten Abend.** *gooten ahbend*
Good night.	**Gute Nacht.** *gooteh nakht*
Good-bye.	**Auf Wiedersehen.** *owf veederzayn*
Excuse me! *(getting attention)*	**Entschuldigen Sie bitte!** *ent-shuhldigen zee bitteh*
Excuse me. *(May I get past?)*	**Darf ich?** *dahrf ikh*
Excuse me!/Sorry!	**Entschuldigung!/Verzeihung!** *entshuhldigoong /fehrtsayoong*
It was an accident.	**Es war ein Versehen.** ← *ess vaar ine fehrzayn* ←
Don't mention it.	**Keine Ursache.** ← *kineh oorzakheh*

10

COMMUNICATION DIFFICULTIES

Do you speak English?
Sprechen Sie Englisch?
sprekhen zee english

Does anyone here speak English?
Spricht hier jemand Englisch?
shprikht heer yaymant english

I don't speak much German.
Ich spreche kaum Deutsch.
ikh shprekheh kowm doych

Can you speak more slowly?
Können Sie langsamer sprechen?
kurnen zee lahngzahmer shprekhen

Can you repeat that?
Können Sie das wiederholen?
kurnen zee dass veederhohlen

Excuse me? [Pardon?]
Wie bitte? *vee bitteh*

I didn't catch that.
Ich habe das nicht verstanden. ←
ikh hahbeh dass nikht fehrshtanden

What was that?
Was haben Sie gesagt? ← *hast du*
vass hahben zee gehzahgt

Can you spell it?
Können Sie das buchstabieren? ←
kurnen zee dass bookhshtahbeeren

Please write it down.
Bitte schreiben Sie es auf. ←
bitteh shriben zee ess owf

Can you translate this for me?
Können Sie mir das übersetzen? ←
kurnen zee meer dass ewberzetsen

What does this / that mean?
Was bedeutet das?
vass bedoytet dass

Please point to that in the book.
Bitte zeigen Sie mir das im Buch. ←
bitteh tsaigen zee meer dass im bookh

I (don't) understand.
Ich verstehe (nicht).
ikh fehrshtayeh (nikht)

Do you understand?
Verstehen Sie? *fehrshtayn zee*

ON THE STREET

Hallo! Wie geht's? *hahloh vee gehts (Hi. How's it going?)*
Gut. Und selbst? *goot oond selbst (Fine. And yourself?)*
Auch gut. Danke. *owkh goot dankeh (I'm fine too. Thanks.)*

Where?

Where is it?	**Wo ist es?** *voa ist ess*
above the bank	**über der Bank** *ewber dehr bank*
across the road	**auf der anderen Straßenseite** *owf dehr anderen shtrahsensiteh*
here/there	**hier/dort** *heer/dort*
in the car	**im Auto** *im owto*
in the town	**in der Stadt** *in dehr shtat*
in Germany	**in Deutschland** *in doytchlahnt*
near the post office	**in der Nähe der Post** *in dehr naieh dehr post*
by the bank	**bei der Bank** *by dehr bank*
on the left/right	**links/rechts** *links/rekhts*
in front of the café	**vor dem Café** *foar daym kahfay*
under the bridge	**unter der Brücke** *oonter dehr brewkeh*

Where to?

Where are you going? [walking]	**Wohin gehen Sie?** *voahin gayen zee*
across the road	**über die Straße** *ewber dee shtrahse*
into the museum	**ins Museum** *ins moozayoom*
into town	**in die Stadt** *in dee shtat*
to the hotel	**zum Hotel** *tsoom hohtel*
Where are you going? [driving]	**Wohin fahren Sie?** *voahin fahren zee*
up to the traffic light	**bis zur Ampel** *biss tsoor ahmpel*
toward Berlin	**in Richtung Berlin** *in rikhtoong behrleen*

When ...?

When does the train arrive?	**Wann kommt der Zug an?** *van komt dehr tsoog an*
in 10 minutes	**in zehn Minuten** *een tsayn minooten*
always	**immer** *immer*
around midnight	**gegen Mitternacht** *gaygen mittehrnakht*
at 7 o'clock	**um sieben Uhr** *um zeeben oor*
before Friday	**vor Freitag** *foar frietaag*
by tomorrow	**bis morgen** *biss morgen*
daily	**täglich** *taiglikh*
during the summer	**während des Sommers** *vairent des zommers*
early	**früh** *frew*
every week	**jede Woche** *yaydeh vokheh*
for 2 hours	**zwei Stunden** *tsvie shtunden*
from 9 a.m. to 6 p.m.	**von neun bis achtzehn Uhr** *von noyn biss akhtsayn oor*
immediately	**sofort** *zofoart*
in 20 minutes	**in zwanzig Minuten** *in tsvantsikh minooten*
never	**nie** *nee*
not yet	**noch nicht** *nokh nikht*
now	**jetzt** *yetst*
often	**oft** *oft*
on March 8	**am achten März** *am akhten mehrts*
on weekdays	**an Werktagen** *an vehrktaagen*
once a week	**einmal in der Woche** *ienmaal in dehr vokheh*
sometimes	**manchmal** *mankhmaal*
soon	**bald** *balt*
then	**dann** *dan*
within 2 days	**innerhalb von zwei Tagen** *innehalp fon tsvie taagen*

What kind of ...?

I'd like something ...	**Ich möchte etwas ...** *ikh murkhteh etvass*
It's ...	**Es ist ...** *ess ist*
beautiful/ugly	**schön/hässlich** *shurn/hehsslikh*
better/worse	**besser/schlechter** *besser/shlekhter*
big/small	**groß/klein** *groass/klien*
cheap/expensive	**billig/teuer** *billikh/toyer*
clean/dirty	**sauber/schmutzig** *zowber/shmutsikh*
dark/light	**dunkel/hell** *dunkel/hel*
delicious/revolting	**köstlich/scheußlich** *kurstlikh/shoysslikh*
early/late	**früh/spät** *frew/shpait*
easy/difficult	**einfach/schwierig** *ienfakh/shveereegh*
empty/full	**leer/voll** *layr/fol*
good/bad	**gut/schlecht** *goot/shlekht*
heavy/light	**schwer/leicht** *shvayr/liekht*
hot/warm/cold	**heiß/warm/kalt** *hiess/varm/kalt*
modern/old-fashioned	**modern/altmodisch** *modayrn/altmoadish*
narrow/wide	**eng/weit** *eng/viet*
next/last	**nächste/letzte** *naikhsteh/letsteh*
old/new	**alt/neu** *alt/noy*
open/closed	**geöffnet/geschlossen** *geurfnet/geshlossen*
pleasant/nice/ unpleasant	**freundlich/nett/unfreundlich** *froyndlikh/net/unfroyndlikh*
quick/slow	**schnell/langsam** *shnell/langzaam*
quiet/noisy	**leise/laut** *liezeh/lowt*
right/wrong	**richtig/falsch** *rikhtikh/falsh*
tall/short	**groß/klein** *groass/klien*
thick/thin	**dick/dünn** *dik/dewn*
vacant/occupied	**frei/besetzt** *frie/bezetst*
young/old	**jung/alt** *yung/alt*

How much/many?

How much is that?	**Wie viel kostet das?** *vee feel kostet dass*
How many are there?	**Wie viele gibt es?** *vee feeler gipt ess*
1, 2, 3	**eins, zwei, drei** *ienss, tsvie, drie*
4, 5	**vier, fünf** *feer, fewnf*
none	**keine** *kieneh*
about 20 euros	**etwa zwanzig Euro** *etvaa tsvantsikh oyroh*
a little	**ein wenig** *ien vaynikh*
a lot of money	**viel Geld** *veel gelt*
enough	**genug** *genook*
few	**wenige** *vayniggeh*
a few of them	**einige von ihnen** *ienigger fon eenen*
many people	**viele Leute** *feeleh loyteh*
more/less	**mehr/weniger** *mayr vaynigger*
much more	**viel mehr** *feel mayr*
nothing else	**sonst nichts** *zonst nikhts*
some bread	**etwas Brot** *etvass broat*
too much	**zu viel** *tsoo feel*

Why?

Why is that?	**Warum (ist das so)?** *varum (ist dass zoa)*
Why not?	**Warum nicht?** *varum nikht*
because of the weather	**wegen des Wetters** *vaygen dess vetterss*
because I'm in a hurry.	**weil ich es eilig habe** *viel ikh ess* *ielikh haabeh*
I don't know why.	**Ich weiß nicht, warum.** *ikh* *viess nikht varum*

Who?/Which?

Which one do you want?	**Welches möchten Sie?** *velkhess murkhten zee*
one like that	**so eins** *zoa ienss*
that one/this one	**jenes/dieses** *yayness/deezess*
not that one	**nicht das da** *nikht dass daa*
none	**keiner/keine/keines** *kiener/kieneh/kieness*
someone	**jemand** *yaymant*
something	**etwas** *etvass*

Whose?

Whose is that?	**Wem gehört das?** *vaym gehurt dass*
It belongs to …	**Es gehört …** *ess gehurt*
her/him	**ihr/ihm** *eer/eem*
me, you, them	**mir, Ihnen [dir], ihnen** *meer, eenen [deer], eenen*
no one	**niemandem** *neemandem*
This is … bag.	**Das ist … Tasche.** *dass ist … tasheh*
my	**meine** *mieneh*
our	**unsere** *unzereh*
your	**Ihre [deine]** *eereh [dieneh]*
his/her	**seine/ihre** *zieneh/eereh*
their	**ihre** *eereh*

IN THE STORE

Wie möchten Sie zahlen? *vee murkhten zee tsahlen* (How would you like to pay?)

In bar, bitte. *een bar bitteh* (Cash, please.)

16

Is it …?/Is there …?

Is it …?	**Ist es …?** *ist ess*
Is it free? (unoccupied)	**Ist es frei?** *ist ess frie*
It isn't ready.	**Es ist nicht fertig.** *ess ist nikht fehrtikh*
Is/Are there …?	**Gibt es …?** *gipt ess*
Are there buses into town?	**Gibt es Busse in die Stadt?** *gipt ess busseh in dee shtat*
There isn't any hot water.	**Es gibt kein warmes Wasser.** *ess gipt kien varmess vasser*
Here/There it is.	**Hier/Da ist es.** *heer/daa ist ess*
Here/There they are.	**Hier/Da sind sie.** *heer/daa zint zee*

How?

How would you like to pay?	**Wie möchten Sie zahlen?** *vee murkhten zee tsaalen*
by credit card/ by cash	**mit Kreditkarte/in bar** *mit kredeetkarteh/een bar*
How are you getting here?	**Wie kommen Sie hierher?** *vee kommen zee heerhayr*
by car	**mit dem Auto** *mit daym owto*
on foot	**zu Fuß** *tsoo fooss*
with a friend	**mit einem Freund/einer Freundin** *mit ienem froynt/iener froyndin*
by chance	**durch Zufall** *doorkh tsoofal*
entirely	**ganz** *gants*
equally	**gleich** *gliekh*
extremely	**äußerst** *oysserst*
quickly	**schnell** *shnel*
slowly	**langsam** *langzaam*
too fast	**zu schnell** *tsoo shnel*
totally	**völlig** *furllikh*
very	**sehr** *zayr*
without a passport	**ohne Reisepass** *oaneh riezepass*

Can ...?

Can I have ...?
Kann ich ... haben?
kan ikh ... haaben

Can we have...?
Können wir ... haben?
kurnen veer ... haaben

Can you show me ...?
Können Sie mir ... zeigen?
kurnen zee meer ... tsiegen

Can you tell me ...?
Können Sie mir sagen ...?
kurnen zee meer zaagen

Can you help me?
Können Sie mir helfen?
kurnen zee meer helfen

Can you direct me to ...?
Können Sie mir den Weg nach ... zeigen?
kurnern zee meer dayn vayk naakh ... tsiegen

Sorry, I can't.
Leider nicht. *lieder nikht*

What would you like?

I'd like ...
Ich hätte gern ... *ikh hehtteh gehrn*

We'd like ...
Wir hätten gern ... *veer hehtten gehrn*

Give me ...
Geben Sie mir ... *gayben zee meer*

I'm looking for ...
Ich suche ... *ikh zookheh*

I would like to ...
Ich möchte gern ...
ikh murkhteh gehrn

go to ...
nach ... gehen *naakh ... gayen*

find ...
... finden *... finden*

see ...
... sehen *... zayen*

speak to ...
mit ... sprechen
mit ... shprekhen

IN THE POST OFFICE

Wem gehört dieser Schirm? *vaym gehhurt deeser sheerm (Whose umbrella is that?)*

Mir. Danke. *meer dahnkeh (Mine. Thanks.)*

Bitte. *bitteh (You're welcome.)*

OTHER USEFUL WORDS

hopefully	**hoffentlich** *hoffentlikh*
of course	**natürlich** *natewrlikh*
perhaps	**vielleicht** *veelliekht*
fortunately	**glücklicherweise** *glewglikherviezeh*
unfortunately	**leider** *lieder*
also	**auch** *owkh*
and	**und** *unt*
but	**aber** *aaber*
or	**oder** *oader*

EXCLAMATIONS

At last!	**Endlich!** *endlikh*
Damn!	**Verdammt!** *fehrdamt*
I don't mind.	**Es ist mir egal.** *ess ist meer aygaal*
No way!	**Auf keinen Fall!** *owf kienen fal*
Nonsense.	**Unsinn.** *unzin*
Quite right too!	**Richtig so!** *rikhtikh zoa*
Really?	**Wirklich?** *veerklikh*
Rubbish!	**Quatsch!** *kvach*
That's enough.	**Das reicht.** *dass riekht*
That's true.	**Das stimmt.** *dass shtimt*
You're joking!	**Das soll wohl ein Witz sein!** *dass zoll voal ien vits zien*
How are things?	**Wie geht's?** *vee gayts*
great/brilliant	**ausgezeichnet** *owsgetsiekhnet*
great	**großartig** *groassaartikh*
fine	**gut** *goot*
not bad	**nicht schlecht** *nikht shlekht*
so so	**einigermaßen** *ienigermaassen*
not good	**nicht gut** *nikht goot*
terrible	**schrecklich** *shreklikh*
awful	**furchtbar** *foorkhtbaar*

Accommodations

It's best to book in advance and to confirm your stay. If you haven't booked, you're more likely to find accommodations available outside of towns and city centers.

Hotel *hottel*
Hotel; simple or fancy, your room will be spotless, usually with luxurious duck or goose-down quilts.

Hotel garni *hottel garni*
A hotel with comfortable accommodations that serves only breakfast. Usually beverages and snacks will be available.

Schlosshotel *shlosshottel*
Castle converted into a hotel; most are located in the countryside.

Rasthof/Motel *rasthoaf/mottel*
Roadside lodge, motel; most are located just off an expressway [motorway] or principal route.

Gasthaus/Gasthof *gasthowss/gasthoaf*
Inn providing lodging, food and drink.

Pension/Fremdenheim *penzioan/fremdenhiem*
Small family-style hotel; full/half board. Meals are usually served to house guests only.

Zimmer frei *tsimmer frie*
Where you see this sign (it means "vacancy"), you'll find the equivalent of bed and breakfast.

Jugendherberge *yoogent hehrbehrgeh*
Youth hostel; in Austria, Germany and Switzerland, they are of a very high standard. A variation is the Youth Guest House, which usually has a later closing time.

Ferienwohnung *fayreeenvoanung*
Furnished apartment in holiday resorts; you'll probably have to reserve it in advance. Otherwise, contact the local tourist office.

RESERVATIONS/BOOKING

In advance

Can you recommend a hotel in …?	**Können Sie ein Hotel in … empfehlen?** *kurnen zee ien hottel in … empfaylen*
Is it near the center of town?	**Liegt es in der Nähe des Stadtzentrums?** *leegt ess in dehr naieh dess shtattsentrumz*
How much is it per night?	**Was kostet es pro Nacht?** *vass kostet ess proa nakht*
Is there anything cheaper?	**Gibt es nichts Billigeres?** *gipt ess nikhts billigeress*
Could you reserve/book me a room, please?	**Können Sie mir bitte ein Zimmer reservieren?** *kurnen zee meer bittch ien tsimmer rezehrveeren*

At the hotel

Do you have any vacancies?	**Haben Sie noch Zimmer frei?** *haaben zee nokh tsimmer fry*
I'm sorry, we're full.	**Wir sind leider voll belegt.** *veer zint lyder fol belaygt*
Is there another hotel nearby?	**Gibt es ein anderes Hotel in der Nähe?** *gipt ess ien anderess hottel in dehr naieh*
I'd like a single/double room.	**Ich hätte gern ein Einzel/Doppelzimmer** *ikh hehtter gehrn ien ientsel/doppeltsimmer*
A room with …	**Ein Zimmer mit …** *ien tsimmer mit*
twin beds	**zwei Einzelbetten** *tsvie ientselbeten*
a double bed	**einem Doppelbett** *ienem doppelbet*
a bath/shower	**Bad/Dusche** *baat/dusheh*

AT THE HOTEL RECEPTION

Haben Sie noch Zimmer frei? *haaben zee nokh tsimmer fry* (*Do you have any vacancies?*)
Leider nein. *lyder nine* (*No. I'm sorry.*)
Danke. Auf Wiedersehen. *dahnkeh owf veederzayn* (*Thank you. Good bye.*)

RECEPTION

I have a reservation.
Ich habe reservieren lassen.
ikh haabeh rezehrveeren lassen.

My name is …
Mein Name ist … *mien naameh ist*

We've reserved a double and a single room.
Wir haben ein Doppelzimmer und ein Einzelzimmer reserviert lassen.
veer haaben ien doppeltsimmer unt ien ientseltsimmer rezehrveeren lassen

I confirmed my reservation by mail.
Ich habe meine Reservierung schriftlich bestätigt. *ikh haabeh mieneh rezehrveerung shriflikh beshtaitigt*

Could we have adjoining rooms?
Könnten wir nebeneinander liegende Zimmer haben? *kurnten veer naybenienander leegendeh tsimmer haaben*

AMENITIES AND FACILITIES

Is there … in the room?
Gibt es … im Zimmer? *gipt ess … im tsimmer*

air conditioning
eine Klimaanlage *ieneh kleemaanlaageh*

TV
einen Fernseher *ienen fehrnzayer*

telephone
ein Telefon *ien taylayfoan*

Does the hotel have …?
Hat das Hotel …? *hat dass hottel*

fax facilities
einen Telefaxdienst *ienen taylayfaksdeenst*

laundry service
einen Wäschedienst *ienen vehshedeenst*

satellite/cable TV
Satellitenfernsehen/Kabelfernsehen
zatelleetenfehrnzayen/kaabelfehrnzayen

sauna
eine Sauna *ieneh zowna*

swimming pool
ein Schwimmbad *ien shvimbaat*

Could you put … in the room?
Könnten Sie … ins Zimmer stellen?
kurnten zee … ins tsimmer shtellen

an extra bed
ein zusätzliches Bett *ien tsoozehtslikhess bet*

a crib/child's cot
ein Kinderbett *ien kinderbet*

Do you have facilities for …?
Haben Sie Einrichtungen für …?
haaben zee ienrikhtungen fewr

the disabled
Behinderte *behinderteh*

children
Kinder *kinder*

22

YOU MAY SEE

ZIMMER FREI	Room vacant
FRÜHSTÜCK INBEGRIFFEN	Breakfast included
MAHLZEITEN ERHÄLTLICH	Meals available
NAME/VORNAME	Name/first name
WOHNORT/STRASSE/NR.	Home address/street/ number
NATIONALITÄT/BERUF	Nationality/Profession
GEBURTSDATUM	Date of birth
GEBURTSORT	Place of birth
PASSNUMMER	Passport number
KRAFTFAHRZEUGKENNZEICHEN	License plate number
ORT/DATUM	Place/date
UNTERSCHRIFT	Signature

How Long?

We'll be staying …	**Wir bleiben …** *veer blieben*
overnight only	**nur eine Nacht** *noor ieneh nakht*
a few days	**ein paar Tage** *ien paar taageh*
a week (at least)	**(mindestens) eine Woche** *(meendestens) iener vokheh*
I'd like to stay an extra night.	**Ich möchte noch eine Nacht bleiben.** *ikh murkhteh nokh ieneh nakht blieben*

YOU MAY HEAR

Kann ich bitte Ihren Pass sehen?	May I see your passport, please?
Bitte füllen Sie dieses Formular aus.	Please fill out this form.
Bitte unterschreiben Sie hier.	Please sign here.
Was ist Ihr Kraftfahrzeugkennzeichen?	What is your car license plate number?

PRICES

How much is it …?	**Was kostet es …?** *vass kostet ess*
per night/ week	**pro Nacht/Woche** *proa nakht/vokheh*
for bed and breakfast	**für Übernachtung mit Frühstück** *fewr ewbernakhtung mit frewshtewk*
excluding meals	**ohne Mahlzeiten** *oaneh maaltsieten*
for American Plan (A.P.) [full board]	**mit Vollpension** *mit folpenzioan*
for Modified American Plan [half board]	**mit Halbpension** *mit halppenzioan*
Does the price include …?	**Ist … im Preis inbegriffen?** *ist … im pries inbegriffen*
breakfast	**das Frühstück** *dass frewshtewk*
service	**die Bedienung** *dee bedeenung*
sales tax [VAT]	**die Mehrwertsteuer** *dee mayrvayrtshtoyer*
Do I have to pay a deposit?	**Muss ich eine Anzahlung leisten?** *muss ikh ieneh antsaloonk liessten*
Is there a discount for children?	**Gibt es eine Ermäßigung für Kinder?** *gipt ess ieneh ehrmaissigung fewr kinder*

DECISION

May I see the room?	**Kann ich das Zimmer sehen?** *kan ikh dass tsimmer zayen*
That's fine. I'll take it.	**Gut, ich nehme es.** *goot ikh naymeh ess*
It's too …	**Es ist zu …** *ess ist tsoo*
cold/hot	**kalt/warm** *kalt/varm*
dark/small	**dunkel/klein** *dunkel/klien*
noisy	**laut** *lowt*
Do you have anything …?	**Haben Sie nichts …?** *haaben zee nikhts*
bigger/cheaper	**größeres/billigeres** *grursseress/billigeress*
quieter	**ruhigeres** *rooigeress*
No, I won't take it.	**Nein, ich nehme es nicht.** *nien ikh naymer ess nikht*

COMPLAINTS

The … doesn't work.	**… funktioniert nicht.** *… funktsionneert nikht*
air conditioning	**die Klimaanlage** *dee kleema-anlaageh*
heat [heating]	**die Heizung** *dee hietsung*
light	**das Licht** *dass likht*
television	**der Fernseher** *dehr fehrnzayer*
I can't turn the heat (heating) on/off.	**Ich kann die Heizung nicht anmachen/aus machen.** *ikh kan dee hietsung nikht anmakhen/owsmakhen*
There is no hot water.	**Es gibt kein heißes Wasser.** *ess gipt kien hiessess vasser*
There is no toilet paper.	**Es ist kein Toilettenpapier da.** *ess ist kien twalettenpapeer daa*
The faucet [tap] is dripping.	**Der Wasserhahn tropft.** *dehr vasserhaan tropft*
The sink/toilet is blocked.	**Das Waschbecken/Die Toilette ist verstopft.** *dass vashbeken/dee twaletteh ist fehrshtopft*
The window/door is jammed.	**Das Fenster/Die Tür klemmt.** *dass fenster/dee tewr klemmt*
My room has not been made up.	**Mein Zimmer ist nicht gemacht.** *mien tsimmer ist nikht gemakht*
The … is broken.	**… ist kaputt.** *… ist kaput*
blind	**das Rollo** *dass rolloa*
lamp	**die Lampe** *dee lampeh*
lock	**das Schloss** *dass shloss*

ACTION

Could you have that taken care of?	**Können Sie sich darum kümmern?** *kurnen zee zikh darum kewmmern*
I'd like to move to another room.	**Ich möchte in ein anderes Zimmer umziehen.** *ikh murkhteh in ien anderess tsimmer umtseeern*
I'd like to speak to the manager.	**Ich möchte mit dem Geschäftsführer sprechen.** *ikh murkhteh mit daym geshehftsfewrer shprekhen*

REQUIREMENTS

The 220-volt, 50-cycle AC is universal in Germany, Austria, and Switzerland. If you bring your electrical appliances, buy an adapter plug (round pins, not square). You may also need a transformer appropriate to the wattage of the appliance.

ABOUT THE HOTEL

Where's the …?	**Wo ist …?** *voa ist*
bar	**die Bar** *dee baar*
bathroom [toilet]	**die Toilette** *dee twaletteh*
parking lot [car park]	**der Parkplatz** *dehr paarkplats*
dining room	**der Speisesaal** *dehr shpiezezaal*
elevator [lift]	**der Aufzug** *dehr owftsoog*
shower	**die Dusche** *dee dusheh*
swimming pool	**das Schwimmbad** *dass shvimbaat*
tour operator's bulletin board	**das Anschlagbrett des Reiseveranstalters** *dass anshlaagbret dess riezefehranshtalterss*
Does the hotel have a garage?	**Gibt es eine Hotelgarage?** *gipt ess iener hottelgaraazheh*
What time is breakfast served?	**Wann wird das Frühstück serviert?** *van veert dass frewstewk zehrveert*
Is there room service?	**Gibt es einen Zimmerservice?** *gipt ess ienen tsimmerzehrvees*

YOU MAY SEE

AMTSANSCHLUSS: WÄHLEN SIE …	dial … for an outside line
KEIN AUSGANG	no exit
BITTE NICHT STÖREN	do not disturb
EMPFANG: WÄHLEN SIE …	dial … for reception
AUFZUG	elevator [lift]
NOTAUSGANG	emergency exit
NUR FÜR RASIERAPPARATE	electric razors only

PERSONAL NEEDS

The key to room …, please.	**Den Schlüssel für Zimmer …, bitte.** *dayn shlewssel fewr tsimer … bitteh*
I've lost my key.	**Ich habe meinen Schlüssel veloren.** *ikh haabeh mienen shlewssel fehrloaren*
I've locked myself out.	**Ich habe mich ausgesperrt.** *ikh haabeh mikh owsgeshpehrt*
Could you wake me at …?	**Können Sie mich um … wecken?** *kurnen zee mikh um … veken*
I'd like breakfast in my room.	**Ich möchte auf meinem Zimmer frühstücken.** *ikh murkhteh owf mienem tsimmer frewshtewkon*
Can I leave this in the safe?	**Kann ich dies in den Safe legen?** *kan ikh deez in dayn "safe" laygen*
Could I have my things from the safe?	**Kann ich meine Sachen aus dem Safe haben?** *kan ikh mieneh zakhen ows daym safe haaben*
Where can I find the…?	**Wo kann ich … finden?** *voa kan ikh … finden*
tour guide	**den Reiseleiter** *dayn rieserlieter*
May I have …?	**Kann ich … haben?** *kan ikh … haaben*
a bath towel	**ein Badetuch** *ien baadetookh*
an (extra) blanket	**eine (zusätzliche) Decke** *ieneh (tsoozehtslikheh) dekeh*
(more) hangers	**(noch) einige Kleiderbügel** *(nokh) ienigeh kliederbewgel*
a pillow	**ein Kopfkissen** *ien kopfkissen*
soap	**Seife** *ziefeh*

MAIL AND TELEPHONE

Avoid high costs when telephoning from hotel rooms by buying a **Telefonkarte** (phonecard) and making calls from a public phone.

Is there any mail for me?	**Ist Post für mich da?** *ist posst fewr mikh daa*
Are there any messages?	**Hat jemand eine Nachricht hinterlassen?** *hat yaymant ieneh naakhrikht hinterlassen*

LODGING

We've reserved in the name of …	**Wir haben auf den Namen … reserviert.** *veer haaben owf dayn naamen … rezehrveert*
an apartment	**eine Ferienwohnung** *iener fayreeenvoanung*
a cottage	**ein Ferienhaus** *ien fayrienhowss*
Where do we pick up the keys?	**Wo bekommen wir die Schlüssel?** *voa bekommen veer dee shlewssel*
Where is the…?	**Wo ist …?** *voa ist*
electric meter	**der Stromzähler** *dehr shtroamtsailer*
fuse box	**der Sicherungskasten** *dehr zikherungskasten*
water heater	**das Heißwassergerät** *dass hiessvassergerait*
Are there any spare fuses?	**Sind Ersatzsicherungen da?** *zint ehrzatszikherungen daa*
Are there any spare gas bottles?	**Gibt es Gasflaschen als Reserve?** *gipt ess gaassflashen als rayzehrveh*
Are there any spare sheets?	**Sind noch zusätzliche Bettlaken da?** *zint nokh tsoozehtslikheh betlaaken daa*
Which day does the cleaner come?	**An welchem Tag kommt die Putzfrau?** *an velkhem taag komt dee putsfrow*

PROBLEMS?

Where can I contact you?	**Wo kann ich Sie erreichen?** *voa kan ikh zee ehrriekhen*
How does the … work?	**Wie funktioniert …?** *vee funktsionneert*
water heater	**das Heißwassergerät?** *dass hiessvassergerait*
The … has broken down.	**… ist kaputtgegangen.** *… ist kaputgegangen*
That was already damaged when we arrived.	**Das war schon bei unserer Ankunft beschädigt.** *dass vaar shoan bie unzerer ankunft beshaidigt*

28

USEFUL TERMS

boiler	**der Boiler** *dehr boyler*
stove [cooker]	**der Herd** *dehr hehrt*
utensils [cutlery]	**das Besteck** *dass beshtek*
freezer	**der Gefrierschrank** *dehr gefreershrank*
refrigerator	**der Kühlschrank** *dehr kewlshrank*
kettle	**der Kessel** *dehr kessel*
pot	**der Kochtopf** *dehr kokhtopf*
toaster	**der Toaster** *dehr toaster*
toilet paper	**das Toilettenpapier** *dass twalettenpapeer*
washing machine	**die Waschmaschine** *dee vashmasheeneh*

ROOMS

balcony	**der Balkon** *dehr balkoan*
bathroom	**das Badezimmer** *dass baadetsimmer*
bedroom	**das Schlafzimmer** *dass shlaaftsimmer*
dining room	**das Esszimmer** *dass esstsimmer*
kitchen	**die Küche** *dee kewkheh*
living room	**das Wohnzimmer** *dass voantsimmer*
toilet	**die Toilette** *dee toaletteh*

YOUTH HOSTEL

Youth hostels in Germany, Austria and Switzerland are of a very high standard.

Do you have any beds left for tonight?	**Haben Sie heute Nacht noch Plätze frei?** *haaben zee hoyteh nakht nokh plehtseh frie*
Do you rent bedding?	**Verleihen Sie Bettzeug?** *fehrlieen zee bettsoyg*
What time are the doors locked?	**Wann werden die Türen abgeschlossen?** *van vehrden dee tewren apgeshlossen*
I have an International Student Card.	**Ich habe einen internationalen Studentenausweis.** *ikh haabeh ienen internatsioanaalen shtuddentenowsvies*

CAMPING

Camping is very popular in German-speaking countries and sites tend to be of a high standard.

Booking

Is there a camp site near here?	**Gibt es hier in der Nähe einen Campingplatz?** *gipt ess heer in dehr naieh ienen kempingplats*
Do you have space for a trailer [caravan]?	**Haben Sie Platz für einen Wohnwagen?** *haaben zee plats fewr iienen voanvaagen*
What is the charge …?	**Wie hoch sind die Gebühren …?** *vee hoakh zint dee gebewren*
per day/week	**pro Tag/Woche** *proa taag/vokheh*
for a tent/car	**für ein Zelt/ein Auto** *fewr ien tselt/ien owto*
for a trailer	**für einen Wohnwagen** *fewr ienen voanvaagen*
Can we camp anywhere on the campground?	**Können wir überall auf dem Platz zelten?** *kurnen veer ewberal owf daym plats tselten*
Can we park the car next to the tent?	**Können wir das Auto neben dem Zelt parken?** *kurnen veer dass owto nayben daym tselt parken*

Facilities

Are there cooking facilities on site?	**Gibt es auf dem Platz Kochgelegenheiten?** *gipt ess owf daym plats kokhgelaygenhieten*
Are there any electric outlets?	**Gibt es hier Stromanschlüsse?** *gipt ess heer shtroamanshlewsseh*
Where is/are the …?	**Wo ist/sind** *voa ist/zint*
drinking water	**das Trinkwasser** *dass trinkvasser*
trash cans [dustbins]	**die Mülleimer** *dee mewlliemer*
showers	**die Duschen** *dee dushen*
Where are the laundry facilities?	**Wo kann man Wäsche waschen?** *voa kan man vehsheh vashen*

YOU MAY SEE

ZELTEN VERBOTEN	no camping
TRINKWASSER	drinking water

Complaints

It's too sunny/shady/crowded here.
Hier ist es zu sonnig/schattig/überfüllt.
heer ist tsoo zonnikh/shattikh/ewberfewlt

The ground's too hard/uneven.
Der Boden ist zu hart/uneben.
dehr boaden ist tsoo hart/unayben

Do you have a more level spot?
Haben Sie eine ebenere Stelle?
haaben zee ieneh aybenereh shteleh

Camping equipment

backpack	**der Rucksack** *dehr rukzak*
butane gas	**das Butangas** *dass butaangaass*
charcoal	**die Holzkohle** *dee holtskoaleh*
cooler	**die Kühlbox** *dee kewlboks*
cot	**die Campingliege** *dee kempingleegeh*
firelighter	**der Feueranzünder** *dehr foyerantsewnder*
flashlight [torch]	**die Taschenlampe** *dee tashenlampeh*
folding chair/table	**der Klappstuhl/Klapptisch** *dehr klapshtool/klaptish*
hammer	**der Hammer** *dehr hamer*
ice pack	**der Kälteakku** *dehr kehlteakoo*
kerosene	**das Kerosin** *dass kehroseen*
knapsack	**der Rucksack** *dehr rukzak*
matches	**die Streichhölzer** *dee shtriekhhurltser*
(air) mattress	**die (Luft)matratze** *dee (luft)matratseh*
paraffin	**das Paraffin** *dass parafeen*
pocket knife	**das Taschenmesser** *dass tashenmesser*
pump	**die Pumpe** *dee pumpeh*
pot	**der Kochtopf** *dehr kokhtopf*
sleeping bag	**der Schlafsack** *dehr shlaafzak*
tent	**das Zelt** *dass tselt*
tent floor	**der Zeltboden** *dehr tseltboaden*
tent pegs	**die Heringe** *dee hayringeh*
tent pole	**die Zeltstange** *dee tseltshtangeh*
water jug	**der Wasserkanister** *dehr vasserkanister*

CHECKING OUT

What time do we need to vacate the room?	**Bis wann müssen wir das Zimmer räumen?** *biss van mewssen veer dass tsimmer roymen*
Could we leave our baggage here until ... o'clock?	**Können wir unser Gepäck bis ... Uhr hier lassen?** *kurnen veer unzer gepehk biss ... oor heerlassen*
I'm leaving now.	**Ich reise jetzt ab.** *ikh rieze yetst ap*
Could you order me a taxi, please?	**Könnten Sie mir bitte ein Taxi bestellen?** *kurnten zee meer bitteh ien taksi beshtelen*
It's been a very enjoyable stay.	**Es war ein sehr angenehmer Aufenthalt.** *ess vaar ien zayr angenaymer owfenthalt*

PAYING

May I have my bill, please?	**Kann ich bitte die Rechnung haben?** *kan ikh bitteh dee rekhnung haaben*
How much is my telephone bill?	**Wie hoch ist meine Telefonrechnung?** *vee hoakh ist mieneh taylayfoanrekhnung*
I think there's a mistake in this bill.	**Ich glaube, Sie haben sich verrechnet.** *ikh glowbeh zee haaben zikh fehrrekhnet*
I've made ... phone calls.	**Ich habe ... Anrufe gemacht.** *ikh haabeh ... anroofer gemakht*
Can I have my passport back?	**Kann ich meinen Pass zurückhaben?** *kan ikh mienen pas tsoorewkhaaben*
Can I have a receipt, please?	**Kann ich bitte eine Quittung haben?** *kan ikh bitteh ieneh kvittung haaben*

Tipping

A service charge is generally included in hotel and restaurant bills. If the service has been particularly good, you may want to leave an extra tip. The following chart is a guide:

	Germany & Austria	Switzerland
Bellman	€1–2	1–2 SF
Hotel maid, p/wk	€5–8	10 SF
waiter/waitress	round up (optional)	optional

EATING OUT

RESTAURANTS

Beisel *biezel*
The Austrian equivalent to a **Gasthaus**.

Bierhalle *beerhalleh*
Beer hall; besides beer you'll also be able to order hot dishes, salads and pretzels. The best-known beer halls are in Munich, which has a giant beer festival (**Oktoberfest**) in late September.

Bierstube *beershtoobeh*
The nearest equivalent to a pub or a bar though the atmosphere may be very different; usually only serves a few "dishes of the day."

Café *kafay*
Coffee shop offering pastries, snacks and drinks. Many have quite extensive breakfast menus. A **Tanzcafé** will have a small dance floor.

Gasthaus/Gasthof *gasthowss/gasthoaf*
Inn, usually in the country. It offers home cooking and a folksy atmosphere.

Gaststätte *gaststetteh*
Another word for restaurant.

Konditorei *kondeetoarie*
Pastry shop, often with a café

Milchbar *milkhbaar*
Bar serving mainly plain and flavored milk drinks with pastries. Also called a **Milchstübl** in some regions.

Raststätte *rastshtetteh*
Roadside restaurant; also called a **Rasthof** in Austria. Usually found on highways/motorways with lodging and service-station facilities.

Ratskeller *raatskeller*
Restaurant in the cellar of the town hall (often an historic building).

Restaurant *restorang*
Restaurants are usually up-scale establishments with a menu to match, ranging from local specialties to international cuisine.

Schnellimbiss *shnelimbiss*
Snack bar; the English term is also seen. The principal fare is beer and sausages. A sausage stand **(Würstchenstand)** is often similar.

Weinstube *vienshtoobeh*
Cozy restaurant found not only in wine-producing areas, where you can also order simple hot dishes and snacks.

bar	**die Bar**	take-away/out	**zum Mitnehmen**
hot-dog stall	**die Wurstbude**	coffee shop	**der Kaffeekaden**
ice-cream parlor	**die Eisdiele**	snack bar	**die Imbisstube**
pizza parlor	**die Pizzeria**	pub/inn	**das Wirsthaus**

MEAL TIMES

Frühstück *frewshtewk*
Breakfast: from 7–10 a.m. More substantial than the Continental breakfast: you'll be offered a selection of cold meats, cheeses, pâtés, jams and marmalades, accompanied by a variety of breads, together with tea, coffee or hot chocolate. Boiled eggs are also popular.

Mittagessen *mittaagessen*
Lunch: from 11.30 a.m. – 2 p.m. Many Germans eat their main meal in the middle of the day and most restaurants will offer their set menus **(Menü** or **Gedeck)** at midday as well as in the evening. If you want something smaller, look under **Kleine Gerichte**.

Abendessen/Abendbrot *aabentessen/aabentbroat*
Dinner: standard evening meals in German homes consist of a variety of bread with cold meats, cheeses, and maybe salad. You'll be able to get a full menu in restaurants which tend to serve between 6:30 and 9:30 p.m; larger restaurants may serve until 10 or 11 p.m.

Most restaurants will offer several fixed-price menus **(Tagesgedeck)** at different price points. These usually change every day and provide typical German dishes at a reasonable price. Or you can choose from the à la carte menu **(Speisekarte)**. Service is always included.

It's quite common to drink beer with most German meals, but if you want to try some of the local wine ask for **eine Flasche** (bottle), **eine halbe Flasche** (half-bottle) or **eine Karaffe** (carafe).

ESSENTIAL

A table for	**Ein Tisch für** *ien tish fewr*
2/3/4	**zwei/drei/vier** *tsvie/drie/feer*
Waiter/waitress!	**Bedienung!** *behdeenoong*
The bill, please.	**Die Rechnung, bitte.** *dee rekhnung bitteh*
A receipt, please.	**Eine Quittung, bitte.** *ine-eh queetoong bitteh*
Thank you.	**Danke.** *dankeh*

FINDING A PLACE TO EAT

Can you recommend a good restaurant?	**Können Sie ein gutes Restaurant empfehlen?** *kurnen zee ien gootess restorrang empfaylen*
Is there a(n) … restaurant near here?	**Gibt es hier in der Nähe ein … Restaurant?** *gipt ess heer in dehr naieh ien … restorrang*
traditional local	**traditionelles gutbürgerliches** *traditsionnelless gootbewrgerlikhess*
Chinese	**chinesisches** *khinayzishess*
Greek	**griechisches** *greekhishess*
Italian	**italienisches** *italyaynishess*
inexpensive	**preiswertes** *pricevayrtess*
Turkish	**türkisches** *tewrkishess*
vegetarian	**vegetarisches** *vegetaarishess*
Where can I find a(n) …?	**Wo finde ich …?** *voa findeh ikh*
sausage stand	**einen Würstchenstand** *ienen vewrstkhenshtant*
café	**ein Café** *ien kafay*
café/restaurant with a beer garden	**ein Café/Restaurant mit Biergarten** *ien kafay/restorrang mit beergarten*
fast-food restaurant	**einen Schnellimbiss** *ienen shnelimbiss*
ice cream parlor	**eine Eisdiele** *ieneh iesdeeleh*
pizzeria	**eine Pizzeria** *ieneh peetseree-ah*
snack bar	**eine Imbissstube** *ieneh imbiss-shtoobe*
steak house	**ein Steakhaus** *ien shtaykhowss*

RESERVATIONS

I'd like to reserve a table for 2.

Ich möchte einen Tisch für zwei Personen bestellen. *ikh murkhteh ienen tish fewr tsvie pehrzoanen beshtelen*

For this evening/ tomorrow at …

Für heute Abend/Morgen um … *fewr hoyteh aabent/morgen um*

We'll come at 8:00.

Wir kommen um acht Uhr. *veer kommen um akht oor*

A table for 2, please.

Einen Tisch für zwei Personen, bitte. *ienen tish fewr tsvie pehrzoanen bitteh*

We have a reservation.

Wir haben einen Tisch bestellt. *veer haaben ienen tish beshtelt*

YOU MAY HEAR

Ihr Name, bitte?	What's the name, please?
Es tut mir leid. Wir sind völlig ausgebucht.	I'm sorry. We're completely booked.
In … Minuten wird ein . Tisch frei	We'll have a table in … minutes.
Sie müssen in … Minuten	You'll have to come back in … minutes.

WHERE TO SIT

Could we sit …?

Können wir … sitzen? *kurnen veer … zitsen*

outside

im Freien *im frie-en*

by the window

am Fenster *am fenster*

smoking/non-smoking

Raucher/Nichtraucher *rowkher/nikhtrowkher*

IN A RESTAURANT

Haben Sie einen Tisch im Freien? *haaben zee ienen tish im frieen (Do you have a table outside?)*

Aber sicher. *ahber seekher (But of course.)*

Vielen Dank. *veelen dank (Thank you very much.)*

Haben Sie gewählt?	Are you ready to order?
Was nehmen Sie?	What would you like?
Ich empfehle Ihnen …	I recommend …
… haben wir nicht.	We haven't got …
Guten Appetit.	Enjoy your meal.

ORDERING

Excuse me, please!	**Entschuldigen Sie, bitte!** *entshuldiggen zee bitteh*
The wine list, please.	**Die Weinkarte, bitte.** *dee vienkarteh bitteh*
Do you have a set menu?	**Haben Sie ein Menü?** *haaben zee ien maynew*
Can you recommend some typical local dishes?	**Können Sie etwas typisch Deutsches empfehlen?** *kurnen zee etwas tewpish doytshes empfaylen*
Could you tell me what … is?	**Können Sie mir sagen, was … ist?** *kurnen zee meer zaagen vass … ist*
What is in it?	**Was ist darin?** *vass ist daarin*
I'd like …	**Ich hätte gern …** *ikh hetteh gehrn*
I'll have …	**Ich nehme …** *ikh naymeh*
a bottle/glass/carafe of …	**eine Flasche/ein Glas/eine Karaffe …** *iener flasheh/ien glaass/ieneh karaffeh*

IN A RESTAURANT

Was möchten Sie trinken? *vaas murkhten zee drinken*
(What would you like to drink?)

Ein Bier, bitte. *ien beer bitteh (A beer, please.)*

Sofort. *sofohrt (Right away.)*

Side dishes

Could I have ... without ...?	**Kann ich ... ohne ... haben?** *kan ikh ... oaneh ... haaben*
With a side order of ...	**Mit ... als Beilage.** *mit ... als bielaageh*
Could I have salad instead of vegetables, please?	**Kann ich bitte Salat statt Gemüse haben?** *kan ikh bitteh zalaat shtat gemewzeh haaben*
Does the meal come with vegetables/ potatoes?	**Ist Gemüse/Sind Kartoffeln bei dem Essen dabei?** *ist gemewzeh/zint kartoffeln bie daym essen dahbie*
Do you have any sauces?	**Haben Sie Soßen?** *haaben zee zoassen*
Would you like ... with that?	**Möchten Sie ... dazu haben?** *murkhten zee ... dahtsoo haaben*
vegetables	**Gemüse** *gemewzeh*
salad	**Salat** *zalaat*
potatoes	**Kartoffeln** *kartoffeln*
French fries	**Pommes frites** *pom frit*
sauce	**Soße** *zoasseh*
ice	**Eis** *iess*
May I have some ...?	**Könnte ich etwas ... haben?** *kurnteh ikh etvass ... haaben*
bread	**Brot** *broat*
butter	**Butter** *butter*
lemon	**Zitrone** *zitroaneh*
mustard	**Senf** *zenf*
pepper	**Pfeffer** *pfefer*
salt	**Salz** *zalts*
seasoning	**Würze** *vewrtseh*
sugar	**Zucker** *tsukker*
artificial sweetener	**Süßstoff** *sewsshtof*

General questions

Could I/we have …, please?	**Kann ich/Können wir bitte … haben?** *kan ikh/kurnen veer bitteh … haaben*
ashtray	**einen Aschenbecher** *ienen ashenbekher*
cup/glass	**eine Tasse/ein Glas** *ieneh tasseh/ien glas*
fork/knife	**eine Gabel/ein Messer** *ieneh gaabel/ien messer*
napkin	**eine Serviette** *ieneh zehrvietteh*
plate/spoon	**einen Teller/Löffel** *ienen teller/lurfel*
I'd like some more …, please.	**Ich hätte gern noch etwas … , bitte.** *ikh hetteh gehrn nokh etvuas … bitteh*
Nothing more, thanks.	**Nichts mehr, danke.** *nikhts mayr dankeh*
Where is the bathroom [toilet]?	**Wo sind die Toiletten?** *voa zint dee twaletten*

Special requirements

I can't eat food containing …	**Ich darf nichts essen, was … enthält.** *ikh darf nikhts essen vass … enthehlt*
salt/sugar	**Salz/Zucker** *zalts/tsukker*
Do you have meals/drinks for diabetics?	**Haben Sie Gerichte/Getränke für Diabetiker?** *haaben zee gerikhteh/getrehnkeh fewr dee-abaytiker*
Do you have vegetarian meals?	**Haben Sie vegetarische Gerichte?** *haaben zee vegetaarisheh gerikhteh*

For the children

Do you have children's portions?	**Haben Sie Kinderportionen?** *haaben zee kinderpoartsioaen*
Could we have a child's seat, please?	**Können wir bitte einen Kinderstuhl haben?** *kurnen veer bitteh ienen kindershtool haaben*
Where can I warm the baby's bottle?	**Wo kann ich das Fläschchen wärmen?** *voa kan ikh dass flehshkhen vehrmen*
Where can I feed/change the baby?	**Wo kann ich das Baby füttern/wickeln?** *voa kan ikh dass baby fewttern/vikeln*

39

FAST FOOD

Something to drink

I'd like …	**Ich hätte gern …** *ikh hetteh gehrn*
(hot) chocolate	**(heiße) Schokolade** *(hiesseh) shokolaadeh*
coffee	**Kaffee** *kafay*
black/with milk	**schwarz/mit Milch** *shvarts/mit milkh*
tea	**Tee** *tay*
I'd like a … of red/ white wine.	**Ich hätte gern … Rotwein/Weißwein.** *ikh hetteh gehrn … roatvien/viessvien*
bottle	**eine Flasche** *ieneh flasheh*
glass	**ein Glas** *ien glas*

YOU MAY HEAR

Bitte schön?	Can I help you?
… haben wir nicht mehr.	We've run out of …
Sonst noch etwas?	Anything else?

And to eat …

A piece of …, please.	**Ein Stück …, bitte.** *ien shtewk … bitteh*
I'd like two of those.	**Ich hätte gern zwei davon.** *ikh hetteh gehrn tsvie dahfon*
burger	**Hamburger** *hamboorger*
cake	**Kuchen** *kookhen*
French fries	**Pommes frites** *pom frit*
sandwich	**belegtes Brot** *belaygtess broat*
sausage	**Wurst** *voorst*

Ice cream

Some common flavors are **Erdbeereis** (strawberry), **Schokoladeneis** (chocolate), **Vanilleeis** (vanilla).

A … portion, please.	**Eine … Portion, bitte.** *ieneh … poartsioan bitteh*
small	**kleine** *klieneh*
medium/regular	**mittlere/normale** *mitlereh/normaaleh*
large	**große** *groasseh*

IN A CAFÉ

Was hätten Sie gern? *vaas hetten zee gehrn (What would you like?)*

Zwei Kaffee, bitte. *tzvi cahfeh bitteh (Two coffees, please.)*

Sonst noch etwas? *sonst nokh etvass (Anything else?)*

Danke, das ist alles. *dankeh dass ist aless (That's all, thanks.)*

COMPLAINTS

I have no knife/ fork/spoon.	**Ich habe kein Messer/keine Gabel/keinen Löffel.** *ikh haabeh kien messer/ kieneh gaabel/kienen lurfel*
There must be some mistake.	**Es muss ein Irrtum vorliegen.** *ess muss ien irtoom foarleegen*
That's not what I ordered.	**Das habe ich nicht bestellt.** *dass haabeh ikh nikht beshtelt*
I asked for ...	**Ich wollte ...** *ikh volteh*
The meat is ...	**Das Fleisch ist ...** *dass fliesh ist*
overdone	**zu stark gebraten** *tsoo shtark gebraaten*
underdone	**zu roh** *tsoo roa*
too tough	**zu zäh** *tsoo tsai*
This is too ...	**Das ist zu ...** *dass ist tsoo*
bitter/sour	**bitter/sauer** *bitter/zower*
The food is cold.	**Das Essen ist kalt.** *dass essen ist kalt*
This isn't fresh.	**Das ist nicht frisch.** *dass ist nikht frish*
How much longer will our food be?	**Wie lange dauert unser Essen noch?** *vee langeh dowert unzer essen nokh*
Have you forgotten our drinks?	**Haben Sie unsere Getränke vergessen?** *haaben zee unzereh getrehnkeh fehrgessen*
This isn't clean.	**Das ist nicht sauber.** *dass ist nikht zowber*
I'd like to speak to the manager.	**Ich möchte mit dem Geschäftsführer sprechen.** *ikh murkhteh mit daym geshehftsfewrer shprekhen*

PAYING

Tipping: Service is generally included in the bill, but if you are happy with the service, a personal tip for the waiter is appropriate and appreciated – it's usual to round up the bill.

The bill, please.	**Zahlen, bitte.** *tsaalen bitteh*
We'd like to pay separately.	**Wir möchten getrennt bezahlen.** *veer murkhten getrent betsaalen*
It's all together, please.	**Alles zusammen, bitte.** *aless tsoozammen bitteh*
I think there's a mistake in this bill.	**Ich glaube, Sie haben sich verrechnet.** *ikh glowbeh zee haaben zikh fehrrekhnet*
What is this amount for?	**Wofür ist dieser Betrag?** *voafewr ist deezer betraag*
I didn't have that. I had …	**Das hatte ich nicht. Ich hatte …** *dass hatteh ikh nikht. ikh hatteh*
Is service included?	**Ist die Bedienung inbegriffen?** *ist dee bedeenung inbegriffen*
Can I pay with this credit card?	**Kann ich mit dieser Kreditkarte bezahlen?** *kan ikh mit deezer kredeetkarteh betsaalen*
Could I have a receipt, please?	**Kann ich bitte eine Quittung haben?** *kan ikh bitteh ieneh kvittung haaben*
Can I have an itemized bill, please?	**Kann ich eine detaillierte Rechnung haben?** *kan ikh ieneh daytayeerteh rekhnoong haaben*
That was a very good meal.	**Das Essen war sehr gut.** *dass essen vaar zayr goot*

IN A RESTAURANT

Zahlen bitte. *tzahlen bitteh* (The bill please.)
Hier bitte. Hat's geschmeckt? *heer bitteh hahts gehshmeckt*
(Here you are. Did you like the food?)
Ja, sehr. *yah sehr* (Yes, very much.)

COURSE BY COURSE

Breakfast (Frühstück)

No trip to Germany would be complete without sampling some of the breads:
Weißbrot (white), **Vollkornbrot** (whole grain), **französisches Weißbrot/
Baguette** (French), **Zwiebelbrot** (onion), **Rosinenbrot** (raisin), **Roggenbrot** (rye).

I'd like …	**Ich hätte gern …** *ikh hetteh gehrn*
bread/rolls	**Brot/Brötchen** *broat/brud-khen*
toast	**Toast** *toast*
butter	**Butter** *butter*
cereal	**Müsli/Cornflakes** *mewsli/cornflakes*
cheese	**Käse** *kaizeh*
cold meats	**Aufschnitt** *owfshnit*
eggs	**Eier** *ie-er*
boiled egg	**ein gekochtes Ei** *ien gekokhtes ie*
fried eggs	**Spiegeleier** *shpeegelie-er*
scrambled eggs	**Rühreier** *rewrie-er*
honey	**Honig** *hoanikh*
jam	**Marmelade** *marmelaadeh*
milk	**Milch** *milkh*
orange juice	**Orangensaft** *orangshenzaft*

Appetizers (Vorspeisen)

Aufschnittplatte *owfshnitplatteh*
assorted cold cuts served with gherkins and bread

Bauernomelett *bowern omlett*
diced bacon and onion omelet

Bündnerfleisch *bewndnerfliesh*
cured, dried beef served in thin slices (Swiss)

Fleischpastete *flieshpastayteh* meat paté

Matjesfilet nach Hausfrauenart *matyehsfillay nakh howsfrowenart*
fillets of herring with apples and onions

Russische Eier *russisheh ie-er*
hard-boiled eggs with mayonnaise

Stolzer Heinrich *stoalzer hienrikh*
fried pork sausage in beer sauce (Bavarian)

Soups (Suppen)

Soups appear on menus in two main forms: **Suppe** (soup) and **Brühe** (broth). Look for these specialties.

Backerbsensuppe	*bakehrpsenzuppeh*	type of split-pea soup
Bauernsuppe	*bowernzuppeh*	cabbage and frankfurter soup
Champignonsuppe	*shampinyongzuppeh*	mushroom soup
Erbsensuppe	*ehrpzenzuppeh*	pea soup
Flädlesuppe	*flaydlezuppeh*	broth with pancake strips
Gemüsesuppe	*gemewsezuppeh*	vegetable soup
Gulaschsuppe	*goolashzuppeh*	spiced soup of stewed beef
Hühnerbrühe	*hoonerbreweh*	chicken broth
Leberknödelsuppe	*layberknurdelzuppeh*	liver-dumpling soup
Nudelsuppe	*noodelzuppeh*	noodle soup
Ochsenschwanzsuppe	*okhsenshvantszuppeh*	oxtail soup
Tomatensuppe	*tomaatenzuppeh*	tomato soup

Fish and seafood (Fisch und Meeresfrüchte)

You'll recognize **Hering, Karpfen** and **Makrele;** other popular fish and seafood are listed below or appear in the Menu Reader.

Dorsch	*dorsh*	young cod
Forelle	*forelleh*	trout
Garnelen	*garnaylen*	prawns/shrimps
Kabeljau	*kaabelyow*	cod
Lachs	*laks*	salmon
Languste	*langoosteh*	crayfish
Muscheln	*musheln*	clams/mussels
Salm	*zalm*	salmon
Scholle	*sholleh*	plaice/flounder
Tintenfisch	*tintenfish*	squid, octopus

Meat (Fleisch)

Ich hätte gern …	*ikh hetteh gehrn*	I'd like some …
Rindfleisch	*rintfliesh*	beef
Hähnchen	*hainkhen*	chicken
Ente	*enteh*	duck
Schinken	*shinken*	ham
Lammfleisch	*lammfliesh*	lamb
Schweinefleisch	*shvienefliesh*	pork
Kaninchen	*kaneenkhen*	rabbit
Würste	*vewrsteh*	sausages
Truthahn	*troothaan*	turkey
Kalbfleisch	*kalpfliesh*	veal
Reh	*ray*	venison

To find out what type of cut you'll be getting, look to the end of the word: the meat comes first (e.g. **Schweine-**), followed by the cut (**-kotelett**)

-braten	*braaten*	joint, roast
-brust	*brust*	breast
-hachse/haxe	*hakseh*	shank
-herz	*herts*	heart
-kotelett	*kotlett*	cutlet, chop
-klößchen	*klurskhen*	little dumplings
-leber	*layber*	liver
-schnitzel	*shnitsel*	cutlet
-zunge	*tsungeh*	tongue

Meat dishes (Fleischgerichte)

Eisbein	*iesbien*	pickled pig's knuckle
Faschiertes	*fasheertes*	minced meat
Fleischkäse	*flieshkaizeh*	meat loaf
Gehacktes	*gehaktes*	minced meat
Kalbshaxen	*kalpshaksen*	roast shank of veal
Leberkäse	*layberkaizeh*	type of meat loaf
Wiener Schnitzel	*veener shnitsel*	breaded veal cutlet

Bauernschmaus
sauerkraut garnished with boiled bacon, smoked pork, sausages, dumplings, potatoes (Austrian)

Berner Platte
sauerkraut or green beans liberally garnished with pork chops, boiled bacon and beef, sausages, tongue and ham (Swiss)

Holsteiner Schnitzel
breaded veal cutlet topped with fried egg, garnished with vegetables and usually accompanied by bread and butter, anchovies, mussels and smoked salmon

Kohlroulade cabbage leaves stuffed with minced meat

Maultaschen
Swabian-style ravioli filled with meat, vegetables and seasoning

Rouladen
slices of beef or veal filled, rolled and braised (in brown gravy)

Sauerbraten beef roast, marinated with herbs and braised in a rich sauce

Schlachtplatte platter of various sausages and cold meats

Sausages (Würste)

Bierwurst	*beervoorst*	pork and beef, smoked
Blutwurst	*blootvoorst*	blood sausage
Bockwurst	*bokvoorst*	large frankfurter
Bratwurst	*braatvoorst*	pork, fried or grilled
Fleischwurst	*flieshvoorst*	mildly seasoned, popular with children
Jagdwurst	*yaagtvoorst*	smoked pork, similar to salami
Leberwurst	*laybervoorst*	liver sausage
Katenrauchwurst	*kaatenrowkhvoorst*	country-style, smoked
Regensburger	*raygensburger*	highly spiced, smoked
Rotwurst	*roatvoorst*	blood sausage/ black pudding
Weißwurst	*viesvoorst*	veal and bacon with parsley and onion
Zervelatwurst	*tservelaatvoorst*	pork, beef and bacon, seasoned and smoked
Zwiebelwurst	*tsveebelvoorst*	pork and onion

Side dishes (Beilagen)

Kartoffeln *kartoffeln* potatoes, which may appear as: **Bratkartoffeln/ Röstkartoffeln** (fried), **Rösti** (hash-brown), **Kartoffelbrei/-püree** (mashed), **Kartoffelsalat** (potato salad), **Salzkartoffeln** (boiled).

Klöße/Knödel *klursseh/knurdel* dumplings – they are often served with soups or meat dishes. Some varieties are **Grießklöße** (semolina), **Kartoffelklöße** (potato), **Leberknödel** (liver), **Mehlklöße** (flour), **Nockerl** (small), **Semmelknödel** (Bavarian bread dumplings). Dumplings are called **Klöße** in northern Germany, but **Knödel** in the south.

Teigwaren *tiegwaaren* pasta; some varieties include **Nudeln** (noodles), **Spätzle** and **Knöpfli** (types of gnocchi).

You'll recognize these vegetables: **Brokkoli, Karotten, Sauerkraut, Sellerie, Tomaten.**

Blumenkohl	*bloomenkoal*	cauliflower
Bohnen	*boanen*	beans
Erbsen	*ehrpsen*	peas
Gurke	*goorkeh*	cucumber
Karfiol	*karfioal*	cauliflower
Kopfsalat	*kopfzalaat*	head of lettuce
Mohrrüben	*moarrewben*	carrots
Zwiebeln	*tsveebeln*	onions
gemischter Salat	*gemishter zalaat*	mixed salad
grüner Salat	*grewner zalaat*	green salad
Rettichsalat	*rettichzalaat*	white radish salad
Rotkrautsalat	*roatkrowtzalaat*	red cabbage salad
Tomatensalat	*tomaatenzalaat*	tomato salad

Kohl/Kraut *koal/krowt* cabbage – variations: **Grünkohl** (kale), **Krautsalat** (cole-slaw), **Rotkohl/-kraut** (red cabbage), **Sauerkraut** (pickled, shredded cabbage), **Weißkohl/-kraut** (white cabbage).

Pilze *piltseh* mushrooms. Common varieties include **Champignons** (white) and **Pfifferlinge** (chanterelle).

Cheese (Käse)

Most of the cheeses from Germany, Austria and Switzerland are mild, but there are some strong cheeses – classified in three grades: **würzig**, **pikant** and **scharf**.

hard cheeses	(mild)	**Allgäuer Bergkäse** (like Swiss cheese), **Appenzeller**, **Räucherkäse** (smoked), **Tilsiter**
	(sharp)	**Handkäse**, **Harzer Käse**, **Schabzieger**
soft cheeses	(mild)	**Allgäuer Rahmkäse**, **Altenburger** (goat's milk cheese), **Edelpilz** (blue cheese), **Frischkäse** (curd cheese), **Kümmelkäse** (with caraway seeds), **Sahnekäse** (cream cheese), **Schichtkäse**
Swiss cheeses	(mild)	**Emmentaler**, **Greyerzer**

Fruit (Obst)

Apfelsine	*apfelzeeneh*	orange
Birne	*beerneh*	pear
rote/schwarze Johannisbeeren	*roateh/shvartseh yohanisbayren*	red/black currants
Kirschen	*keershen*	cherries
Pflaumen	*pflowmen*	plums, prunes
Zitrone/Limone	*tsitroaneh/limoaneh*	lemon/lime
Zwetschgen	*tsvetshgen*	plums

Dessert (Nachtisch)

And you'll recognize: **Apfel, Banane, Mandarine, Melone, Aprikosen, Datteln, Kokosnuss, Orange, Rhabarber**.

Apfelkuchen	*apfelkookhen*	apple tart
Dampfnudeln	*dampfnoodeln*	sweet dumplings
gemischtes Eis	*gemishtes iess*	mixed ice cream portion
Germknödel	*gehrmknurdel*	sweet dumpling
Obstsalat	*oabstzalaat*	fruit salad
Rote Grütze	*roater grewtseh*	red berry compote
Zwetschgenkuchen	*zvetshgenkookhen*	plum tart

DRINKS

Beer (Bier)

Beer is the most popular drink in Germany and Austria – and it's not all lager! For easy ordering, ask for **Bier vom Fass** (draft beer). To be more specific, ask for **ein Helles** (light beer) or **ein Dunkles** (dark beer). And look out for:

Alkoholfreies Bier: alcohol-free
Altbier: high hops content; similar to British ale
Berliner Weiße mit Schuss: pale beer with a shot of raspberry syrup
Bockbier, Doppelbock, Starkbier: high alcoholic and malt content
Export: pale, higher in alcohol and less bitter than Pilsener
Hefeweizen/Hefeweißbier: pale, brewed from wheat
Kölsch: golden and light, brewed in Cologne
Kulmbacher Eisbock: highest alcohol content of all German beer
Malzbier: dark and sweet, very low in alcohol
Pilsener (Pils): pale and strong with an aroma of hops
Radlermaß/Alsterwasser: lager shandy (beer with lemonade)
Weißbier: light, brewed from wheat grain

Wine (Wein)

The Association of German Wine Estates (VDP) acts as a quality control and ensures that wines carrying the VDP label are of superior quality. The wine seal **(Weinsiegel)** on the neck of the wine bottle is color-coded for easy recognition: yellow seal for dry **(trocken)**, green for medium-dry **(halbtrocken)** and red for sweet **(lieblich)**.

Kabinett: light, dry wine
Spätlese: riper, more full-bodied, often sweeter
Auslese: slightly dry wine, richer than Spätlese
Beerenauslese: slightly sweet wine, honeyed and rich
Trockenbeerenauslese: sweet, dessert wine
Eiswein: intensely sweet, fairly scarce and expensive
Tafelwein: table wine; lowest quality
Qualitätswein bestimmter Anbaugebiete: medium-quality wine
Qualitätswein mit Prädikat: highest quality wine

Wine regions

Ahr (region south of Bonn) The region's pale red wines are the best in Germany; produced around the towns of Ahrweiler, Neuenahr and Walporzheim.

Rheingau (area producing highly reputed wines)

Riesling (Schloss Johannisberger, Hattenheimer, Kloster Eberbacher, Rüdesheimer); **Sekt** (sparkling wine) from Eltville and Hochheim; reds, produced in Assmannshausen and Ingelheim.

Niersteiner, Domtal, Oppenheimer Wine of lesser quality is sold under the name of Liebfraumilch. Towns producing wines of exceptional quality include Alsheim, Bingen, Bodenheim, Dienheim, Guntersblum, Ingelheim, Nackenheim, Nierstein, Oppenheim and Worms.

Rheinpfalz (further south of Rheinhessen; mainly produces white wines) Dürkheimer, Deidesheimer, Forster, Ruppertsberger, Wachenheimer.

Mittelrhein (wine-growing area between Rüdesheim and Koblenz) Vineyards in Bingen, Bacharach, Boppard and Oberwesel.

Mosel (Moselle Valley) The best are produced in the vineyards of Bernkastel, Brauneberger, Graach, Piesport, Wehlen, Zeltingen. Names to look for: Bernkasteler, Graacher, Piesporter, Zeltinger.

Baden (mostly whites, a few light reds; south-west Germany) Markgräfler, Mauerwein, Seewein, Rulander, Gutedel, Kaiserstuhl,

Württemberg (good wine-growing region of red wines) Trollinger (red), Schillerwein (rosé) and Stettener Brotwasser. The best wine is produced at Cannstatt, Feuerbach and Untertürckheim.

Franken (Franconia: region around Würzburg producing dry, strong, white wines) Wine-growing areas: Iphofen, Eschendorf, Andersacker, Rödelsee, Würzburg. Names to look for: Bocksbeutel, Steinwein.

Nahe (full-bodied white wines) Look for Schloss Böckelheim or areas such as Bad Kreuznach, Bretzenheim, Münster, Niederhausen, Nordheim, Roxheim and Winzerheim for some excellent wines.

Austria (good white wines) Gumpoldskirchner (south of Vienna); Dürnsteiner, Loibner, Kremser (Wachau area); table wines such as Nussberger, Grinzinger, Badener (Vienna region).

Switzerland (red and white table wines) German-speaking cantons produce mainly light red wines: Hallauer, Maienfelder, Stammheimer.

Other drinks

You'll recognize **Cognac, Rum, Wodka, Whisky.** Other drinks you may want to order in German-speaking countries include **Apfelwein** (fermented cider), **Bowle** (punch), **Glühwein** (mulled wine), **Portwein** (port), **Weinbrand** (brandy).

More common are the many liqueurs and brandies, typical of Germany, Austria and Switzerland. Try some of the following:

Schnaps *shnaps*

The generic term for spirits/brandies. Varieties include **Apfel-schnaps** (apple); **Birnenschnaps** (pear); **Bommerlunder** (caraway-flavored brandy); **(Doppel) korn** (aqua vitae); **Dornkaat/Steinhäger** (similar to gin); **Heidelbeergeist** (blueberry brandy); **Kirschwasser** (cherry brandy); **Obstler** (fruit brandy); **Zwetschgen-wasser** (plum brandy); **Träsch** (pear and apple brandy); **Weizenkorn** (aqua vitae).

Likör *likur*

Liqueur; look for varieties such as **Aprikosenlikör** (apricot), **Eierlikör** (eggnog), **Himbeerlikör** (raspberry), **Kirschlikör** (cherry), **Kümmel** (caraway-flavored).

You'll have no trouble finding your favorite soft drinks or sodas such as *Coca-Cola®, Fanta®, Pepsi®.* Also popular is **Kaffee und Kuchen** (coffee and cakes) in the afternoon.

I'd like …	**Ich hätte gern …** *ikh hetteh gehrn*
(hot) chocolate	**eine (heiße) Schokolade** *ieneh (hiesseh) shokkolaadeh*
(glass of) milk	**(ein Glas) Milch** *(ien glas) milkh*
mineral water	**Mineralwasser** *minneraalvasser*
carbonated	**mit Kohlensäure** *mit koalenzoyreh*
non-carbonated	**ohne Kohlensäure** *oaner koalenzoyreh*
fruit juice	**Fruchtsaft** *frukhtzaft*
coffee	**Kaffee** *kafay*
tea	**Tee** *tay*

MENU READER

A

Aal eel
Aalsuppe eel soup
Abendbrot supper
Abendessen dinner
alkoholfrei non-alcoholic
alkoholfreies Bier non-alcoholic beer
alkoholfreies Getränk non-alcoholic drink
alle Preise inklusive Bedienung und Mehrwertsteuer (MwSt.) service charge and VAT (sales tax) included
Allgäuer Käsesuppe cheese soup from the Allgäu
Alsterwasser beer with lemonade
Altbier similar to British ale
Ananas pineapple
Anis aniseed
Aperitif aperitif
Apfel apple
Apfelcreme apple cream dessert
Apfelkuchen apple tart
Apfelküchlein apple fritters
Apfelsaft apple juice
Apfelschnaps apple brandy
Apfelsine orange
Apfelsinensaft orange juice
Apfelstrudel apple strudel
Apfelwein cider
Appetithäppchen canapés

Aprikosen apricots
Aprikosenlikör apricot liqueur
... Art ...-style
Auberginen eggplant
auf Bestellung made to order
-auflauf soufflé
Aufschnitt(platte) cold cuts
auf Vorbestellung advance order
Auslese wine classification
Austern oysters

B

Bachsaibling brook trout
Back- baked
Backerbsensuppe type of pea soup
Backpflaumen prunes
Baguette French bread
Banane banana
Barsch freshwater perch
Basilikum basil
Basler Mehlsuppe flour soup with grated cheese *(Swiss)*
Bauernomelett diced bacon and onion omelet
Bauernschmaus sauerkraut with meats, dumplings/potatoes
Bauernsuppe cabbage and frankfurter soup
(deutsches) Beefsteak hamburger
Beerenauslese wine classification
Beilagen accompaniments
belegtes Brot open-face sandwich

Berliner jelly doughnut

Berliner Weiße pale beer

Berner Platte sauerkraut or green beans with meats

Bete beet

Bethmännchen marzipan balls

Beuschel veal with lemon sauce

Bienenstich honey-almond cake

Bier beer

Bierwurst smoked pork and beef sausage

Birne pear

Birnen, Bohnen & Speck pears, green beans and bacon

Birnenschnaps pear brandy

Bismarckhering pickled herring with onions

blau boiled in bouillon

Blaubeer-Kaltschale chilled blueberry soup

Blaubeeren blueberries

Blaukraut red cabbage

Blindhuhn Westphalian vegetable stew

Blumenkohl cauliflower

blutig rare/underdone

Blutwurst blood sausage

Bockbier strong beer

Bockwurst large frankfurter

Bohnen beans

Bohnensuppe bean soup with bacon

Bommerlunder caraway-flavored brandy

Borretsch borage

Bouillon clear soup

Bowle punch

Brachse/Brasse bream

Brandwein brandy

Brat- roast

-braten joint, roast

Bratkartoffeln fried potatoes

Bratwurst fried pork sausage

Brechbohnen string beans

Brokkoli broccoli

Brombeeren blackberries

Brot bread

Brötchen rolls

-brust breast

Bückling kipper

Buletten meat patties

Bündnerfleisch cured beef

Butterkuchen butter crumble cake

Butterreis buttered rice

C

Cayenne-Pfeffer cayenne pepper

Champignons white mushrooms

Champignonsuppe mushroom soup

Chicorée chicory, endives

Christstollen Christmas fruitcake

Cornichons small pickles

-creme pudding

Cremeschnitte napoleon/millefeuille

Curryreis curried rice

D

Dampfnudeln sweet dumplings

dasselbe mit ... the same served with ...

Datteln dates
Dill dill
Doornkaat German gin, juniper-berry brandy
Doppelbock strong beer
(Doppel)Korn grain-distilled liquor, similar to whisky
Doppelrahm-Frischkäse cream cheese
Dorsch cod
dunkles Bier dark beer
(gut) durchgebraten well-done

E

Edelpilz blue cheese, similar to Stilton
Egli perch
Eier eggs
Eierlikör eggnog
Eierspeisen egg dishes
Eintopfgerichte stews
Eis/-eis ice cream
Eisbein pickled pig's knuckle
Eistee iced tea
Eiswein wine classification
Endivien curly endive
Endiviensalat curly endive salad
Endpreise einschließlich Service und Mehrwertsteuer service and VAT included
Ente duck
Erbsen peas
Erbsensuppe pea soup
Erdbeeren strawberries
Erdnüsse peanuts
Espresso espresso coffee

Essig vinegar
Essiggurken pickles/gherkins
Estragon tarragon
Export strong, pale beer

F

falscher Hase meat loaf
Fasan pheasant
Faschiertes minced meat
Feigen figs
Felchen kind of trout
Fenchel fennel
Filetsteak beef steak
Fisch fish
Fischbeuschelsuppe fish roe and vegetable soup
Fischfrikadellen fish croquettes
Fischgerichte fish dishes
Fischsuppe fish soup
Fisolen French (green) beans
Flädlesuppe broth with pancake strips
Fleisch (gerichte) meat (dishes)
Fleischkäse type of meat loaf
Fleischklößchen meatballs
Fleischpastete type of meat loaf
Fleischsalat diced meat salad with mayonnaise
Fleischwurst mildly seasoned sausage
Fondue bread dipped into melted cheese
Forelle trout
Frankfurter Würstchen frankfurter
französisches Weißbrot French baguette

Fridattensuppe broth with pancake strips
Frikadellen meat patties
frisch geräucherte Gänsebrust auf Toast freshly smoked breast of goose on toast
Frischkäse cream cheese
frittiert deep-fried
Früchtetee fruit tea
Fruchtjogurt fruit yogurt
Fruchtsaft fruit juice
Frühstück breakfast
für unsere kleinen Gäste children's meals
für zwei Personen for two

G

Gans goose
Gänseleberpastete goose liver pâté
Garnelen prawns/shrimps
Gebäck pastries
gebacken baked
(im schwimmenden Fett) gebacken deep-fried
(in der Pfanne) gebraten fried
(im Ofen) gebraten roasted
gebrühter Weißkrautsalat parboiled white cabbage coleslaw
gedämpft steamed
Geflügel poultry
gefüllt stuffed
gegrillt grilled/broiled
gehackt diced
Gehacktes minced meat
gekocht boiled

gekochtes Ei boiled egg
Gelbwurst mildly seasoned sausage
Gelee jelly/jam
gemischter Salat mixed salad
gemischtes Gemüse mixed vegetables
Gemüse vegetables
Gemüse nach Wahl choice of vegetables
geräuchert smoked
Germknödel sweet dumpling
Geröstete hash-brown potatoes
geschmort braised
Geschnetzeltes chopped veal in wine sauce
(in Butter) geschwenkt sautéed (in butter)
Geselchtes salted and smoked meat, usually pork
gespickter Hirsch larded venison
Getränke drinks
Gewürz spice
Glace/-glace ice cream
Glühwein mulled wine
glutenfreies Brot gluten-free bread
Götterspeise fruit jelly (Jell-O)
Grießbrei cream of wheat
Grießklöße semolina dumplings
Grießnockerlsuppe semolina-dumpling soup
grüne Bohnen French (green) beans
grüner Salat green salad
Grünkohl kale
Gugelhupf pound cake

55

Gulasch gulash; chunks of beef stewed in a rich paprika gravy
Gulaschsuppe spiced soup of stewed beef
Gurken cucumber

H

-hachse shank
Hackbraten meat loaf
Hackepeter spiced pork tartare
Haferbrei oatmeal
Hähnchen chicken
halbfester Käse medium-hard cheese
halbtrocken medium-dry
Hammelfleisch mutton
hart hard
Hase hare
Haselnüsse hazelnuts
Hauptgerichte main courses
Häuptlsalat lettuce salad
hausgemacht homemade
-haxe shank
Hecht pike
Hefeklöße yeast dumplings
Hefekranz ring-shaped cake of yeast dough, with almonds and sometimes candied fruit
Hefeweizen pale beer
Heidelbeeren blueberries
Heidelbeergeist blueberry brandy
Heidschnucken mutton from the Lüneburg Heath
Heilbutt halibut
heiß hot
heißer Apfelwein hot apple cider

helles Bier light beer
-hendl chicken
Hering(salat) herring (salad)
-herz heart
Himbeeren raspberries
Himbeerlikör raspberry brandy
hohe Rippe roast ribs of beef
Holsteiner Schnitzel breaded veal cutlet topped with fried egg
Honig honey
Honigkuchen honey biscuits
Hoppel-Poppel scrambled eggs with diced sausages or bacon
Huhn chicken
Hühnerbrühe chicken broth
Hummer lobster
Hummerkrabben large prawns
Hüttenkäse cottage cheese

I

Imbiss snacks
... im Preis inbegriffen ... included in the price
Ingwer ginger

J

Jagdwurst smoked pork sausage, similar to salami
Jakobsmuscheln scallops
Jogurt yogurt
Johannisbeersaft currant juice

K

Kabeljau cod
Kabinett wine classification
Kaffee coffee
Kaffeesahne cream

Kaisergranate kind of shrimp

Kaiserschmarren shredded pancake with raisins served with syrup

Kakao hot chocolate

Kalbfleisch veal

Kalbshaxen roast shank of veal

Kalbsleber veal liver

kalt cold

Kaltschale chilled fruit soup

Kaninchen rabbit

Kapaun capon

Kapern capers

Karamel caramel

Karfiol cauliflower

Karotten carrots

Karpfen carp

Kartoffelauflauf potato casserole

Kartoffelbälle potato balls

Kartoffelbrei mashed potatoes

Kartoffelchips chips

Kartoffelklöße potato dumplings

Kartoffelkroketten potato croquettes

Kartoffelmus mashed potatoes

Kartoffeln potatoes

Kartoffelpuffer potato fritters

Kartoffelsalat (mit Speck) potato salad (with bacon)

Kartoffelstock mashed potatoes

Kartoffelsuppe potato soup

Käse cheese

Käsebrett/Käse nach Ihrer Wahl cheese selection

Käseschnitte open, melted cheese sandwich

Käsestangen cheese sticks

Käsewähe hot cheese tart

Kasseler Rippenspeer smoked pork chops

Katenrauchwurst country-style, smoked sausage

Kekse cookies

Kerbel chervil

-keule haunch

Kirschcreme cherry cream dessert

Kirschen cherries

Kirschlikör cherry liqueur

Kirschwasser cherry brandy

kleine Mahlzeiten light meals/snacks

Klöße dumplings

Knoblauch garlic

Knödel dumplings

Knödelsuppe dumpling soup

Knöpfli kind of gnocchi

koffeinfreier Kaffee decaffeinated coffee

Kognak brandy

Kohl cabbage

Kohlrabi kohlrabi

Kohlroulade cabbage leaves stuffed with minced meat

Kokosnuss coconut

Kompott/-kompott stewed fruit, compote

Königinpastete diced meat and mushrooms in puff-pastry

Königinsuppe soup with beef, sour cream and almonds

Königsberger Klopse meatballs in white caper sauce
Kopfsalat lettuce
-kotelett chop
Krabben shrimps
Kraftbrühe beef consommé
Kräuter herbs
Kräutersalz herb-flavored salt
Kräutertee herb tea
(roher) Krautsalat coleslaw
Krautstiel white beet
Krautwickel braised cabbage rolls
Krebs river crayfish
Kren horseradish
Krenfleisch pork served with shredded vegetables and horseradish
Kresse cress
Kuchen/-kuchen cake
Kulmbacher Eisbock very strong beer
Kümmel caraway; caraway-flavored liquor
Kürbis pumpkin
Kutteln tripe

Labkaus minced/marinated corned beef, pickles, beets, smelts and herring served with mashed potatoes and fried eggs
Lachs salmon
Lammfleisch lamb
Languste spiny lobster
Lauch leeks
Laugenbrötchen pretzel rolls

Leber liver
Leberkäse type of meat loaf
Leberknödel liver dumplings
Leberknödelsuppe liver-dumpling soup
Leberwurst liver sausage
Lebkuchen gingerbread
Leckerli ginger biscuits
leicht light
Leipziger Allerlei peas, carrots and asparagus
Lenden- fillet of beef (tenderloin)
Lendenstück loin
lieblich sweet
Likör liqueur
Limette lime
Limonade soda
Limone lemon
Linsen lentils
Linsensuppe lentil soup
Lorbeer bay leaf

Maibowle white wine punch, flavored with sweet woodruff
Mais sweet corn
Maispoularde corn-fed chicken
Majoran marjoram
Makrele mackerel
Makronen macaroons
Malzbier low-alcohol beer
Mandarine tangerine
Mandeln almonds
Marillen apricots
mariniert marinated
Marmelade jam

Märzen strong beer
Masthühnchen chicken
Matjesfilet nach Hausfrauenart herring fillets
Matjeshering salted young herring
Maultaschen type of ravioli
Meeresfrüchte seafood
Meerrettich horseradish
Mehlklöße flour dumplings
Mehlnockerln small dumplings
Melone melon
Mettwurst spicy smoked pork sausage
Milch milk
Milchkaffee coffee with milk
Milchmixgetränk milk shake
Mineralwasser mineral water
mit Ei with egg
mit Eis on the rocks/with ice
mit Kohlensäure carbonated
mit Milch with milk
mit Sahne with cream
mit Zitrone with lemon
mit Zucker with sugar
Mittagessen lunch
mittel medium
Mohnbrötchen poppy seed rolls
Mohrrüben carrots
Mokka mocha; coffee-flavored
Muscheln clams/mussels
Muskatblüte mace
Muskatnuss nutmeg

N

nach ... Art ... style
nach Wahl with choice of

Nachspeisen/Nachtisch desserts
Nelke clove
Nieren kidneys
Nockerl small dumpling
Nudeln noodles
Nudelsuppe noodle soup
Nürnberger Bratwurst fried, veal and pork
Nürnberger Rostbratwurst Nuremberg-style pork sausage
Nuss- nut-flavored
Nüsse nuts

O

Obst fruit
Obstler fruit brandy
Obstsalat fruit salad
Ochsenschwanzsuppe oxtail soup
ohne Kohlensäure non-carbonated
Öl oil
Oliven olives
Omelett(e) omelet
Orangeade orangeade
Orangen oranges
Orangenmarmelade orange marmalade
Orangensaft orange juice

P

Pulatschinken when listed under desserts, pancakes with a jam or cream cheese filling, but they can also be a main course
Pampelmuse grapefruit

59

paniert breaded
Paradeiser tomatoes
Pellkartoffeln potatoes boiled in their jackets, then peeled
Petersilie parsley
Petersilienkartoffeln parsley potatoes
Pfeffer pepper
Pfefferkörner peppercorns
Pfefferminze peppermint
Pfefferpotthast spicy meat and onion casserole
Pfifferlinge chanterelle mushrooms
Pfirsich peach
Pflaumen plums, prunes
Pflümli(wasser) plum brandy
Pharisäer coffee with rum and whipped cream
Pichelsteiner Eintopf meat and vegetable stew
pikant pungent/hot
Pickelsteiner Franconia casserole with horseradish, garlic, salsify
Pilsener pils
Pilze mushrooms
Piment all-spice
-plätzli cutlet
Pökelfleisch salted meat
Pommes frites French fries
Porree leek
Portwein port
Poulet chicken
Preiselbeeren cranberries
Presskopf pork headcheese
Printen honey biscuits

Prinzessbohnen thick stringbeans
pur straight (neat)
-püree creamed

Quark dairy product similar to plain yogurt
Quitte quince

Raclette melted cheese with potatoes and pickles
Radieschen radishes
Radlermaß beer w/ lemonade
Räucheraal smoked eel
Räucherhering smoked herring
Rebhuhn partridge
Regensburger highly spiced, smoked sausage
Reh(pastete) venison paté
Reibekuchen potato pancake
reif ripe
Reis rice
Reisgerichte rice dishes
Rettichsalat white radish salad
Rhabarber rhubarb
Ribisel currants
Rindfleisch beef
Rindswurst grilled beef sausage
Rippensteak rib steak
Rochen ray
Roggenbrot rye bread
Rohschinken cured ham
Rollmops pickled herring
Rosenkohl brussels sprouts
Rosinen raisins

Rosinenbrot raisin bread
Rosmarin rosemary
Rösti hash-brown potatoes
Röstkartoffeln fried potatoes
rot red
Rotbarsch red sea-bass
Rote Grütze red berry compote
rote Beete beet
rote Johannisbeeren red currants
Rotkohl red cabbage
Rotkrautsalat red cabbage salad
Rotwurst blood sausage
Rouladen slices of rolled and braised beef or veal
Rüben beet
-rücken back
Rüdesheimer Kaffee coffee with brandy and whipped cream
Rüebli carrots
Rührei scrambled eggs
Rum rum
Russische Eier hard-boiled eggs with mayonnaise

S

Safran saffron
saisonbedingt seasonal
Salate salads
Salbei sage
Salm salmon
Salz salt
Salzgurke pickled cucumber
Salzkartoffeln boiled potatoes
Sardinen sardines
Sauerbraten marinated, braised beef

Sauerkirsch-Kaltschale chilled sour cherry soup
Sauerkraut sauerkraut
Sauerkraut und Rippchen sauerkraut and ribs
Schalotten shallots
scharf piquant/hot
Schellfisch haddock
Schillerlocke pastry cornet with vanilla cream filling
Schillerwein type of rosé
Schinken ham
Schinkenröllchen mit Spargel rolled ham filled with asparagus
Schlachtplatte platter of various sausages and cold meats
Schlesisches Himmelreich smoked pork loin cooked with mixed dried fruits
Schmelzkäse spreadable cheese
Schnaps strong spirit or brandy
Schnecken snails
Schnepfe wood cock
Schnittlauch chives
Schnitzel cutlet
(heiße) Schokolade hot chocolate
Schokoladen- chocolate …
Scholle plaice
Schupfnudeln rolled potato noodles
schwarze Johannisbeeren black currants
schwarzer Kaffee black coffee
Schwarzwälder Kirschtorte Black Forest cake
Schwarzwurzeln salsify
Schweinefleisch pork

Schweinekamm pork shoulder
Schweinekotelett pork chop
Schweinshaxe knuckle of pork
Seebarsch sea bass
Seebutt brill
Seehecht hake
Seezunge sole
sehr trocken extra dry
Sekt sparkling wine
selbstgemacht homemade
Sellerie celery
Selleriesalat celeriac root salad
Semmelknödel Bavarian bread dumplings
Semmelsuppe dumpling soup
Senf mustard
Seniorenmenü senior citizens' meals
Serbische Bohnensuppe spiced bean soup
Sesambrötchen sesame seed rolls
Soleier eggs pickled in brine
Spanferkel suckling pig
Spargel(spitzen) asparagus (tips)
Spätlese wine classification
Spätzle kind of noodle
Speck bacon
Speckknödel bread dumplings with bacon
Spekulatius almond cookies
Spezialität des Hauses specialty of the house
Spezialitäten der Region local specialties
Spiegeleier fried eggs
Spiegeleier mit Schinken/Speck ham/bacon and eggs

-spießchen skewered ...
Spinat spinach
Sprotten sprats
Stachelbeeren gooseberries
Starkbier strong beer
Steckrüben turnips
Steinbutt turbot
Steinhäger juniperberry brandy, similar to gin
Steinpilze wild yellow mushrooms
Steinpilze Försterinnenart mushrooms forestiere
Stolzer Heinrich sausage in beer
Stör sturgeon
Strammer Max bread with ham, fried eggs and maybe onions
Streichkäse spreadable cheese
Streuselkuchen coffee cake with crumble topping
Stückchen pastries
Sülze headcheese
Sülzkotelett pork chops in aspic
Suppen soups
süß sweet
Süßspeisen desserts
Süßstoff artificial sweetener

T

Tafelspitz mit Meerrettich boiled beef with horseradish cream sauce
Tagesgedeck set menu of the day
Tagesgericht dish of the day
Taube pigeon, squab
Tee tea
Teewurst soft, spreadable sausage

Teig dough
Teigwaren pasta
Teilchen pastries
Teltower Rübchen baby turnips
Thymian thyme
Tintenfisch squid/octopus
Tomaten tomatoes
Tomatenketchup ketchup
Tomatensaft tomato juice
Tomatensalat tomato salad
Tomatensuppe tomato soup
Topfbraten pot roast
Topfenstrudel flaky pastry filled with vanilla-flavored cream cheese, rolled and baked
Torte/-torte layer cake
Töttchen Westphalian sweet and sour veal stew
Träsch pear and apple brandy
Trauben grapes
Traubensaft grape juice
trocken dry
Trockenbeerenauslese wine classification
Truthahn turkey

U

überbacken oven-browned
ungarisch Hungarian
unser Küchenchef empfiehlt … the chef recommends …

V

Vanille vanilla
VDP (Verband Deutscher Prädikats- & Qualitäts Weingüter) officially recognized wine

Vollkornbrot whole grain bread
Vollmilch whole milk
vollmundig full-bodied
vom Rost grilled/broiled
Vorspeisen appetizers/starters

W

Wacholder juniper
Wachsbohnen yellow wax beans
Wachtel quail
Waldmeister sweet woodruff
Walnüsse walnuts
warme Getränke hot beverages
Wasser water
Wassermelone watermelon
weich soft
Wein wine
Weinbrand brandy
Weincreme wine cream dessert
Weintrauben grapes
weiß white
Weißbier pale, light beer
Weißbrot white bread
weiße Bohnen white beans
Weißherbst type of rosé
Weißkohl/-kraut white cabbage
Weißwurst veal and bacon sausage with parsley and onion
Weizenkorn wheat-distilled liquor, similar to whisky
Wermut vermouth
Whisky whisky
Wiener Schnitzel breaded veal cutlet
Wienerli Vienna-style frankfurter
Wild game

Wildschwein wild boar
Windbeutel cream puff
Wirsing savoy cabbage
Wodka vodka
Würste sausages
Wurstplatte assorted cold cuts
Würze seasoning
würzig aromatic

Z

Zander (giant) pike-perch
Zervelat(wurst) pork, beef and bacon sausage
Zimmertemperatur room temperature
Zimt cinnamon
Zitrone lemon
zu allen Gerichten servieren wir ... all meals are served with ...
Zucchetti zucchini
Zucker sugar
Zuckererbsen young green peas
Zunge/-zunge tongue
Zungenwurst blood sausage with pieces of tongue and diced fat
Zuschlag extra charge/supplement
Zwetschgen plums
Zwetschgenkuchen plum tart
Zwetschgenwasser plum brandy
Zwiebelbrot onion bread
Zwiebeln onions
Zwiebelsuppe onion soup
Zwiebelwurst liver and onion sausage
Zwischengerichte for the small appetite

TRAVEL

Germany, Austria and Switzerland have well-developed public transport systems. You should be able to enjoy trouble-free traveling.

SAFETY

Would you accompany me to the bus stop?	**Würden Sie mich zur Bushaltestelle begleiten?** *vewrden zee mikh tsoor busshalteshteleh beglieten*
I don't want to … on my own.	**Ich möchte nicht allein …** *ikh murkhteh nikht allien*
stay here	**hier bleiben** *heer blieben*
walk home	**zu Fuß nach Hause gehen** *tsoo fooss naakh howzeh gayen*
I don't feel safe here.	**Ich fühle mich hier nicht sicher.** *ikh fewleh mikh heer nikht zikher*
Good evening.	**Guten Abend.** *goo-ten ah-bend*

ESSENTIAL	
A ticket to …	**Eine Fahrkarte nach …** *ieneh faarkarteh naakh*
How much is …?	**Wie viel kostet …?** *Vee feel kostet*
When?	**Wann?** *van*
When will … arrive?	**Wann kommt … an?** *van komt … an*
When will … leave?	**Wann fährt … ab?** *van fairt … ap*

ARRIVAL

Import restrictions between EU countries have been relaxed on items for personal use or consumption that are bought duty-paid within the EU. Suggested maximum: 90*l* wine or 60*l* sparkling wine, 20*l* fortified wine, 10*l* spirits and 110*l* beer.

Passport control

We have a joint passport.	**Wir haben einen gemeinsamen Pass.** *veer haaben ienen gemiensaamen pass*
The children are on this passport.	**Die Kinder sind auf diesem Pass eingetragen.** *dee kinder zint owf deezem pass iengertraagen*
What's the purpose of your visit?	**Was ist der Zweck Ihres Aufenthalts?** *vass ist dehr zvayk eeress owfenthalts*
I'm here on vacation [holiday].	**Ich bin im Urlaub hier.** *ikh bin im oorlowp heer*
I'm here on business.	**Ich bin geschäftlich hier.** *ikh bin geshehftlikh heer*
I'm just passing through.	**Ich bin nur auf der Durchreise.** *ikh bin nur owf dehr durkhriezeh*
I'm ...	**Ich reise ...** *ikh riezeh*
on my own	**allein** *allien*
with my family	**mit meiner Familie** *mit miener fameelieh*
with a group	**mit einer Gruppe** *mit iener gruppeh*

Document Requirements

UK	valid passport; visitor's passport; or British Excursion document (valid 60 hours)
U.S./Can.	valid passport

Duty Free Into:	Cigarettes	Cigars	Tobacco	Spirits	Wine
Germany	200	50	250g	1*l*	or 2*l*
Switz./Austria	1) 200 or	50 or	250g	1*l*	and 2*l*
	2) 400 or	100 or	500g	1*l*	and 2*l*
Canada	200 and	50 and	200g	1*l*	or 1*l*
U.K.	200 or	50 or	250g	1*l*	and 2*l*
U.S.	200 and	100 and	discr.	1*l*	or 1*l*

1) EU residents; 2) non-EU residents

Customs

I have only the normal allowances.	**Ich habe nur die erlaubten Mengen.** *ikh haabeh nur dee ehrlowbten mengen*
It's a gift.	**Es ist ein Geschenk.** *ess ist ien geshenk*
It's for my personal use.	**Es ist für meinen persönlichen Gebrauch.** *ess ist fewr mienen payrzurnlikhen gebrowkh*

YOU MAY HEAR

Haben Sie etwas zu verzollen?	Do you have anything to declare?
Das müssen Sie verzollen.	You must pay duty on this.
Wo haben Sie das gekauft?	Where did you buy this?
Bitte öffnen Sie diese Tasche.	Please open this bag.
Haben Sie noch mehr Gepäck?	Do you have any more luggage?

Duty-free shopping

What currency is this in?	**In welcher Währung ist das?** *in velkher vairung ist dass*
Can I pay in …	**Kann ich mit … bezahlen?** *kan ikh mit … betsaalen*
dollars	**Dollars** *dollarz*
euros	**Euro** *oyroh*
pounds	**Pfund** *pfunt*

YOU MAY SEE

PASSKONTROLLE	passport control
GRENZÜBERGANG	border crossing
POLIZEI	police
ZOLL	customs
ANMELDEFREIE WAREN	nothing to declare
ANMELDEPFLICHTIGE WAREN	goods to declare
ZOLLFREIE WAREN	duty-free goods

PLANE

The national German, Austrian and Swiss airlines all run frequent internal services. There are generally good connections between the airport and downtown.

Tickets and reservations

When is the … flight to Berlin?	**Wann geht der … Flug nach Berlin?** *van gayt dehr … floog naakh behrleen*
first/next/last	**erste/nächste/letzte** *ehrsteh/naikhsteh/letsteh*
I'd like 2 … tickets to …	**Ich hätte gern zwei … nach …** *ikh hetteh gehrn tsvie … naakh*
one-way [single]	**einfache Flugtickets** *ienfakheh floogtikets*
round-trip [return]	**Rückflugtickets** *rewkfloogtikets*
first class	**erste Klasse** *ehrsteh klasseh*
business class	**Businessklasse** *biznessklasseh*
economy class	**Touristenklasse** *tooristenklasseh*
How much is a flight to …?	**Wie viel kostet ein Flug nach …?** *Vee feel kostet ien floog naakh*
Are there any supplements?	**Kommen da noch Zuschläge hinzu?** *kommen daa nokh tsooshlaigeh hinntsoo*
I'd like to … my reservation.	**Ich möchte meine Reservierung …** *ikh murkhteh mieneh rezehrveerung …*
cancel	**stornieren** *shtorneeren*
change	**ändern** *ehndern*
confirm	**bestätigen** *beshtaitigen*

Inquiries about the flight

How long is the flight?	**Wie lange dauert der Flug?** *vee langeh dowert dehr floog*
What time does the plane leave?	**Wann fliegt die Maschine ab?** *van fleegt dee masheeneh ap*
What time will we arrive?	**Wann kommen wir an?** *van kommen veer an*
What time do I have to check in?	**Wann muss ich einchecken?** *van muss ikh ientsheken*

Checking in

Where is the check-in desk
for flight …?

**Wo ist der Abfertigungsschalter
für den Flug …?** *voa ist dehr
apfehrtigungz-shalter fewr
dayn floog …*

I have …

Ich habe … *ikh haabeh*

3 suitcases to check in

drei Koffer für die Abfertigung
drie koffer fewr dee apfehrtigung

1 piece of hand luggage

zwei Stück Handgepäck
tsvie shtewk hantgepehk

YOU MAY HEAR

Ihr Flugticket/Ihren Pass, bitte. Your ticket/passport please.
Möchten Sie am Fenster oder Would you like a window or an
am Gang sitzen? aisle seat?
Raucher oder Nichtraucher? Smoking or non-smoking?
Wie viele Gepäckstücke How many pieces of baggage
haben Sie? do you have?
Sie haben Übergepäck. You have excess baggage.
Sie müssen pro Kilo You'll have to pay a supple-
Übergepäck einen Zuschlag ment of … euros per kilo of
von … Euro zahlen. excess baggage.
Das ist als Handgepäck zu That's too heavy/large for hand
schwer/groß. baggage.
Haben Sie diese Taschen Did you pack these bags
selbst gepackt? yourself?

YOU MAY SEE

ANKUNFT arrivals
ABFLUG departures
SICHERHEITSKONTROLLE security check
LASSEN SIE IHR GEPÄCK Do not leave bags unattended!
NICHT UNBEWACHT!

Information

Is there a delay on the flight?	**Hat der Flug Verspätung?** *hat dehr floog fehrshpaitung*
How late will it be?	**Wie viel Verspätung hat er?** *Vee feel fehrshpaitung hat ehr*
Has the flight from ... landed?	**Ist der Flug aus ... gelandet?** *ist dehr floog owss ... gelandet*
Which gate does the flight to ... leave from?	**An welchem Flugsteig geht der Flug nach ...?** *an velkhem floogshtieg gayrt dehr floog naakh*

Boarding/In-flight

Your boarding card, please.	**Ihre Bordkarte, bitte.** *eerer bortkarteh bitteh*
Could I have something to drink/eat, please?	**Kann ich bitte etwas zu trinken/essen haben?** *kan ikh bitteh etvass tsoo trinken/essen haaben*
Please wake me for the meal.	**Bitte wecken Sie mich zum Essen.** *bitteh veken zee mikh tsum essen*
What time will we arrive?	**Wann kommen wir an?** *van kommen veer an*
I feel airsick.	**Ich bin luftkrank.** *ikh bin luftkrank*
An airsickness bag, please.	**Eine Spucktüte, bitte.** *ieneh shpuktewteh bitteh*

Arrival

Where is/are ...?	**Wo ist/sind ...?** *voa ist/zint*
currency exchange	**die Wechselstube** *dee vekselshtoobeh*
buses	**die Busse** *dee busseh*
car rental	**die Autovermietung** *dee owtofehrmeetung*
exit	**der Ausgang** *dehr owsgang*
taxis	**die Taxis** *dee taksiss*
telephone	**das Telefon** *dass taylayfoan*
Is there a bus into town?	**Gibt es einen Bus in die Stadt?** *gipt ess ienen buss in dee shtat*
How do I get to the ... Hotel?	**Wie komme ich zum ... Hotel?** *vee kommeh ikh tsum ... hottel*

Luggage/Baggage

Where no porters are available, you might find luggage carts (Kofferkulis). In Germany they tend to be coin-operated (€1–2, returnable after use).

Porter! Excuse me!	**Gepäckträger! Entschuldigung.** *gepehktraiger entshuldiggoong*
Could you take my luggage …?	**Können Sie mein Gepäck … tragen?** *kurnen zee mien gepehk … traagen*
to a taxi/bus	**zu einem Taxi/Bus** *tsoo ienem taksi/buss*
Where is/are …?	**Wo ist/sind …?** *voa ist/zint*
luggage carts [trolleys]	**die Kofferkulis** *dee kofferkooliss*
baggage lockers	**die Schließfächer** *dee shleesfehkher*
baggage check [left-luggage office]	**die Gepäckaufbewahrung** *dee gepehkowfbevaarung*
baggage claim	**die Gepäckausgabe** *dee gepehkowsgaabeh*
Where is the luggage from flight …?	**Wo ist das Gepäck vom Flug …?** *voa ist dass gepehk fom floog*

Loss and theft

My luggage has been lost/stolen.	**Mein Gepäck ist verloren gegangen/ gestohlen worden.** *mien gepehk ist fehrloaren gegangen/geshtoalen vorden*
My suitcase was damaged.	**Mein Koffer ist beschädigt worden.** *mien koffer ist beshaidigt vorden*
Our luggage has not arrived.	**Unser Gepäck ist nicht angekommen.** *unzer gepehk ist nikht angekommen*

YOU MAY HEAR

Wie sieht Ihr Gepäck aus?	What does your luggage look like?
Haben Sie den Gepäckschein?	Do you have the claim check?
Ihr Gepäck könnte heute später ankommen.	Your luggage may arrive later today.
Rufen Sie diese Nummer an, um nachzufragen, ob Ihr Gepäck angekommen ist.	Call this number to check if your luggage has arrived.

TRAIN

Children under 4 travel free on German railways, those aged 4–11 pay half fare. Children under 6 travel free in Austria. On most trains you can book a parent-child compartment (**Baby-Kleinkindabteil**), which is designed for parents with children and has a changing table (**Wickeltisch**).

Check out available reductions and travel cards (Eurailpass, Freedom Pass, Inter-Rail, Euro-Minigruppe); children (Puzzle-Ticket Junior); travel for a set number of days in one country (Euro-Domino, Swiss Flexipass, German Rail Pass); groups (Euro-Minigruppe); under 26 (Inter-Rail, Freedom).

InterCityExpress (ICE)	high-speed InterCity within Germany; luxury facilities.
EuroCity/InterCity (EC/IC)	long-distance InterCity connecting German and other European cities.
InterRegio (IR)	local trains connecting with the **IC** train network.
Nahverkehrszug	local train, stopping at all stations; (Austria: **Personenzug;** Switzerland: **Regionalzug).**
RegionalExpress (RE)	medium distance train, connecting outlying areas with the city.
RegionalBahn (RB	local train, stopping at all stations.
StadtExpress (SE)	commuter trains connecting outlying communities to the city.
S-Bahn (S)	fast commuter train covering a shorter distance than the **StadtExpress**.
Nachtzüge	night trains with either sleeping-car compartments (**Schlafwagen**) or berths (**Liegewagen);** supplement payable for bedding; reservations are usually necessary.
Inter-City-Night (ICN)	night train with the comfort of hotel-standard coaches; tourist class available with reclining seats (**Liegesessel**); cars, motorcycles, and bicycles are also transported by the **ICN.**
City-Night-Line (CNL)	similar to the **ICN** running between Vienna and Cologne, Hamburg and Zurich.

To the station

How do I get to the
rail station/main rail station?

**Wie komme ich zum
Bahnhof/Hauptbahnhof?** *vee
kommeh ikh tsum baanhoaf/
howptbaanhoaf*

Do trains to Heidelberg
leave from Mannheim
Station?

**Fahren die Züge nach Heidelberg
vom Mannheimer Bahnhof ab?**
*faaren dee tsewgeh naakh hiedelbehrg
fom manhiemer baanhoaf ap*

Is it far?

Ist es weit? *eest es viet*

Can I leave my car there?

**Kann ich mein Auto dort stehen
lassen?** *kan ikh mien owto dort
shtayenlasen*

At the station

Where is/are the …?

Wo ist/sind …? *voa ist/zint*

currency exchange office

die Wechselstube *dee vekselshtoobeh*

information desk

die Auskunft *dee owskunft*

baggage check
[left-luggage office]

die Gepäckaufbewahrung
dee gepehkowfbevaarung

lost-and-found

das Fundbüro *dass funtbewroa*

luggage lockers

die Schließfächer
dee shleesfehkher

platforms

die Bahnsteige *dee baanshtiegeh*

ticket office

der Fahrkartenschalter
dehr faarkartenshalter

waiting room

der Wartesaal *dehr vartezaal*

YOU MAY SEE

ABFAHRT	departures
ANKUNFT	arrivals
AUSGANG	exit
AUSKUNFT	information
EINGANG	entrance
ZU DEN BAHNSTEIGEN	to the platforms

Tickets

Where can I buy tickets?	**Wo kann ich Fahrkarten kaufen?** *voa kan ikh faarkarten kowfen*
I'd like a … to …	**Ich hätte gern … nach …** *ikh hetteh gehrn … naakh*
one-way [single] ticket	**eine einfache Fahrkarte** *iener ienfakheh faarkarteh*
round-trip [return] ticket	**eine Rückfahrkarte** *ieneh rewkfaarkarteh*
first/second class ticket	**eine Fahrkarte erster/zweiter Klasse** *iener faarkarteh ehrster/tsvieter klasseh*
I'd like to reserve a seat.	**Ich möchte einen Platz reservieren.** *ikh murkhteh ienen plats rezehrveeren*
aisle seat	**einen Platz am Gang** *ienen plats am gang*
window seat	**einen Fensterplatz** *ienen fensterplats*
berth	**einen Liegewagenplatz** *ienen leegevaagenplats*
Is there a sleeping car [sleeper]?	**Gibt es einen Liegewagen?** *gipt ess ienen leegevaagen*
I'd like a(n) … berth.	**Ich möchte … schlafen.** *ikh murkhteh … shlaafen*
upper/lower	**oben/unten** *oaben/oonten*
Can I buy a ticket on board?	**Kann ich im Zug eine Fahrkarte lösen?** *kan ikh im tsoog ieneh faarkarteh lurzen*

Price

How much is that?	**Wie viel kostet das?** *vee feel kostet dass*
Is there a discount for …?	**Gibt es eine Ermäßigung für …?** *gipt ess ieneh ehrmaissigung fewr*
children/families	**Kinder/Familien** *kinder/fameelien*
senior citizens	**Senioren** *zenioaren*
students	**Studenten** *shtudenten*
There is a supplement of …	**Sie müssen einen Zuschlag von … zahlen.** *zee mewssen ienen tsooshlaahkh fon … tsaalen*

Queries

Do I have to change trains?
Muss ich umsteigen?
muss ikh umshtiegen

You have to change at …
Sie müssen in … umsteigen. *zee mewssen in … umshtiegen*

How long is this ticket valid for?
Wie lange ist diese Fahrkarte gültig?
vee langeh ist deezeh faarkarteh gewltikh

Can I take my bicycle on the train?
Kann ich mein Fahrrad im Zug mitnehmen? *kan ikh mien faarraat im tsoog mitnaymen*

Can I return on the same ticket?
Kann ich mit derselben Fahrkarte zurückfahren? *kan ikh mit dehrzelben faarkarteh tsoorewkfaaren*

In which car [coach] is my seat?
In welchem Wagen ist mein Platz?
in velkhem vaagen ist mien plats

Is there a dining car on the train?
Führt der Zug einen Speisewagen?
fewrt dehr tsoog ienen shpiezevaagen

Train times

Could I have a timetable?
Kann ich einen Fahrplan haben?
kan ikh ienen faarplaan haaben

When is the … train to Berne?
Wann fährt der … Zug nach Bern?
van fairt dehr … tsoog naakh behrn

first/next/last
erste/nächste/letzte
ehrsteh/naikhsteh/letsteh

How frequent are the trains to...?
Wie oft fahren die Züge nach …?
vee oft faaren dee tsewgeh naakh

once/twice a day
einmal/zweimal am Tag
ienmaal/tsviemaal am taag

5 times a day
fünfmal am Tag *fewnfmaal am taag*

every hour
jede Stunde *yaydeh shtundeh*

What time do they leave?	**Wann fahren sie ab?** *van faaren zee ap*
on the hour	**zur vollen Stunde** *tsoor follen shtundeh*
20 minutes past the hour	**um zwanzig Minuten nach** *um tsvantsikh minooten naakh*

What time does the train stop at …?	**Wann hält der Zug in …?** *van hehlt dehr tsoog in*
What time does the train arrive in …?	**Wann kommt der Zug in … an?** *van komt dehr tsoog in … an*
How long is the trip? [journey]	**Wie lange dauert die Fahrt?** *vee langeh dowert dee faart*
Is the train on time?	**Ist der Zug pünktlich?** *ist dehr tsoog pewnktlikh*

Departures

Which platform does the train to … leave from?	**Auf welchem Bahnsteig fährt der Zug nach … ab?** *owf velkhem baanshtieg fairt dehr tsoog naakh … ap*
Where is platform 4?	**Wo ist Bahnsteig vier?** *voa ist baanshtieg feer*
over there	**dort drüben** *dort drewben*
on the left/right	**auf der linken/rechten Seite** *owf dehr linken/rekhten zieteh*
under the underpass	**durch die Unterführung (hindurch)** *doorkh dee unterfewrung (hinndoorkh)*
Where do I change for …?	**Wo muss ich nach … umsteigen?** *voa muss ikh naakh … umshtiegen*
How long will I have to wait for a connection?	**Wie lange muss ich auf einen Anschluss warten?** *vee langer muss ikh owf ienen anshluss varten*

IN A TRAIN STATION

Zweimal nach Berlin, bitte. *tzwiemahl nakh berleen bitteh*
(Two tickets to Berlin, please.)
Einfach oder hin und zurück? *ienfakh ohder hin oond tzoorewk* *(One way or round trip?)*
Hin und zurück, bitte. *hin oond tzoorewk bitteh*
(Round trip, please.)

Boarding

Is this the platform for the train to …?
Ist das der Bahnsteig für den Zug nach …?
ist dass der baanshtieg fewr dayn tsoog naakh

Is this the train to …?
Ist dies der Zug nach …?
ist deez dehr tsoog naakh

Is this seat free?
Ist dieser Platz frei?
ist deezer plats frie

I think that's my seat.
Ich glaube, das ist mein Platz.
ikh glowbeh dass ist mien plats

Are there any seats/ berths available?
Sind noch Plätze/Schlafplätze frei?
zint nokh plehtseh/shlaafpletseh frie

Do you mind …?
Stört es Sie, …? *shturt ess zee*

  if I sit here?
  wenn ich hier sitze? *ven ikh heer zitseh*

  if I open the window?
  wenn ich das Fenster öffne?
  ven ikh dass fenster urfneh

During the trip

How long are we stopping here?
Wie lange halten wir hier?
vee langeh halten veer heer

When do we get to …?
Wann kommen wir in … an?
van kommen veer in … an

Have we passed …?
Sind wir schon an … vorbeigekommen?
zint veer shoan ahn …foarbiegekommen

Where is the dining/ sleeping car?
Wo ist der Speisewagen/Schlafwagen?
voa ist dehr shpiezevaagen/shlaafvaagen

Where is my berth?
Wo ist mein Schlafplatz?
voa ist mien shlaafplats

I've lost my ticket.
Ich habe meine Fahrkarte verloren.
ikh haabeh mieneh faarkarteh fehrloaren

YOU MAY SEE

BUSHALTESTELLE	Bus stop
RAUCHEN VERBOTEN	No smoking
NOTAUSGANG	Emergency exit

LONG-DISTANCE BUS [COACH]

Where is the
bus station?

Wo ist der Busbahnhof?
voa ist dehr bussbaanhoaf

When's the next
bus to …?

**Wann fährt der nächste Bus
nach …?** *van fairt dehr naikhsteh
buss naakh*

Which stop does it
leave from?

Von welcher Haltestelle fährt er ab?
fon velkher halteshteleh fairt ehr ap

Where are the bus
stops?

Wo sind die Bushaltestellen?
voa zint dee busshalteshtelen

Does the bus stop at …?

Hält der Bus in …?
hehlt dehr buss in

BUS/STREETCAR [TRAM]

Look for travel cards or booklets (for a day, week/ month) valid on buses,
streetcars and subways. Booklets of 10 tickets (**10er Karten**) are another
cheap way to travel. Always validate your ticket in the machine marked with
the sign **Hier Fahrschein entwerten**. If you get caught without a ticket
you'll have to pay a hefty fine.

Where is the bus station?

Wo ist der Busbahnhof?
voa ist dehr bussbaanhoaf

Where can I get a bus/
streetcar [tram] to …?

**Wo hält der Bus/die Straßenbahn
zum …?** *voa hehlt dehr buss/dee
shtraassenbaan tsum*

the airport

Flughafen
flooghaafen

the railway station

Bahnhof
baanhoaf

the town center

Stadtzentrum
shtat-tsentrum

YOU MAY HEAR	
Gehen Sie zu der Haltestelle dort drüben.	Go to that stop over there.
Nehmen Sie die Linie zehn.	Take bus number 10.
Sie müssen in … umsteigen.	You must change buses at …

78

Buying tickets

Where can I buy tickets?

Wo kann ich Fahrscheine kaufen?
voa kan ikh faarshieneh kowfen

A one-way [single]
ticket to…

Eine einfache Fahrt nach …
ieneh ienfakheh faart naakh …

A round-trip [return]
ticket to …

Einmal nach … und zurück.
ienmaal naakh … unt tsoorewk

A booklet of tickets,
please.

Ein Fahrscheinheft, bitte.
ien faarshienheft bitteh

How much is
the fare to …?

Wie viel kostet die Fahrt nach …?
vee feel kostet dee faart naakh

Traveling

Is this the right bus
to the town hall?

Ist dies der richtige Bus zum Rathaus?
*ist deez dehr rikhtigeh buss tsum
raathowss*

Could you tell me
when to get off?

**Können Sie mir sagen, wann ich
aussteigen muss?** *kurnen zee meer
zaagen van ikh ows-shtiegen muss*

Do I have to change
buses?

Muss ich umsteigen?
muss ikh umshtiegen

How many stops
are there to …?

Wie viele Haltestellen sind es bis …?
vee feeleh halteshtelen zint ess biss

It's 3 stops from here.

Es sind drei Haltestellen von hier.
ess zint drie halteshtelen fon heer

Next stop, please!

Die nächste Haltestelle, bitte!
dee naikhsteh halteshteleh bitteh

AT THE BUS STOP

Entschuldigung, welcher Bus fährt in die Stadt?
entshuhldigoong velkher buss fairt in dee shtaht
(Excuse me, which bus goes downtown?)
Die Linie 17. *dee leenyeh zeebtzehn (Bus number 17.)*
Vielen Dank. *tveelen dahnkh (Thank you very much.)*
Bitte bitte. *bitteh bitteh (You're very welcome.)*

79

SUBWAY [METRO]

There are excellent subway systems in Berlin, Bonn, Düsseldorf, Cologne, Frankfurt, Hamburg and Munich and a smaller system in Vienna. Large maps outside each station make the systems easy to use. Tickets should be purchased from the vending machines at all **U-Bahn** stations before you board a train. Ticket inspection is common and there are hefty fines for invalid tickets.

Look for multiple tickets and day or month passes that make traveling cheaper.

General inquiries

Where's the nearest subway station?
Wo ist die nächste U-Bahnstation?
voa ist dee naikhsteh oo-baanshtatsioan

Where do I buy a ticket?
Wo kann ich eine Fahrkarte kaufen?
voa kan ikh ieneh faarkarteh kowfen

Could I have a map?
Kann ich einen Plan haben?
kan ikh ienen plaan haaben

Traveling

Which line should I take for the main station?
Welche Linie fährt zum Hauptbahnhof?
velkheh leenieh fairt tsum howptbaanhoaf

Is this the right train for …?
Ist dies die richtige U-Bahn nach …?
ist deez dee rikhtiggeh oo-baan naakh

Which stop is it for …?
An welcher Haltestelle muss ich für … aussteigen? *an velkher halteshteleh muss ikh fewr … owsshtiegen*

How many stops is it to …?
Wie viele Haltestellen sind es bis …?
vee feeleh halteshtelen zint ess biss

Is the next stop …?
Ist die nächste Haltestelle …?
ist dee naikhsteh halteshteleh

Where are we?
Wo sind wir? *voa zint veer*

Where do I change for …?
Wo muss ich nach … umsteigen?
voa muss ikh naakh … umshtiegen

What time is the last train to …?
Wann fährt die letzte U-Bahn nach …?
van fairt dee letsteh oo-baan naakh

FERRY

Companies operating services from the UK to the Continent include Stena Sealink, Hoverspeed, Brittany Ferries, P&O, Sally Ferries, North Sea Ferries, Scandinavian Seaways. Ferry services to the islands of the North Sea and Baltic Sea are popular, and reservations are advisable.

first/next/last	**erste/nächste/letzte** *ehrsteh/naikhsteh/letster*
A round-trip [return] ticket for …	**Eine Rückfahrkarte für …** *iener rewkfaarkarteh fewr*
1 car and 1 trailer [caravan]	**ein Auto und einen Wohnwagen** *ien owto unt ienen voanvaagen*
I want to reserve a …	**Ich möchte eine … buchen.** *ikh murkhteh ieneh … bookhen*
single/double cabin	**Einzelkabine/Doppelkabine** *ientselkabeeneh/doppelkabeeneh*

YOU MAY SEE

RETTUNGSRING	life preserver [life belt]
RETTUNGSBOOT	life boat
SAMMELPLATZ	muster station
KEIN ZUGANG ZU DEN	no access to
AUTODECKS	car decks

BOAT TRIPS

Is there a …?	**Gibt es …?** *gipt ess*
boat trip	**eine Schiffsfahrt** *ieneh shifsfaart*
river cruise	**eine Flussfahrt** *ieneh flussfaart*
What time does the boat leave?	**Wann fährt das Schiff ab?** *van fairt dass shif ap*
What time does the boat return?	**Wann kommt das Schiff wieder?** *van komt dass shif veeder*
Where does the boat stop?	**Wo hält das Schiff?** *voa hehlt dass shif*
Where can we buy tickets?	**Wo können wir Fahrkarten kaufen?** *voa kurnen veer faarkarten kowfen*

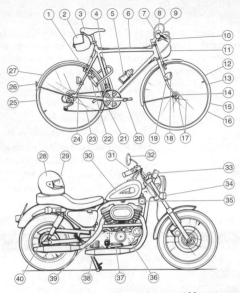

1	brake pad **Bremsbelag** m	21	lock **Schloss** nt
2	bicycle bag **Fahrradtasche** f	22	generator **Dynamo** m
3	saddle **Sattel** m	23	chain **Kette** f
4	pump **Luftpumpe** f	24	rear light **Rücklicht** nt
5	water bottle **Wasserflasche** f	25	rim **Felge** f
6	frame **Rahmen** m	26	reflectors **Rückstrahler** mpl
7	handlebars **Lenker** m	27	fender [mudguard] **Schutzblech** nt
8	bell **Klingel** f	28	helmet **Helm** m
9	brake cable **Bremskabel** nt	29	visor **Visier** nt
10	gear lever [shift] **Schalthebel** m	30	fuel tank **Tank** m
11	gear [control cable] **Schaltkabel** nt	31	clutch lever **Kupplungshebel** m
12	inner tube **Schlauch** m	32	mirror **Spiegel** m
13	front/back wheel **Vorderrad** nt/ **Hinterrad** nt	33	ignition **Zündung** f
14	axle **Achse** f	34	turn signal [indicator] **Blinker** m
15	tire [tyre] **Reifen** m	35	horn **Hupe** f
16	wheel **Rad** nt	36	engine **Motor** m
17	spokes **Speichen** fpl	37	gear **Schalthebel** m
18	bulb **Glühbirne** f	38	kick stand **Ständer** m
19	headlamp **Scheinwerfer** m	39	exhaust pipe **Auspuff** m
20	pedal **Pedal** nt20	40	chain **Kette** f

BICYCLE/MOTORBIKE

I'd like to rent a …	**Ich möchte … mieten.** *ikh murkhteh … meeten*
3/10 gear bicycle	**ein drei/zehn-Gang-Rad** *ien drie-/tsayn-gang-raat*
moped	**ein Moped** *ien moapet*
mountain bike	**ein Mountainbike** *ien mountainbike*
motorbike	**ein Motorrad** *ien moatorraat*
How much does it cost per day/week?	**Wie viel kostet es pro Tag/Woche?** *vee feel kostet ess proa taag/vokheh*
Do you require a deposit?	**Muss ich eine Kaution hinterlegen?** *muss ikh ieneh kowtsioan hinterlaygern*
The brakes don't work.	**Die Bremsen funktionieren nicht.** *dee bremzen funktsionneeren nikht*
There are no lights.	**Die Beleuchtung fehlt.** *dee beloykhtung faylt*
The front/rear tire has a flat [puncture].	**Der Vorderreifen/Hinterreifen hat einen Platten.** *dehr forder-riefen/hinter-riefen hat ienen platen*

HITCHHIKING

Hitchhiking is permitted everywhere except on expressways [motorways] and their access roads, but is not recommended for anyone. Alternatively, go to the **Mitfahrzentrale** (usually found in large towns) that matches drivers with those looking for lifts; you pay a fee to the **Mitfahrzentrale** and make a contribution for the gasoline [petrol].

Where are you heading?	**Wohin fahren Sie?** *voahinn faaren zee*
I'm heading for …	**Ich fahre nach …** *ikh faareh naakh*
Could you drop me off …?	**Können Sie mich … absetzen?** *kurnen zee mikh … apzetsen*
here	**hier** *heer*
at the … exit	**an der … Ausfahrt** *an dehr … owsfaart*
in the center	**im Zentrum** *im tsentrum*
Thanks for the lift.	**Danke für's Mitnehmen.** *dankeh fewrs mitnehmen*

TAXI/CAB

Catch a taxi at a taxi stand (**Taxistand**) or phone from wherever you are; numbers are listed under **Taxi** in the local phone book or advertised in phone booths. Taxis in Germany are beige-colored and all have meters.

Tipping suggestions:

Germany: round up bill; Austria: 10%; Switzerland: 15%.

Where can I get a taxi?	**Wo finde ich ein Taxi?** *voa findeh ikh ien taksi*
I'd like a taxi …	**Ich hätte gern … ein Taxi.** *ikh hetteh gehrn … ien taksi*
now	**sofort** *zofoart*
in an hour	**in einer Stunde** *in iener shtundeh*
for tomorrow at 9:00	**für morgen um neun Uhr** *fewr morgen um noyn oor*
The address is …	**Die Adresse ist …** *dee adresseh ist …*
Please take me ….	**Bitte bringen Sie mich …** *bitteh bringen zee mikh*
to the airport	**zum Flughafen** *tsum flooghaafen*
to the railway station	**zum Bahnhof** *tsum baanhoaf*
to the … Hotel	**zum … Hotel** *tsum … hottel*
to this address	**zu dieser Adresse** *tsoo deezer adresseh*
How much will it cost?	**Wie viel kostet das?** *vee feel kostet dass*
Please stop here.	**Bitte halten Sie hier.** *bitteh halten zee heer*
How much is that?	**Was kostet das?** *vass kostet dass*
Keep the change.	**Der Rest ist für Sie.** *dehr rest ist fewr zee*

AT A TAXI STAND

Was kostet es zum Flughafen? *vass kostet ess tsoom flooghaafen (How much is it to the airport?)*
Dreißig Euro. *driessikh oyroh (30 euros.)*
Dann fahren Sie uns, bitte. *dann faaren zee oons bitteh (Then take us, please.)*

CAR

While driving, the following documents must be carried: valid driver's license (**Führerschein**), registration (**Kraftfahrzeugzulassung**) and insurance documentation (**Versicherungsschein**). Insurance for minimum third-party risks is compulsory in Europe. It is recommended that you take out international motor insurance through your insurer.

Speed conversion chart

km	1	10	20	30	40	50	60	70	80	90	100	110	120	130
miles	0.6	6	12	19	25	31	37	44	50	56	62	68	75	81

Road network

Germany & Austria   **E** – international expressway (green – no tolls); **A** (**Autobahn**) – national expressway (white numbers, blue background); **B** (**Bundesstraße**) – main road; **L** (**Landstraße**) – secondary road; **G** (**Gemeindestraße**) – local road

Switzerland   **A** – expressway/motorway (toll free); **N** – main road; **E** – secondary road

Speed limits mph (km/h)	Built-up area	Outside built-up area	motorway
Germany	31 (50)	62 (100)	81 (130)
Austria	31 (50)	62 (100)	81 (130)
Switzerland	31 (50)	50 (80)	62-74 (100-120)

Essential equipment: warning triangle, nationality plate and first-aid kit; headlight beams must be adjusted for right-hand drive vehicles; wearing seat belts is compulsory (front and back).

Minimum driving age: Austria, Switzerland, Germany – 18;

Tolls are payable on some Austrian roads, mainly mountain passes. All roads are toll free in Germany, but for travel on Swiss motorways, a pass/vignette is required – available from tourist offices, customs, post offices and garages. It is valid for 1 year, non-transferable and to be attached to your windshield. An additional pass/vignette is required for trailers [caravans]. Vehicles "flash" to warn of their approach – it's not a signal for you to go. Note that the use of horns is prohibited in built-up areas. Alcohol limit in blood: max. 50mg/ 100ml. Note that any alcohol impairs concentration.

Car rental

You will need to produce a valid driver's license held for at least a year for Austria or Switzerland, or for 6 months for Germany.

Children's safety seats (**Kindersitze**) are compulsory for children under 12 and are available from car rental agencies; advance reservations recommended.

Minimum rental age: Germany, Austria, Switzerland – 21 (25 with some firms).

Where can I rent a car?	**Wo kann ich ein Auto mieten?** *voa kan ikh ien owto meeten*
I'd like to rent a car.	**Ich möchte ein Auto mieten.** *ikh murkhteh ien owto meeten*
a 2-/4-door car	**ein zweitüriges/viertüriges Auto** *ien tsvietewrigess/feertewriggess owto*
an automatic	**einen Automatikwagen** *ienen owtommaatikvaagen*
with 4-wheel drive	**mit Vierradantrieb** *mit feeraatantreeb*
with air conditioning	**mit Klimaanlage** *mit kleema-anlaageh*
I'd like it for a day/a week.	**Ich möchte es für einen Tag/eine Woche.** *ikh murkhteh ess fewr ienen taag/ieneh vokheh*
How much does it cost per day/week?	**Wie viel kostet es pro Tag/Woche?** *vee feel kostet ess proa taag/vokheh*
Is insurance included?	**Ist die Versicherung inbegriffen?** *ist dee fehrzikherung inbegriffen*
unlimited milage	**ohne Kilometerbegrenzung** *oahneh killommayterbegrentzoong*
What sort of fuel does it take?	**Welchen Treibstoff braucht es?** *velkhen triebshtoff browkht ess*
Could I have full insurance, please?	**Kann ich bitte eine Vollkaskoversicherung haben?** *kan ikh bitteh ieneh folkaskofehrzikherung haaben*

YOU MAY HEAR	
Kann ich Ihren Führerschein sehen?	May I see your driver's license?
Wer fährt?	Who will be driving?

Gas [Petrol] station

Where's the next gas station, please?	**Wo ist die nächste Tankstelle, bitte?** *voa ist dee naikhsteh tankshteleh bitteh*
Fill it up, please.	**Volltanken, bitte.** *foltanken bitteh*
liters of …, please.	**… Liter …, bitte.** *… leeter … bitteh*
super/premium	**Super** *zooper*
regular	**Normal** *normaal*
lead-free	**bleifreies Benzin** *bliefrie-ess bentseen*
diesel	**Diesel** *deezel*
I'm pump number …	**Zapfsäule Nummer …** *nummer*
Where is the air pump/ water?	**Wo ist die Luftpumpe/das Wasser?** *voa ist dee luftpumpe/dass vasser*

YOU MAY SEE

PREIS PRO LITER	price per liter

Parking

In most Blue Zones, you may park free for a limited time with a parking disk (available from gas stations, tourist offices and automobile clubs). Except for one-way streets, parking is only permitted on the right-hand side. No parking where you see these signs: **Halten verboten**; **Stationierungsverbot**. Vehicles that are illegally parked may be ticketed or towed.

Is there a parking lot [car park] nearby?	**Gibt es in der Nähe einen Parkplatz?** *gipt ess in dehr naieh ienen parkplats*
What's the charge per hour/per day?	**Wie viel kostet es pro Stunde/Tag?** *vee feel kostet ess proa shtundeh/taag*
Where do I pay?	**Wo muss ich bezahlen?** *voa muss ikh betsaalen*
Do you have some change for the parking meter?	**Haben Sie Kleingeld für die Parkuhr?** *haaben zee kliengelt fewr dee parkoor*
My car has been booted [clamped].	**Mein Auto ist mit einer Parkkralle festgesetzt worden.** *mien owto ist mit iener park-kraleh festgezetst vorden*

Breakdown

In case of a breakdown: refer to your breakdown assistance documents; or contact the breakdown service: Germany: **ADAC** ☎ 01802/22 22 22; Austria: **ÖAMTC** ☎ 120 or **ARBÖ** ☎ 123; Switzerland: ☎ 140. On German autobahns, the emergency phones connect you to the operator; ask for the **Pannendienst**.

Where is the nearest garage?	**Wo ist die nächste Reparaturwerkstatt?** *voa ist dee naikhsteh rayparatoorvehrkshtat*
I've had a breakdown.	**Ich habe eine Panne.** *ikh haabeh ieneh paneh*
Can you send a mechanic/tow truck?	**Können Sie einen Mechaniker/Abschleppwagen schicken?** *kurnen zee ienen mekhanikker/apshlepvaagen shiken*
I'm a member of ...	**Ich bin Mitglied im ...** *ikh bin mitgleet im*
My license plate number is ...	**Mein Kraftfahrzeugkennzeichen ist ...** *mien kaftfaartsoyk kentsiekhen ist*
The car is ...	**Das Auto steht ...** *dass owto shtayt*
on the highway	**auf der Autobahn** *owf dehr owtobaan*
2 km from ...	**zwei km von ... entfernt** *tsvie killommayter fon ... entfehrnt*
How long will you be?	**Wie lange dauert es, bis Sie kommen?** *vee langeh dowert ess biss zee kommen*

What is wrong?

My car won't start.	**Mein Auto springt nicht an.** *mie owto shpringt nikht an*
The battery is dead.	**Die Batterie ist leer.** *dee batteree ist layr*
I've run out of gasoline.	**Ich habe kein Benzin mehr.** *ikh haabeh kien bentseen mayr*
I have a flat [puncture].	**Ich habe einen Platten.** *ikh haabeh ienen platen*
The ... doesn't work.	**... funktioniert nicht. ...** *funktsioneert nikht*
I've locked the keys in the car.	**Ich habe die Schlüssel im Auto eingeschlossen.** *ikh haabeh dee shlewssel im owto iengeshlossen*

Repairs

Do you do repairs?	**Führen Sie Reparaturen aus?** *fewren zee rayparatooren owss*
Could you have a look at my car?	**Können Sie sich mein Auto ansehen?** *kurnen zee zikh mien owto anzayen*
Can you repair it (temporarily)?	**Können Sie es (provisorisch) reparieren?** *kurnen zee ess (provizoarish) raypareeren*
Please make only essential repairs.	**Bitte reparieren Sie nur das Nötigste.** *bitteh raypareeren zee noor dass nurtiggsteh*
Can I wait for it?	**Kann ich darauf warten?** *kan ikh dahrowf varten*
Can you repair it today?	**Können Sie es heute reparieren?** *kurnen zee ess hoyteh raypareeren*
When will it be ready?	**Wann wird es fertig?** *van veert ess fehrtikh*
How much will it cost?	**Wie viel wird das kosten?** *vee feel veert dass kosten*
That's outrageous!	**Das ist unverschämt!** *dass ist unfehrshaimt*
Can I have a receipt for the insurance?	**Kann ich eine Quittung für die Versicherung haben?** *kan ikh ieneh kvittung fewr dee fehrzikherung haaben*

YOU MAY HEAR

... funktioniert nicht.	The ... isn't working.
Ich habe die Ersatzteile nicht.	I don't have the parts.
Ich muss die Ersatzteile bestellen.	I will have to order the parts.
Ich kann es nur provisorisch reparieren.	I can only repair it temporarily.
Es kann nicht repariert werden.	It can't be repaired.
Es wird ... fertig.	It will be ready ...
heute noch	later today
morgen	tomorrow
in ... Tagen	in ... days

15 headlights **Scheinwerfer** mpl
16 license plate
   Nummernschild nt
17 fog lamp **Nebelscheinwerfer** m
18 turn signals [indicators]
   Blinker mpl
19 bumper **Stoßstange** f
20 tires [tyres] **Reifen** mpl
21 hubcap [wheel cover]
   Radkappe f
22 valve **Ventil** nt
23 wheels **Räder** ntpl
24 outside [wing] mirror
   Außenspiegel m
25 automatic locks [central
   locking] **Zentralverriegelung** f
26 lock **Schloss** nt
27 wheel rim **Felge** f
28 exhaust pipe **Auspuffrohr** nt
29 odometer [milometer]
   Kilometerzähler m

1 tail lights [back lights]
   Rücklichter ntpl
2 brakelights **Bremslichter** ntpl
3 trunk [boot] **Kofferraum** m
4 gas tank door [petrol cap]
   Tankdeckel m
5 window **Fenster** nt
6 seat belt **Sicherheitsgurt** m
7 sunroof **Schiebedach** nt
8 steering wheel **Lenkrad** nt
9 ignition **Zündung** f
10 ignition key **Zündschlüssel** m
11 windshield [windscreen]
   Windschutzscheibe f
12 windshield [windscreen]
   wipers **Scheibenwischer** mpl
13 windshield [windscreen]
   washer **Scheibenwaschanlage** f
14 hood [bonnet] **Motorhaube** f

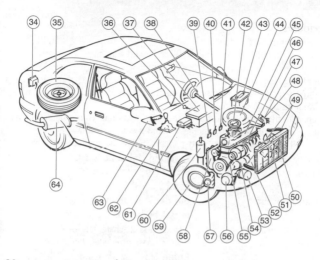

30	warning light **Warnlampe** f
31	fuel gauge **Benzinuhr** f
32	speedometer **Tachometer** m
33	oil gauge **Ölstandsanzeiger** m
34	tail lights **Rückfahrscheinwerfer** mpl
35	spare tire **Ersatzrad** nt
36	choke (in older cars) **Choke** m
37	heater **Heizung** f
38	steering column **Lenksäule** f
39	accelerator **Gaspedal** nt
40	brake pedal **Bremspedal** nt
41	clutch **Kupplung** f
42	carburetor **Vergaser** m
43	battery **Batterie** f
44	air filter **Luftfilter** m
45	camshaft **Nockenwelle** f
46	alternator **Lichtmaschine** f
47	distributor **Verteiler** m
48	points (in older cars) **Unterbrecherkontakte** mpl

49	radiator hose (top/bottom) **Kühlwasserleitung** f
50	radiator **Kühler** m
51	fan **Ventilator** m
52	engine **Motor** m
53	oil filter **Ölfilter** m
54	starter motor **Anlasser** m
55	fan belt **Keilriemen** m
56	horn **Hupe** f
57	brake pads **Bremsbeläge** mpl
58	transmission [gearbox] **Getriebe** nt
59	brakes **Bremsen** fpl
60	shock absorbers **Stoßdämpfer** mpl
61	fuses **Sicherungen** fpl
62	gear shift [lever] **Schaltknüppel** m
63	handbrake **Handbremse** f
64	muffler **Auspufftopf** m

Accidents

In the event of an accident:

1. put your warning triangle about 100 m behind your car;
2. report the accident to the police (compulsory if there is personal injury); don't leave before they arrive;
3. show your driver's license and insurance papers; and give your name, address, insurance company to the other party;
4. report to the insurance office of the third party and your own company;
5. don't make any written statement without advice of a lawyer;
6. note all details of the other party and any independent witnesses.

There has been an accident.	**Es ist ein Unfall passiert.** *ess ist ien unfal passeert*
It's …	**Es ist …** *ess ist*
on the autobahn	**auf der Autobahn** *owf dehr owtobaan*
near …	**in der Nähe von …** *in dehr naieh fon*
Where's the nearest telephone?	**Wo ist das nächste Telefon?** *voa ist dass naikhsteh taylayfoan*
Call …	**Rufen Sie ..** *roofen zee*
the police	**die Polizei** *dee pollitsie*
an ambulance	**einen Krankenwagen** *ienen krankenvaagen*
a doctor	**einen Arzt** *ienen aartst*
the fire department	**die Feuerwehr** *dee foyervehr*
Could you help me, please?	**Können Sie mir bitte helfen?** *kurnen zee meer bitteh helfen*

Injuries

There are people injured.	**Es gibt Verletzte.** *ess gipt fehrletsteh*
No one is hurt.	**Es ist niemand verletzt.** *ess ist neemant fehrletst*
He/She is bleeding.	**Er/Sie blutet.** *ehr/zee blootet*
She's unconscious.	**Sie ist bewusstlos.** *zee ist bevustloass*
He can't breathe.	**Er bekommt keine Luft.** *ehr bekomt kieneh looft*
Don't move him.	**Bewegen Sie ihn nicht.** *bevaygen zee een nikht*

Legal matters

What's your insurance company?	**Ihre Versicherungsgesellschaft, bitte?** *eerer fehrzikherungzgezelshaft bitteh*
What's your name and address?	**Ihr Name und Ihre Anschrift?** *eer naameh unt eereh anshrift*
He ran into me.	**Er ist mit mir zusammengestoßen.** *ehr ist mit meer tsoozammengeshtoassen*
She was driving too fast.	**Sie ist zu schnell gefahren.** *zee ist tsoo shnel gefaaren*
I was (only) driving … km/h.	**Ich bin (nur) … km/h gefahren.** *ikh bin (noor) … kilomayter proa shtunder gefaaren*
I had right of way.	**Ich hatte Vorfahrt.** *ikh hateh foarfaart*
I need an interpreter.	**Ich brauche einen Dolmetscher.** *ikh browkheh ienen dolmecher*
He/She saw everything.	**Er/Sie hat alles gesehen.** *ehr/zee hat alles gezayen*
The license plate number was …	**Das Kraftfahrzeugkennzeichen war …** *dass kraftfaartzoygkentsiekhen vaar*

YOU MAY HEAR

Kann ich bitte Ihren … sehen?	Can I see your … please?
Führerschein	driver's license
Versicherungsschein	insurance certificate
Kraftfahrzeugschein	vehicle registration
Wann ist es passiert?	What time did it happen?
Wo ist es passiert?	Where did it happen?
Gibt es Zeugen?	Are there any witnesses?
Sie sind zu schnell gefahren.	You were speeding.
Ihre Beleuchtung funktioniert nicht.	Your lights aren't working.
Sie müssen (sofort) ein Bußgeld bezahlen.	You'll have to pay a fine (on the spot).
Sie müssen auf der Wache eine Aussage machen.	We need you to make a statement at the station.

ASKING DIRECTIONS

Excuse me.

Where is …?

How do I
get to ...?

Where is …?

Can you show me on
the map where I am?

Can you repeat that,
please?

More slowly, please.

Thanks for your help.

Entschuldigung *entshuldigoong*

Wie komme ich nach …?
ve kommeh ikh naakh

Wo ist …? *voa ist*

**Können Sie mir auf der Karte zeigen, wo
ich bin?** *kurnen zee meer owf dehr karteh
tsiegen voa ikh bin*

Können Sie das bitte wiederholen?
kurnen zee dass bitteh veederhoalen

Langsamer, bitte. *langzaamer bitteh*

Vielen Dank für Ihre Hilfe.
feelen dank fewr eereh hilfeh

Traveling by car

Is this the right road
for …?

How far is it to …?

Where does this road
lead?

How do I get onto the
highway [motorway]?

What's the next town
called?

How long does it take
by car?

Ist dies die richtige Straße nach …?
ist deez dee rikhtigeh shtraasseh naakh

Wie weit ist es nach …?
vee viet ist ess naakh

Wohin führt diese Straße?
voahinn fewrt deezeh shtraasseh

Wie komme ich auf die Autobahn?
vee kommeh ikh owf dee owtobaan

Wie heißt die nächste Stadt?
vee hiest dee naikhsteh shtat

Wie lange dauert es mit dem Auto?
vee langeh dowert ess mit daym owto

ON THE STREET

Entschuldigung, wie weit ist es zum Bahnhof? *entshuhldigoong vee viet ist ess tzoom baanhoaf (Excuse me, how
far is it to the train station?)*

Ungefähr 3 Kilometer. *oonghefair drie killommayter (About
3 kilometers/1.8 miles.)*

Vielen Dank. *tveelen dahnkh (Thank you very much.)*

YOU MAY HEAR

Es ist ...	It's ...
geradeaus	straight ahead
auf der linken/rechten Seite	on the left/right
am Ende der Straße	at the end of the street
an der Ecke	at the corner
um die Ecke	round the corner
in Richtung ...	in the direction of ...
gegenüber .../hinter ...	opposite .../behind ...
neben .../nach ...	next to .../after ...
Gehen Sie die ... entlang.	Go down the ...
Seitenstraße/Hauptstraße	side street/main street
Gehen Sie über ...	Cross the ...
den Platz/die Brücke	square/bridge
Nehmen Sie ...	Take the ...
die dritte Straße rechts	third turn to the right
Biegen Sie ... links ab.	Turn left ...
nach der ersten Ampel	after the first traffic light
an der zweiten Kreuzung	at the second intersection
Es liegt ... von hier.	It's ... of here.
nördlich/südlich	north/south
östlich/westlich	east/west
Nehmen Sie die Straße nach ...	Take the road for ...
Sie sind auf der falschen Straße.	You're on the wrong road.
Folgen Sie den Schildern nach ...	Follow the signs for ...
Es ist ...	It's ...
nah/nicht weit/weit	close/not far/a long way
fünf Minuten zu Fuß	5 minutes on foot
zehn Minuten im Auto	10 minutes by car
etwa zehn Kilometer entfernt	about 10 km away

Road signs

YOU MAY SEE

ANLIEGER FREI	access only
AUSWEICHSTRECKE	alternative route
EINBAHNSTRASSE	one-way street
EINORDNEN	get in lane
GESPERRT	road closed
LICHT AN	use headlights
UMLEITUNG	detour [diversion]
VORFAHRT GEWÄHREN	yield [give way]

Town plans & maps

YOU MAY SEE

Altstadt	old town
Bahnhof	station
Bushaltestelle	bus stop
Buslinie	bus route
Flughafen	airport
Fußgängerüberweg	pedestrian crossing
Fußgängerzone	pedestrian zone [precinct]
Kino	movie theater [cinema]
Kirche	church
öffentliches Gebäude	public building
Park	park
Parkplatz	parking lot [car park]
Polizei	police
Postamt	post office
Sportplatz	playing field [sports ground]
Stadion	stadium
Standort	you are here
Taxistand	taxi stand [rank]
Theater	theater
Toiletten	bathrooms [toilets]
U-Bahnstation	subway [metro] station
Verkehrsbüro	information office

SIGHTSEEING

Tourist information offices are often situated in the town center; look for **Fremdenverkehrsamt** or **Verkehrsbüro.**

Events to look for are wine and beer festivals (e.g. **Oktoberfest** in Munich), **Fasching** (carnival time leading up to Ash Wednesday).

Where's the tourist office?	**Wo ist das Fremdenverkehrsbüro?** *voa ist dass fremdenfehrkayrsbewroa*
What are the main points of interest?	**Welches sind die wichtigsten Sehenswürdigkeiten?** *velkhess zint dee vikhtiggsten zayenzvewrdikhkieten*
We're here for …	**Wir sind … hier.** *veer zint … heer*
only a few hours	**nur ein paar Stunden** *noor ien paar shtunden*
a day	**einen Tag** *ienen taag*
a week	**eine Woche** *ieneh vokheh*
Can you recommend …?	**Können Sie … empfehlen?** *kurnen zee … empfaylen*
a sightseeing tour	**eine Stadtrundfahrt** *ieneh shtatruntfaart*
an excursion	**einen Ausflug** *ienen owsfloog*
a boat trip	**eine Schiffsfahrt** *ieneh shiffsfaart*
Do you have any information on …?	**Haben Sie Informationen über …?** *haaben zee infoarmatsioanen ewber*
Are there any trips to …?	**Gibt es Ausflüge nach …?** *gipt ess owsflewgeh naakh*

ESSENTIAL

Wo bekommt man Karten?	Where do you get tickets?
Wie lange dauert die Führung?	How long does the guided tour last?
Zwei Karten, bitte.	Two tickets, please.
Wo sind die Toiletten?	Where's the bathroom/toilet?
Wo gibt's Souvenirs?	Where can I get souvenirs?
Wann müssen wir zurück sein?	When do we have to be back?

RESERVING AN EXCURSION

How much does the tour cost?	**Wie viel kostet die Rundfahrt?** *vee feel kostet dee runtfaart*
Is lunch included?	**Ist das Mittagessen inbegriffen?** *ist dass mittaagessen inbegriffen*
Where do we leave from?	**Wo fahren wir ab?** *voa faaren veer ap*
What time does the tour start?	**Wann beginnt die Rundfahrt?** *van begint dee runtfaart*
What time do we get back?	**Wann sind wir zurück?** *van zint veer tsoorewk*
Do we have free time in …?	**Haben wir in … Zeit zur freien Verfügung?** *haaben veer in … tsiet tsoor frieen fehrfewgung*
Is there an English-speaking guide?	**Gibt es einen Englisch sprechenden Führer?** *gipt ess ienen english shprekhenden fewrer*

ON TOUR

Are we going to see …?	**Werden wir … sehen?** *vehrden veer … zayen*
We'd like to have a look at the …	**Wir möchten … sehen.** *veer murkhten … zayen*
Can we stop here …?	**Können wir hier anhalten, …?** *kurnen veer heer anhalten*
to take photographs	**um Fotos zu machen** *um foatoas tsoo makhen*
to buy souvenirs	**um Reiseandenken zu kaufen** *um riezeandenken tsoo kowfen*
for the bathrooms [toilets]	**um zur Toilette zu gehen** *um tsoor twoaletteh tsoo gayen*
Would you take a photo of us, please?	**Würden Sie bitte ein Foto von uns machen?** *vewrden zee bitteh ien foatoa fon uns makhen*
How long do we have here/in …?	**Wie viel Zeit haben wir hier/in … zur Verfügung?** *vee feel tsiet haaben veer heer/in … tsoor fehrfewgung*

WHERE IS ...?

Town maps are on display in city centers, train, streetcar stations, and at tourist information offices.

Where is the ...	**Wo ist ...** *voa ist*
abbey	**die Abtei** *dee aptie*
art gallery	**die Kunstgalerie** *dee kunstgalehree*
botanical garden	**der Botanische Garten** *dehr botaanisheh garten*
castle	**das Schloss** *dass shloss*
cathedral	**der Dom** *dehr doam*
cemetery	**der Friedhof** *dehr freet-hoaf*
church	**die Kirche** *dee keerkheh*
downtown area	**die Innenstadt** *dee innenshtat*
fountain	**der Brunnen** *dehr brunnen*
harbor	**der Hafen** *dehr haafen*
market	**der Markt** *dehr markt*
monastery	**das Kloster** *dass kloaster*
museum	**das Museum** *dass muzayum*
old town	**die Altstadt** *dee altshtat*
opera house	**das Opernhaus** *dass oapernhowss*
palace	**der Palast** *dehr palast*
park	**der Park** *dehr park*
parliament building	**das Parlamentsgebäude** *dass parlamentsgeboydeh*
shopping area	**das Geschäftsviertel** *dass geshehftsfeertel*
statue	**die Statue** *dee shtaatueh*
theater	**das Theater** *dass tayaater*
town hall	**das Rathaus** *dass raat-howss*
university	**die Universität** *dee unnivehrzitait*
Can you show me on the map?	**Können Sie es mir auf der Karte zeigen?** *kurnen zee ess meer owf dehr karteh tsiegen*

ADMISSION

Museums are usually closed on Mondays and on important holidays (Christmas, New Year's Day, and so on).Usual opening hours are from 9 a.m. to 4 p.m.

Is the ... open to thepublic?	**Ist ... der Öffentlichkeit zugänglich?** *ist ... dehr urfentlikhkiet tsoogehnglikh*
Can we look around?	**Können wir uns umsehen?** *kurnen veer uns umzayen*
What are the opening hours?	**Was sind die Öffnungszeiten?** *vass zint dee urfnungztsieten*
When does it close?	**Wann schließt er/sie/es?** *van shleest ehr/zee/ess*
Is ... open on Sundays?	**Ist ... sonntags geöffnet?** *ist ... zontaags geurfnet*
When is the next guided tour?	**Wann ist die nächste Führung?** *van ist dee naikhsteh fewrung*
Do you have a guidebook (in English)?	**Haben Sie einen Reiseführer (auf Englisch)?** *haaben zee ienen riezefewrer (owf ennglish)*
Can I take pictures?	**Darf ich fotografieren?** *darf ikh fottografeeren*
Is there access for the disabled?	**Ist es für Behinderte zugänglich?** *ist ess fewr behinderteh tsoogehnglikh*
Is there an audio guide in English?	**Gibt es einen Audio-Führer auf Englisch?** *gipt ess ienen owdiofewrer owf ennglish*

PAYING/TICKETS

How much is the entrance fee?	**Was kostet der Eintritt?** *vass kostet dehr ientrit*
Are there discounts for ...?	**Gibt es Ermäßigungen für ...?** *gipt ess ehrmaissiggoongen fewr*
children	**Kinder** *kinder*
disabled	**Behinderte** *behinderteh*
groups	**Gruppen** *gruppen*
seniors	**Rentner** *rentner*
students	**Studenten** *shtuddenten*
1 adult and 2 children, please.	**Ein Erwachsener und zwei Kinder, bitte.** *ien ehrvaksener unt tsvie kinder bitteh*

YOU MAY SEE

EINTRITT FREI	Admission free
EINTRITT VERBOTEN	No entry
FOTOGRAFIEREN VERBOTEN	No photography
GEÖFFNET	Open
GESCHLOSSEN	Closed
NÄCHSTE FÜHRUNG UM …	Next tour at …
ÖFFNUNGSZEITEN	Visiting hours

IMPRESSIONS

It's …	**Es ist …** *ess ist*
amazing	**erstaunlich** *ehrshtownlikh*
beautiful	**schön** *shurn*
boring	**langweilig** *langvielikh*
breathtaking	**atemberaubend** *atemberowbent*
brilliant	**großartig** *groassartikh*
interesting	**interessant** *interessant*
pretty	**hübsch** *hewbsh*
romantic	**romantisch** *rommantish*
superb	**phantastisch** *fantastish*
terrible	**schrecklich** *shreklikh*
ugly	**hässlich** *hesslikh*
It's good value.	**Es ist preiswert.** *ess ist priesvayrt*
It's a rip off.	**Es ist Wucher.** *ess ist vookher*
I (don't) like it.	**Es gefällt mir (nicht).** *ess gefehlt meer (nikht)*
It's great fun.	**Es macht Spaß.** *ess makht shpaass*

AT THE TICKET COUNTER

Zwei Erwachsene, bitte. *tsvie ehrvakseneh bitteh* (Two adults, please.)
Das macht acht Euro. *dass makht akht oyroh* (That's 8 euros.)
Hier, bitte. *heer bitteh* (Here you are.)

TOURIST GLOSSARY

Altarbild altarpiece
Altertum antiquity
Aquarell watercolor
ausgeliehen an on loan to
Ausgrabungen excavations
Ausstellung display, exhibition
Ausstellungsstück exhibit
Backsteingotik Gothic style brick buildings
Badeanlagen baths
begonnen started in
Bernstein amber
Bibliothek library
Bild picture
Bildhauer(in) sculptor
Bogen arch
Bronzezeit bronze age
Bühne stage
Burg castle
Chor(stuhl) choir (stall)
Dach roof
Dom cathedral
Druck print
Edelstein gemstone
Ehrenmal cenotaph
Eingang doorway
Einzelheit detail
Elfenbein ivory
Empore/Galerie gallery
entdeckt discovered in
entworfen von designed by
Entwurf design
erbaut erected/built in
Erker oriel window
fertiggestellt completed in
Fachwerk half-timber
Festung fort/fortress
Friedhof cemetery

Flohmarkt flea market
Flügel wing (of building)
Gartenanlage formal garden
Gasse alley
Gebäude building
Geburtshaus von birthplace of
geboren born in
Gefäß vessel
gegründet founded in
Gemächer apartments (*royal*)
Gemälde canvas (*painting*)
Gemälde painting
gemalt von painted by
gestiftet von donated by
gestorben died in
Gewölbe vault
Grab grave
Grabmal tomb
Grabstein headstone
Gründerzeit Founders' Period
Grundriss plan
Hallenkirche hall church
Hauptschiff nave
Herrenhaus manor house
Herrschaft reign
Hof courtyard
im Stil des/der in the style of
in Auftrag gegeben von commissioned by
interaktives Ausstellungsstück interactive exhibit
Jahrhundert century
Jugendstil Art Nouveau
Jungsteinzeit Neolithic Period
Kaiser emperor
Kaiserin empress
Kanzel pulpit
Kapelle chapel
Keramik ceramics
König king

Königin	queen
Kreuz	cross
Kreuzzug	crusade
Krone	crown
Kunst	art
Kunsthandwerk	crafts
Künstler(in)	artist
Kupferstich	etching
Kuppel	dome
Landschaft	landscape
lebte	lived
Leinwand	canvas (*material*)
Leuchtturm	lighthouse
Maler(in)	painter
Marmor	marble
Maßstab 1:100	scale 1:100
Mauer	wall
Meisterwerk	masterpiece
Mittelalter	Middle Ages
mittelalterlich	medieval
Mittelschiff	nave
Möbel	furniture
Münze	coin
Ölfarben	oils
Orgel	organ
Pfeiler	pillar
Plastik	sculpture
Platz	square
Portal	portal entry
Prunkzimmer	stateroom
Rathaus	town/city hall
Romanik	Romanesque
Römer	Romans
Querhaus	transept
Sammlung	collection
Säule	pillar
Schloss	castle
Schmuck	decoration, jewelry
Schiefer	slate
Schnitzerei	carving
Schule des/der	school of

Seitenschiffe	side aisles
silbern	silver
Sims	sill
Skizze	sketch
Sockel	base
Spätgotik	late Gothic
Stadtmauer	city wall
Stein	stone
Steinzeit	Stone Age
Stich	engraving
Stil	style
Strebepfeiler	buttress
Tafel	plaque
Taufstein	font
Ton	clay
Töpferwaren	pottery
Tor	gate
Treppe	staircase
Turm	tower, spire
Uhr	clock
vergoldet	gilded
versilbert	silver plated
Vierung	crossing (architecture)
von	by (person)
Vortrag	lecture
vorübergehend	temporary
Wachsfigur	waxwork
Waffe	weapon
Wand	wall
Wandgemälde	mural
Wandteppich	tapestry
Wassergraben	moat
Wasserleitung	aqueduct
Wasserspeier	gargoyle
wieder aufgebaut	rebuilt in
Zeichnung	drawing
zeitgenössische Kunst	contemporary art
zerstört von	destroyed by
Ziegel	brick
Zinne	battlement

WHAT ...?

What's that building?	**Was ist das für ein Gebäude?** *vass ist dass fewr ien geboydeh*
What style is that?	**Was ist das für ein Stil?** *vas ist das fewr ien stil?*
What period is that?	**Aus welcher Zeit ist das?** *owss velkher tsiet ist dass*

Karolinger/karolingisch (mid 8–10 century)

Pre-romanesque architectural style characterized by round polygonal churches (e.g. the Palatine Chapel in Aachen Cathedral) and churches with two chancels (e.g. The Benedictine Abbey Church of Corvey).

Romanik (mid 11–mid 13 century)

A somewhat geometric style in church architecture and sculpture and in manuscript illumination (e.g. the Cologne region, Speyer, Mainz).

Gotik/Spätgotik (mid 13–mid 16 century)

Characterized by slender towers, lofty pointed vaulting, flying buttresses and sculptural decoration (e.g. the cathedrals of Cologne, Regensburg and Freiburg-im-Breisgau).

Barock/Rokoko (1630–1780)

This style was characterized by irregularity of form and great variety, aiming to give the overall effect of movement. The Rococo was the extreme form of this and resulted in elaborate decoration.

Biedermeier (1816–1848)

Style of art and furniture design characterized by comfortable, lightweight furniture with flowing lines and glass-fronted cupboards. Painters of this style were Ferdinand Waldmüller and Karl Spitzweg.

Jugendstil (1890–1905)

This equivalent of Art Nouveau developed in Germany and Austria as a reaction against the extravagance of contemporary interior decoration. It first appeared in painting, later in furniture, vases and building façades. An example used in interior design is at the Schauspielhaus in Munich. Architects: Peter Behrens, Hans Poelzig; painter: Gustav Klimt.

Bauhaus (1920–1930)

Architectural school inspired by the fundamental theme of the marriage of art and technique (e.g. the Bauhaus, Dessau; sections of the Weissenhof Siedlung; the Hauptbahnhof in Stuttgart; Chilehaus, Hamburg).

Rulers

das Fränkische Reich (481–919)

The Frankish dynasty, founded by Clovis I, saw the development of Christianity amid a period of colonization. In 800 Charlemagne was crowned Emperor of the Holy Roman Empire and he expanded the Empire over Europe.

die Reformation (1500–1550)

In 1517, Martin Luther published his "95 theses" in Wittenberg.

Friedrich der Große (1740–1786)

Under Frederick the Great, Prussia's borders were expanded.

das Deutsche Reich (1871–1918)

This period was characterized by Prussian domination and struggles between church and state. The First World War was the culmination and downfall of this empire.

Weimarer Republik (1918–1933)

After the abdication of the Kaiser, Germany adopted a Republican Constitution and made its first attempt at democracy.

das Dritte Reich (1933–1945)

Hitler founded a totalitarian state, led by his dictatorship, or Third Reich, the aim of which was world domination. Defeat for Germany in the Second World War finally resulted in Hitler's fall from power.

Wiedervereinigung (1989–1990)

The Berlin Wall came down in 1989 and in March 1990 East Germans held free elections for the first time. The reunification treaty was signed in August 1990 and took effect in October 1990.

Churches/Religious services

Although large churches are normally open to the public during the day, services should be respected and most churches request that bare shoulders are covered before entering.

Catholic church	**katholische Kirche** *katoalisheh keerkheh*
Protestant church	**evangelische Kirche** *evangaylisheh keerkheh*
mosque	**Moschee** *moshay*
synagogue	**Synagoge** *zewnagoageh*
What time is …?	**Wann ist …?** *van ist*
mass/the service	**die Messe/der Gottesdienst** *dee messeh/dehr gottesdeenst*

IN THE COUNTRYSIDE

I'd like a map of …	**Ich hätte gern eine Karte …** *ikh hetteh gehrn ieneh karteh*
this region	**von dieser Gegend** *fon deezer gaygent*
walking routes	**mit Wanderwegen** *mit vandervaygen*
bicycle routes	**mit Radwegen** *mit raatvaygen*
How far is it to …?	**Wie weit ist es nach …?** *vee viet ist ess naakh*
Is there a right of way?	**Darf man dort hingehen?** *darf man dort heengayen*
Is there a trail to …?	**Gibt es einen Wanderweg nach …?** *gipt ess ienen vandervayk naakh*
Can you show me on the map?	**Können Sie es mir auf der Karte zeigen?** *kurnen zee ess meer owf dehr karteh tsiegen*
I'm lost (on foot/driving).	**Ich habe mich verlaufen/verfahren.** *ikh haabeh mikh fehrlowfen/fehrfaaren*

Organized walks/hikes

When does the guided walk start?	**Wann beginnt die geführte Wanderung?** *van begint dee gefewrteh vanderung*
When will we return?	**Wann kommen wir zurück?** *van kommen veer tsoorewk*
What is the walk/hike like?	**Wie ist die Wanderung?** *vee ist dee vanderung*
gentle/medium	**leicht/mittel** *liekht/mittel*
tough	**anstrengend** *anshtrengent*
I'm exhausted.	**Ich bin erschöpft.** *ikh bin ehrshurpft*
How high is that mountain?	**Wie hoch ist dieser Berg?** *vee hoakh ist deezer behrg*
What kind of … is that?	**Was für … ist das?** *vass fewr … ist dass*
animal/bird	**ein Tier/ein Vogel** *ien teer/ien foagel*
flower/tree	**eine Blume/ein Baum** *iener bloomeh/ien bowm*

GEOGRAPHIC FEATURES

bridge	**Brücke**	*brewkeh*
cave	**Höhle**	*hurleh*
cliff	**Klippe**	*klippeh*
field	**Feld**	*felt*
footpath	**Fußweg**	*foosvayg*
forest	**Wald**	*valt*
glacier	**Gletscher**	*glecher*
gorge	**Schlucht**	*shlukht*
hill	**Hügel**	*hewgel*
lake	**See**	*zay*
mountain	**Berg**	*berg*
mountain range	**Gebirge**	*gebeergeh*
nature reserve	**Naturschutzgebiet**	*natoorshutsgebeet*
panorama	**Panorama**	*panoraama*
park	**Park**	*park*
pass	**Pass**	*pass*
path	**Weg**	*vayg*
peak	**Gipfel**	*gipfel*
picnic area	**Picknickplatz**	*piknikplats*
pond	**Teich**	*tiekh*
rapids	**Stromschnellen**	*shtroamshnellen*
river	**Fluss**	*fluss*
sea	**Meer**	*mayr*
spa	**Heilbad**	*hielbahd*
spring	**Quelle**	*kwelleh*
stream	**Bach**	*bakh*
track	**Weg**	*vayg*
valley	**Tal**	*taal*
viewpoint	**Aussichtspunkt**	*owssikhtspunkt*
winery [vineyard]	**Weinberg**	*vienbehrg*
waterfall	**Wasserfall**	*vasserfal*
woods	**Wald**	*valt*

LEISURE

EVENTS

Local papers and, in large cities, weekly entertainment guides will tell you what's on. In many larger cities such as Berlin, Frankfurt, and Munich, you'll even find publications in English.

Do you have a program of events?	**Haben Sie einen Veranstaltungskalender?** *haaben zee ienen fehranshtaltungzkalender*
Can you recommend a …?	**Können Sie … empfehlen?** *kurnen zee … empfaylen*
Is there a/n … somewhere?	**Wird irgendwo … gegeben?** *veert eergentvoa … gegayben*
ballet	**ein Ballett** *ien ballet*
concert	**ein Konzert** *ien kontsehrt*
Is there a good movie on somewhere?	**Wird irgendwo ein guter Film gezeigt?** *veert eergentvoa ien gooter film getsiegt*
opera	**eine Oper** *eineh oaper*
theater	**das Theater** *dass tayaater*

Tickets for concerts, theater, and other cultural events are on sale at special ticket agencies. In small towns these may be in kiosks, book or music stores: ask at the local tourist office.

AT THE BOX OFFICE

Zwei Karten für "Faust", bitte. *tsvie karten fewr fowst bitteh* (*Two tickets for "Faust", please.*)
Vierundsechzig Euro, bitte. *feeruntzekhtsikh oyroh bitteh* (*64 euros, please.*)
Nehmen Sie Kreditkarten? *naymen zee kredeetkarten* (*Do you take creditcards?*)
Aber ja. *ahber yaa* (*But of course.*)

YOU MAY SEE

VORVERKAUF	advance reservations
AUSVERKAUFT	sold out
KARTEN FÜR HEUTE	tickets for today
GARDEROBE	coat check

AVAILABILITY

Where can I get tickets?	**Wo kann ich Karten kaufen?**
	voa kan ikh karten kowfen
Are there any seats for tonight?	**Gibt es für heute Abend noch Karten?**
	gip ess fewr hoytoh aabent nokh karten
There are … of us.	**Wir sind … Personen.**
	veer zint … pehrzoanen
When does it start/end?	**Wann fängt es an/hört es auf?**
	van fehngt ess an/hurt ess owf

TICKETS

I'd like to reserve …	**Ich möchte … vorbestellen.**
	ikh murkhteh … foarbeshtelen
3 for Sunday evening	**drei für Sonntagabend**
	drie fewr sontaagaabent
1 for Friday matinée	**eine für die Nachmittagsvorstellung am Freitag** *ieneh fewr dee naakhmittaagsfoarstehlung am frietaag*
How much are the seats?	**Wie viel kosten diese Plätze?**
	vee feel kosten deezeh plehtseh
Do you have anything cheaper?	**Haben Sie etwas Billigeres?**
	haaben zee etvass billigeress

YOU MAY HEAR

Ihre Kreditkartennummer, bitte.	Your credit card number, please
Welche Kreditkarte ist es?	What's your credit card type?
Bis wann ist Ihre Kreditkarte gültig?	What's the expiration date?
Holen Sie die Karten … ab.	Pick up the tickets …
vor neunzehn Uhr	by 7 p.m.
an der Vorverkaufskasse	at the reservation desk

MOVIES [CINEMA]

Foreign films are usually dubbed into German, but more theaters are also showing films in their original version.

Is there a movie theater [cinema] near here?	**Gibt es hier in der Nähe ein Kino?** *gipt ess heer in dehr naieh ien keeno*
What's playing at the movies?	**Was läuft im Kino?** *vass loyft im keeno*
Is the film dubbed?	**Ist der Film synchronisiert?** *ist dehr film zewnkronizeert*
Is the film subtitled?	**Hat der Film Untertitel?** *hat dehr film unterteetel*
Is the film in the original English?	**Ist der Film in der englischen Originalfassung?** *ist dehr film in dehr englishen originaalfassung*
Who's the main actor?	**Wer spielt die Hauptrolle?** *vayr shpeelt dee howptroleh*
A ..., please.	**Ein/Eine ... bitte.** *ien/ieneh bitteh*
box [carton] of popcorn	**eine Schachtel Popcorn** *ieneh shakhtel popcorn*
chocolate ice cream	**ein Schokoladeneis** *ien shokkolaadenies*
soft drink/soda	**ein Erfrischungsgetränk** *ien ehrfrishungzgetrehnk*
small/regular/large	**klein/mittel/groß** *klien/mittel/groass*

THEATER

What's playing at the ... Theater?	**Was wird im ...-Theater gegeben?** *vass veert im ... -tayaater gegayben*
Who's the playwright?	**Wer ist der Autor?** *vayr ist dehr owtor*
Do you think I'd enjoy it?	**Glauben Sie, dass es mir gefallen würde?** *glowben zee dass ess meer gefallen vewrdeh*
I don't know much German.	**Ich spreche nicht viel Deutsch.** *kh shprekheh nikht feel doych*

OPERA/BALLET/DANCE

All major cities have an opera house and you'll find concerts going on in even the smallest towns. The annual **Bayreuther Festspiele** (Wagner operas) is a spectacular event.

Who's the composer?	**Wer ist der Komponist?** *vayr ist dehr komponist*
Who's the soloist?	**Wer ist der Solist/die Solistin?** *vayr ist dehr zollist/dee zollistin*
Is formal dress required?	**Ist Abendgarderobe Pflicht?** *ist aabentgarderoabeh pfleekht*
Where's the opera house?	**Wo ist das Opernhaus?** *voa ist dass oapernhowss*
I'm interested in contemporary dance.	**Ich interessiere mich für modernen Tanz.** *ikh interesseereh mikh fewr modehrnen tants*

MUSIC/CONCERTS

Where's the concert hall?	**Wo ist die Konzerthalle?** *voa ist dee kontsehrthalleh*
Which orchestra/band is playing?	**Welches Orchester/Welche Band spielt?** *velkhess orkester/velkheh bant shpeelt*
What are they playing?	**Was wird gespielt?** *vass veert geshpeelt*
Who is the conductor?	**Wer ist der Dirigent?** *vayr ist dehr dirigent*
I really like …	**Ich höre gern …** *ikh hurreh gehrn …*
country music	**Countrymusik** *countrymuzeek*
folk music	**Volksmusik** *folksmuzeek*
jazz	**Jazz** *dzhaiss*
music of the '60s	**Musik aus den Sechzigern** *muzeek owss dayn zekhtsiggern*
rock music	**Rockmusik** *rokmuzeek*
soul music	**Soul** *soul*
Are they popular?	**Sind sie beliebt?** *zint zee beleebt*

111

NIGHTLIFE

What is there
to do in the evenings?

Was kann man abends unternehmen?
vass kan man aabents unternaymen

Can you
recommend a ...?

Können Sie ein ... empfehlen?
kurnen zee ien ... empfaylen

Is there a ... in town?

Gibt es in der Stadt ...?
gipt ess in dehr shtat

bar

eine Bar *ieneh baar*

casino

ein Spielkasino
ien shpeelkazeeno

disco

eine Diskothek *ieneh diskotayk*

gay club

einen Gay Club *ienen gay club*

nightclub

einen Nachtklub
ienen nakhtklub

Is there a
cabaret?

Wird dort ein Varieté gezeigt?
veert dort ien variaytay getsiegt

What music do
they play?

Welche Musik wird dort gespielt?
velkheh muzeek veert dort geshpeelt

How do I get there?

Wie komme ich dahin?
vee kommeh ikh dahin

ADMISSION

What time does the
show start?

Wann fängt die Show an?
van fehngt dee shoa an

Is evening dress
required?

Wird Abendgarderobe verlangt?
veert aabentgarderoabeh fehrlangt

Is there an admission
charge?

Muss man Eintritt bezahlen?
muss man ientritt bertsaalen

Is a reservation
necessary?

Muss man reservieren?
muss man rezehrveeren

How long will we have
to stand in line [queue]?

**Wie lange müssen wir Schlange
stehen?** *vee langeh mewssen veer
shlangeh shtayen*

I'd like a good table.

Ich hätte gern einen guten Tisch.
ikh hetteh gehrn ienen gooten tish

CHILDREN

Can you recommend something for the children?	**Können Sie etwas für die Kinder empfehlen?** *kurnen zee etvass fewr dee kinder empfaylen*
Can I take a baby carriage [pram] in?	**Kann ich mit einem Kinderwagen hinein?** *kan ikh mit ienem kindervaagen hinien*
Are there changing facilities here for babies?	**Gibt es hier einen Wickelraum für Babys?** *gipt ess heer ienen vikkelrowm fewr baybis*
kiddie [paddling] pool	**das Planschbecken** *dass planshbeken*
playground	**der Spielplatz** *dehr shpeelplats*
play group	**die Spielgruppe** *dee shpeelgruppeh*
puppet show	**das Puppenspiel** *dass puppenshpeel*
zoo	**der Zoo** *dehr tsoa*

Child care

Can you recommend a reliable babysitter?	**Können Sie eine zuverlässige Kinderbetreuung empfehlen?** *kurnen zee iener tsoofehrlehssigeh kinderbetroyung empfaylen*
Is there constant supervision?	**Werden die Kinder ständig beaufsichtigt?** *vayrden dee kinder shtehndikh beowfzikhtigt*
Are the helpers properly trained?	**Sind die Helfer ausgebildet?** *zint dee helfer owsgebeeldet*
When/Where can I drop them off?	**Wann/Wo kann ich sie abliefern?** *vann/voa kan ikh zee apleefern*
I'll pick them up at …	**Ich hole sie um … ab.** *ikh hoaleh zee um … ap*
We'll be back by …	**Wir sind spätestens um … wieder da.** *veer zint shpaitestenss um … veeder daa*
What age is he/she?	**Wie alt ist er/sie?** *vee alt ist ehr/zee*
She's 3 and he's 18 months.	**Sie ist drei Jahre und er ist achtzehn Monate alt.** *zee ist drie jaareh unt ehr ist akhtsayn moanaateh alt*

SPORTS

Soccer is by far the most popular sport, though you'll find almost all sports well represented. Hiking and cycling are popular actitivites: in most rural areas there are **Wanderwege** (marked paths) and there are designated bicycle paths alongside most roads. Water sports, golf, tennis, fishing and horseback riding are also popular and skiing conditions can be among the best in the world.

Watching

Is there a soccer game [football match] this Saturday?	**Findet diesen Samstag ein Fußballspiel statt?** *findet deezen zamstaag ien foosbalshpeel shtat*
Which teams are playing?	**Welche Mannschaften spielen?** *velkheh manshaften shpeelen*
Can you get me a ticket?	**Können Sie mir eine Karte besorgen?** *kurnen zee meer ieneh karteh bezoargen*
What's the admission charge?	**Was kostet der Eintritt?** *vass kostet dehr ientrit*
Where's the racetrack [race course]?	**Wo ist die Pferderennbahn?** *voa ist dee pfayrderenbaan*
Where can I place a bet?	**Wo kann ich eine Pferdewette abschließen?** *voa kan ikh ieneh pfayrdevetteh apshleesen*
What are the odds on …?	**Wie stehen die Chancen für …?** *vee shtayen dee shangsen fewr*

athletics	**Leichtathletik** *liekhtatlayteek*
basketball	**Basketball** *baasketbal*
cycling	**Rad fahren** *raat faaren*
golf	**Golf** *golf*
horse racing	**Pferderennen** *pfayrderenen*
ping pong	**Tischtennis** *tishtenniss*
soccer [football]	**Fußball** *foosbal*
swimming	**Schwimmen** *shvimmen*
tennis	**Tennis** *tenniss*
volleyball	**Volleyball** *vollibal*

Playing

Where's the nearest …?	**Wo ist der nächste …?** *voa ist dehr naikhsteh*
golf course	**Golfplatz** *golfplats*
tennis court	**Tennisplatz** *tennisplehts*
What's the charge per …?	**Wie viel kostet es pro …?** *vee feel kostet ess proa*
day/round/hour	**Tag/Runde/Stunde** *taag/rundeh/shtundeh*
Do I need to be a member?	**Muss man Mitglied sein?** *muss man mitgleet zien*
Where can I rent …?	**Wo kann ich … mieten?** *voa kan ikh … meeten*
shoes	**Schuhe** *shooeh*
clubs	**Schläger** *shlayger*
equipment	**die Ausrüstung** *dee owsrewstung*
a racket	**einen Schläger** *ienen shlayger*
Can I get lessons?	**Kann ich Stunden nehmen?** *kan ikh shtunden naymen*
Do you have a fitness room?	**Haben Sie einen Fitness-Raum?** *haaben zee ienen fitness-rowm*

YOU MAY SEE

UMKLEIDERÄUME	Changing rooms
ANGELN VERBOTEN	No fishing
ANGELN NUR MIT ANGELSCHEIN	Fishing for permit holders only

YOU MAY HEAR

Wir sind leider ausgebucht.	I'm sorry, we're booked.
Sie müssen eine Kaution von … hinterlegen.	There is a deposit of …
Welche Größe haben Sie?	What size are you?

AT THE BEACH

Try the North Sea and Baltic coast for swimming and sailing; the Frisean and Baltic Islands offer quieter beaches for those not bothered by a brisk wind.

The lakes in the area surrounding the Alps provide good sailing and fishing and will often have small secluded beaches.

Is the beach pebbly/ sandy?	**Ist es ein Kiesstrand/Sandstrand?** *ist ess ien kees-shtrant/zantshtrant*
Is there a ... here?	**Gibt es hier ...?** *gipt ess heer*
children's pool	**ein Kinderbecken** *ien kinderbekken*
swimming pool	**ein Schwimmbad** *ien shvimbaat*
Is it safe to swim here?	**Kann man hier gefahrlos baden?** *kan man heer gefaarloass baaden*
Is it safe for children?	**Ist es für Kinder ungefährlich?** *ist ess fewr kinder ungefairlikh*
Is there a lifeguard?	**Gibt es einen Rettungsschwimmer?** *gipt ess ienen rettungzshvimmer*
I want to rent a/ some ...	**Ich möchte ... mieten.** *ikh murkhteh ... meeten*
deck chair	**einen Liegestuhl** *i enen leegeshtool*
jet ski	**Jet-Ski** *jet-ski*
motorboat	**ein Motorboot** *ien moatorboat*
rowboat	**ein Ruderboot** *ien rooderboat*
sailboat	**ein Segelboot** *ien zaygelboat*
diving equipment	**eine Taucherausrüstung** *ieneh towkherowsrewstung*
umbrella [sunshade]	**einen Sonnenschirm** *ienen zonnenshirm*
surfboard	**ein Surfbrett** *ien "surf"bret*
waterskis	**Wasserskier** *vassershee-er*
windsurfer	**einen Windsurfer** *ienen vint"surfer"*
For ... hours.	**Für ... Stunden.** *fewr ... shtunden*

SKIING

Austria and Switzerland are at the heart of Europe's skiing, with great slopes and often a traditional atmosphere. Resorts vary from the very fashionable and expensive to the cozy conviviality often found in small resorts.

Is there much snow?	**Liegt viel Schnee?** *leegt veel shnay*
What's the snow like?	**Wie ist der Schnee?** *vee ist dehr shnay*
I'd like to rent/hire …	**Ich möchte … mieten.** *ikh murkhteh … meeten*
poles	**Skistöcke** *sheeshturkeh*
skates	**Schlittschuhe** *shlitshooeh*
ski boots	**Skischuhe** *sheeshooeh*
skis	**Skier** *shee-eh*
These are too …	**Sie sind zu …** *zee zint tsoo*
big/small	**groß/klein** *groass/klien*
loose/tight	**locker/eng** *loker/eng*
uncomfortable	**unbequem** *unbekvaym*
A lift pass for a day/ 5 days, please.	**Eine Liftkarte für einen Tag/fünf Tage, bitte.** *ieneh liftkarteh fewr ienen taag/fewnf taageh bitteh*
I'd like to join the ski school. I'm …	**Ich möchte Skiunterricht nehmen. Ich bin …** *ikh murkhteh sheeunterikht naymen ikh bin*
a beginner	**Anfänger** *anfehnger*
experienced	**fortgeschritten** *fortgeshritten*

YOU MAY SEE

DRAHTSEILBAHN/GONDEL	cable car/gondola
SESSELLIFT	chair lift
SCHLEPPLIFT	drag lift

Making Friends

Introductions

Greetings vary according to how well you know someone:

It's polite to shake hands, both when you meet and say good-bye; when being introduced into a group, men will shake hands with women and then with men.

There are three forms for "you" (taking different verb forms): **du** (informal/singular) and **ihr** (informal/plural) are used when talking to relatives, close friends, and children and between young people; **Sie** (formal) is used in all other cases (singular and plural). It's polite to address adults as Mr. and Mrs. (**Herr und Frau**) and to speak to them using the formal form of "you" (**Sie**) until you are asked to use the familiar **du.**

My name is …	**Ich heiße …** *ikh hiesseh*
May I introduce …?	**Darf ich … vorstellen?** *darf ikh … foarshtehlen*
John, this is …	**John, das ist …** *John dass ist*
Pleased to meet you.	**Sehr angenehm.** *zayr angenaym*
The pleasure is all mine.	**Ganz meinerseits.** *gahnz minersites*
What's your name?	**Wie heißen Sie?** *vee hiessen zee*
I'm sorry, I didn;t catch your name.	**Es tut mir leid, ich habe Ihren Namen nicht verstanden.** *ess toot meer liet ikh haabeh eeren naamen nikht fehrstanden*
How are you?	**Wie geht es Ihnen?** *vee gayt ess eenen*
Fine, thanks. And you?	**Danke, gut. Und Ihnen?** *danker goot. unt eenen*

AT A RECEPTION

Ich heiße Sheryl Borg. *ikh hiesseh sheryl borg* (My name is Sheryl Borg.)

Jürgen Lorenz. Sehr angenehm. *yurgen lorenz szayr angenaym* (Jürgen Lorenz. My pleasure.)

Ganz meinerseits. *ghanz minersites* (The pleasure is all mine.)

118

WHERE ARE YOU FROM?

Where do you come from?	**Woher kommen Sie?** *voahayr kommen zee*
Where were you born?	**Wo sind Sie geboren?** *voa zint zee geboaren*
I'm from …	**Ich komme aus …** *ikh kommeh owss*
Australia	**Australien** *owstraalien*
Britain	**Großbritannien** *groasbritanien*
Canada	**Kanada** *kanada*
England	**England** *englant*
Ireland	**Irland** *eerlant*
New Zealand	**Neuseeland** *noyzaylant*
Scotland	**Schottland** *shotlant*
the U.S.	**den USA** *dayn oo-ess-aa*
Wales	**Wales** *"Wales"*
Where do you live?	**Wo wohnen Sie?** *voa voanen zee*
What part of … are you from?	**Aus welchem Teil von … kommen Sie?** *owss velkhem tiel fon … kommen zee*
Austria	**Österreich** *ursteriekh*
Germany	**Deutschland** *doychlant*
Switzerland	**die Schweiz** *dehr shviets* (Reg: Franzi!)
We come here every year.	**Wir kommen jedes Jahr hierher.** *veer kommen yaydess yaar heerhayr*
It's my/our first visit.	**Ich bin/Wir sind zum ersten Mal hier.** *ikh bin/veer zint tsum ehrsten maal heer*
Have you ever been to the U.K./the U.S.?	**Waren Sie schon einmal in Großbritannien/ in den USA?** *vahren zee shoan ienmaal in groasbrittanien/in dayn oo ess aa*
I love (the) … here.	**… hier gefällt mir sehr gut.** *heer gefehlt meer zayr goot*
countryside	**die Landschaft** *dee lantshaft*
cuisine	**die Küche** *dee kewkher*

WHO ARE YOU WITH?

I'm on my own.	**Ich bin allein hier.** *ikh bin alien heer*
I'm with my …	**Ich bin mit … hier.** *ikh bin mit … heer*
wife	**meiner Frau** *miener frow*
husband	**meinem Mann** *mienem man*
family	**meiner Familie** *miener fameelieh*
children	**meinen Kindern** *mienen kindern*
parents	**meinen Eltern** *mienen eltern*
boyfriend/girlfriend	**meinem Freund/meiner Freundin** *mienem froynt/miener froyndin*
father/mother	**der Vater/die Mutter** *dehr faater/dee mutter*
son/daughter	**der Sohn/die Tochter** *dehr zoan/dee tokhter*
brother/sister	**der Bruder/die Schwester** *dehr brooder/dee shvester*
uncle/aunt	**der Onkel/die Tante** *dehr onkel/dee tanteh*
What's your son's/ wife's name?	**Wie heißt Ihr Sohn/Ihre Frau?** *vee hiesst eer zoan/eereh frow*
I'm …	**Ich bin …** *ikh bin*
married/single	**verheiratet/unverheiratet (ledig)** *fehrhieraatet/unfehrhieraatet (lehdikh)*
divorced	**geschieden** *gesheeden*
I'm separated.	**Ich lebe getrennt.** *ikh laybeh getrent*
We live together.	**Wir leben zusammen.** *veer layben tsoozamen*
Do you have any children?	**Haben Sie Kinder?** *haaben zee kinder*
2 boys and a girl.	**Zwei Jungen und ein Mädchen.** *tsvie yungen unt ien maitkhen*
How old are they?	**Wie alt sind sie?** *vee alt zint zee*
They're ten and twelve.	**Sie sind zehn und zwölf.** *zee zint tsayn unt tsvurlf*

WHAT DO YOU DO?

What are you studying?	**Was studieren Sie?** *vass shtuddeeren zee*
I'm studying …	**Ich studiere …** *ikh shtudeereh*
science	**Naturwissenschaften** *natoorvissenshaften*
the arts	**Geisteswissenschaften** *giestesvissenschaften*
I'm a businessman/ woman.	**Ich bin Geschäftsmann/Geschäftsfrau.** *ikh bin geshehftsman/geshehftsfrow*
I'm in …	**Ich bin im … tätig.** *ikh bin im … taitikh*
engineering	**Ingenieurwesen** *insheniurvayzen*
retail	**Einzelhandel** *ientselhandel*
sales	**Verkauf** *fehrkowf*
Who do you work for?	**Bei welcher Firma arbeiten Sie?** *bie velkher feerma aarbieten zee*
I work for …	**Ich arbeite bei …** *ikh aarbieteh bie*
I'm a/an …	**Ich bin …** *ikh bin*
accountant [*fem.*]	**Buchhalter[in]** *bookhhalter[in]*
housewife	**Hausfrau** *howsfrow*
student [*fem.*]	**Student[in]** *shtudent[in]*
I'm …	**Ich bin …** *ikh bin*
retired	**pensioniert** *pensioaneert*
self-employed	**selbständig** *zelbshtehndikh*
What are your hobbies?	**Was haben Sie für Hobbys?** *vass haaben zee fewr hobbiss*
I like music.	**Ich höre gern Musik.** *ikh horer gehrn muzeek*
I like reading.	**Ich lese gern.** *ikh layzehgehrn*
I like sports.	**Ich treibe gern Sport.** *ikh triebeh gehrn shport*
I play …	**Ich spiele …** *ikh shpeeleh*
chess/cards	**Schach/Karten** *shakh/karten*

121

WHAT WEATHER!

What a lovely day!	**Was für ein herrlicher Tag!** *vass fewr ien hehrlikher taag*
What awful weather!	**Was für ein schreckliches Wetter!** *vass fewr ien shreklikhess vetter*
Isn't it cold/hot today!	**Was für eine Kälte/Hitze heute!** *vass fewr ieneh kehlteh/hitseh hoyteh*
Is it usually as warm/cold as this?	**Ist es immer so warm/kalt?** *ist ess immer zoa varm/kalt*
Do you think it's going to … tomorrow?	**Glauben Sie, es wird morgen …?** *glowben zee ess veert morgen*
be a nice day	**schön** *shurn*
rain	**regnen** *raygnen*
snow	**schneien** *shnieen*
What is the weather forecast?	**Was sagt der Wetterbericht?** *vass zaagt dehr vetterberikht*
It's …	**Es ist …** *ess ist*
cloudy	**bewölkt** *bevurlkt*
foggy	**neblig** *nayblikh*
frosty	**frostig** *frostikh*
icy	**eisig** *iezikh*
rainy	**regnerisch** *raygnerish*
windy	**windig** *vindikh*
thundering	**gewitterig** *gevitterikh*
It's snowy.	**Es schneit.** *ess shniet*
Has the weather been like this for long?	**Ist das Wetter schon lange so?** *ist dass vetter shoan langeh zoa*
What's the pollen count?	**Wie hoch ist der Pollenflug?** *vee hoakh ist dehr pollenfloog*
high/medium/low	**hoch/mittel/niedrig** *hoakh/mittel/needrikh*
What's the forecast for skiing?	**Wie ist der Wintersportbericht?** *vee ist dehr vintershportberikht*

ENJOYING YOUR TRIP?

I'm here on …	**Ich bin … hier.** *ikh bin … heer*
a business trip	**geschäftlich** *geshehftlikh*
vacation [holiday]	**im Urlaub** *im oorlowp*
We came by …	**Wir sind mit … gekommen.** *veer zint mit … gekomen*
train/bus/plane	**der Bahn/dem Bus/dem Flugzeug** *dehr baan/daym buss/ daym floogtsoyg*
car/ferry	**dem Auto/der Fähre** *daym owto/dehr faireh*
We're staying in …	**Wir wohnen …** *veer voanen*
an apartment	**in einer Ferienwohnung** *in iener fayrienvoanung*
a hotel	**in einem Hotel** *in ienem hottel*
with friends	**bei Freunden** *bie froynden*
We've visited …	**Wir haben … besichtigt.** *veer haaben … bezikhtiggt*
We're staying at a campsite.	**Wir sind auf einem Campingplatz.** *veer zint owf ienem kempingplats*
Can you suggest …?	**Können Sie vorschlagen, …?** *kurnen zee foarshlaagen*
things to do	**was wir unternehmen können** *vass veer unternaymen kurnen*
places to eat	**wo wir essen können** *voa veer essen kurnen*
places to visit	**was wir besichtigen können** *vass veer bezikhtigen kurnen*
We're having a great/ an awful time.	**Es gefällt uns sehr gut/ überhaupt nicht.** *ess gefehlt uns zayr goot/ewberhowpt nikht*

123

Sind Sie im Urlaub?	Are you on vacation?
Wie sind Sie hergekommen?	How did you get here?
Wo wohnen Sie?	Where are you staying?
Wie lange sind Sie schon hier?	How long have you been here?
Wie lange bleiben Sie?	How long are you staying?
Gefällt Ihnen Ihr Urlaub?	Are you enjoying your vacation?

INVITATIONS

May I invite you to lunch?
Darf ich Sie zum Mittagessen einladen? *darf ikh zee tsum mittaagessen ienlaaden*

Can you come for a drink this evening?
Kommen Sie heute Abend auf ein Gläschen? *kommen zee hoyteh aabent owf ien glaiskhen*

We are having a party. Can you come?
Wir geben eine Party. Können Sie kommen? *veer gayben ieneh paartee. kurnen zee kommen*

May we join you?
Dürfen wir uns zu Ihnen setzen? *dewrfen veer uns tsoo eenen zetsen*

Would you like to join us?
Möchten Sie sich zu uns setzen? *murkhten zee zikh tsoo uns zetsen*

Going out

What are your plans for …?
Was haben Sie … vor? *vass haaben zee … foar*

today/tonight
heute/heute Abend *hoyteh/hoyteh aabent*

tomorrow
morgen *morgen*

Are you free this evening?
Sind sie heute Abend frei? *zint zee hoyteh aabent frie*

Would you like to …?
Möchten Sie gern …? *murkhten zee gehrn*

go dancing
tanzen gehen *tantsen gayen*

go for a drink
ein Gläschen trinken gehen *ien glaiskhen trinken gayen*

go for a meal
essen gehen *essen gayen*

Where would you like to go?
Wohin möchten Sie gehen? *voahin murkhten zee gayen*

Accepting/Declining

| Great. I'd love to. | **Danke, sehr gern.**
dankeh zayr gehrn |
|---|---|
| Thank you, but I'm busy. | **Vielen Dank, aber ich habe keine Zeit.** *feelen dank aaber ikh haabeh kiener tsiet* |
| May I bring a friend? *(male/female)* | **Darf ich einen Freund/eine Freundin mitbringen?** *darf ikh ienen froynt/ieneh froyndin mitbringen* |
| Where shall we meet? | **Wo treffen wir uns?**
voa treffen veer uns |
| I'll meet you … | **Wir treffen uns …** *veer treffen uns* |
| in the bar | **in der Bar** *in dehr baar* |
| in front of your hotel | **vor Ihrem Hotel** *foar eerem hottel* |
| I'll pick you up at 8. | **Ich hole Sie um acht Uhr ab.** *ikh hoaleh zee um akht oor ap* |
| Could we make it a bit later/earlier? | **Geht es etwas später/früher?** *gayt ess etvass shpaiter/frewer* |
| How about another day? | **Vielleicht ein andermal?** *feelliekht ien andermaal* |
| That will be fine. | **Das ist in Ordnung.** *dass ist in ordnung* |

Dining out/in

If you are invited home for a meal, always take a gift – a bottle of wine, sparkling wine, chocolates or, preferably, flowers (but not roses).

Would you like a drink?	**Möchten Sie etwas zu trinken?** *murkhten zee etvass tsoo trinken*
Do you like …?	**Mögen Sie …?** *murgen zee*
What are you going to have?	**Was nehmen Sie?** *vass naymen zee*
Are you enjoying your meal?	**Schmeckt Ihnen das Essen?** *shmekt eenen dass essen*
That was a lovely meal.	**Das war ein herrliches Essen.** *dass vaar ien hehrlikhess essen*

SOCIALIZING

Are you waiting for someone?	**Warten Sie auf jemanden?** *vaarten zee owf yaymanden*
Do you mind if I …?	**Stört es Sie, wenn ich …?** *shturt ess zee ven ikh*
sit here/smoke	**hier sitze/rauche** *heer zitseh/rowkheh*
Can I get you a drink?	**Möchten Sie etwas zu trinken?** *murkhten zee etvass tsoo trinken*
Why are you laughing?	**Warum lachen Sie?** *varum lakhen zee*
Is my German that bad?	**Ist mein Deutsch so schlecht?** *ist mien doych zoa shlekht*
Shall we go somewhere quieter?	**Sollen wir irgendwohin gehen, wo es ruhiger ist?** *zollen veer eergentvoahin gayen voa ess roo-iger ist*
Leave me alone, please!	**Lassen Sie mich bitte in Ruhe!** *lassen zee mikh bitteh in rooeh*
You look great!	**Du siehst wunderbar aus!** *doo zeest vunderbaar owss*
I'm afraid we've got to leave now.	**Wir müssen jetzt leider gehen.** *veer mewssen yetst lieder gayen*
Thanks for the evening.	**Danke für den Abend.** *dankeh fewr dayn aabent*
Can I see you again tomorrow?	**Kann ich Sie morgen wiedersehen?** *kan ikh zee morgen veederzayen*
See you soon.	**Bis bald.** *biss balt*
Can I have your address?	**Kann ich Ihre Adresse haben?** *kan ikh eereh adresseh haaben*

IN A BAR

Stört es Sie, wenn ich hier sitze? *shturt ess zee ven ikh heer zitseh (Do you mind if I sit here?)*

Aber nein. *ahber nine (Of course not.)*

Danke. *dankeh (Thanks.)*

TELEPHONING

Telephone booths take either phonecards or coins. Phonecards **(Telefonkarten)** are available at the post office, some newsstands and currency exchange offices.

To phone home from German-speaking countries, dial 00 followed by: Australia 61; Canada 1; Ireland 353; New Zealand 64; South Africa 27; UK 44; U.S. 1.

Phone numbers are given in pairs, and note that in telephoning **zwei** becomes **zwo**.

Can I have your telephone number?	**Kann ich Ihre Telefonnummer haben?** *kan ikh eereh taylayfoan-numer haaben*
Here's my number.	**Das ist meine Nummer.** *dass ist mieneh numer*
Please call me.	**Bitte rufen Sie mich an.** *bitteh roofen zee mikh an*
I'll give you a call.	**Ich rufe Sie an.** *ikh roofeh zee an*
Where's the nearest telephone booth?	**Wo ist die nächste Telefonzelle?** *voa ist dee naikhsteh taylayfoantseleh*
May I use your phone?	**Darf ich Ihr Telefon benutzen?** *darf ikh eer taylayfoan benutsen*
It's an emergency.	**Es handelt sich um einen Notfall.** *ess handelt zikh um ienen noatfal*
I'd like to call someone in England/U.S./Canada.	**Ich möchte nach England/USA/Kanada telefonieren.** *ikh murkhteh naakh englant/oo-es-aa/kanada taylay-foneeren*
What's the area [dialling] code for …?	**Was ist die Vorwahl von …?** *vass ist dee foarvaal fon*
I'd like a phonecard, please.	**Ich hätte gern eine Telefonkarte.** *ikh hetteh gehrn ieneh taylayfoankarteh*
What's the number for Information?	**Welche Nummer hat die Auskunft?** *velkheh nummer hat dee owskunft*
I'd like the number for …	**Ich möchte die Nummer für …** *ikh murkhteh dee nummer fewr*
I'd like to call collect [reverse the charges].	**Ich möchte ein R-Gespräch anmelden.** *ikh murkhteh ien ehr-geshpraikh anmelden*

SPEAKING ON THE PHONE

Hello. This is …	**Hallo. Hier spricht …** *halloa heer shprikht*
I'd like to speak to … .	**Ich möchte mit … sprechen.** *ikh murkhteh meet … shprekhen*
Extension …	**Apparat …** *aparaat*
Speak louder/more slowly, please.	**Sprechen Sie bitte etwas lauter/langsamer.** *shprekhen zee bitteh etvass lowter/langzaamer*
Could you repeat that, please?	**Können Sie das bitte wiederholen.** *kurnen zee dass bitteh veederhoalen*
I'm afraid he/she's not in.	**Er/Sie ist leider nicht da.** *ehr/zee ist lieder nikht daa*
You've got the wrong number.	**Sie sind falsch verbunden.** *zee zint falsh fehrbunden*
Just a moment.	**Einen Augenblick, bitte.** *ienen owgenblik bitteh*
When will he/she be back?	**Wann ist er/sie wieder da?** *van ist ehr/zee veeder daa*
Will you tell him/her that I called?	**Würden Sie ihm/ihr sagen, dass ich angerufen habe?** *vewrden zee eem/eer zaagen dass ikh angeroofen haabeh*
My name is …	**Mein Name ist …** *mien naameh ist*
Would you ask him/her to phone me?	**Würden Sie ihn/sie bitten, mich anzurufen?** *vewrden zee een/zee bitten mikh antsooroofen*
Would you take a message, please?	**Würden Sie bitte etwas ausrichten?** *vewrden zee bitteh etvass owsrikhten*
I must go now.	**Ich muss jetzt aufhören.** *ikh muss yetst owfhuren*
Nice to speak to you.	**Es war nett, mit Ihnen zu sprechen.** *ess vaar net mit eenen tsoo shprekhen*
I'll be in touch.	**Ich melde mich wieder.** *ikh meldeh mikh veeder*
Bye.	**Auf Wiederhören.** *owf veederhuren*

STORES & SERVICES

Germany still places the emphasis on small, traditional, specialist shops, offering a more personal experience, although modern shopping malls (**Einkaufszentrum**) are to be found on the outskirts of most towns; in these malls credit cards are often accepted.

Local markets can be found everywhere, from big cities to the smallest regional towns.

While shopping, take time out to head to a **Café** or **Kaffeehaus** to enjoy the traditional afternoon coffee break (**Kaffee und Kuchen**).

I'd like …	**Ich hätte gern …** *ikh hetteh gehrn*
Do you have …?	**Haben Sie …?** *haaben zee*
How much is that?	**Was kostet das?** *vass kostet dass*
Thank you.	**danke** *dankeh*

STORES AND SERVICES
Where is …?

Where's the nearest …?	**Wo ist der/die/das nächste …?** *voa ist dehr/dee/dass naikhsteh*
Where's there a …?	**Wo gibt es einen/eine/ein …?** *voa gipt ess ienen/ieneh/ien*
Where's the shopping mall [centre]?	**Wo ist das Einkaufszentrum?** *voa ist dass ienkowfstsentrum*
Is it far from here?	**Ist es weit von hier?** *ist ess viet fon heer*
How do I get there?	**Wie komme ich dorthin?** *vee kommeh ikh dorthin*

Stores

antiques store	**das Antiquitätengeschäft** *dass antikvitaitengesehehft*
bakery	**die Bäckerei** *dee behkerie*
bookstore	**die Buchhandlung** *dee bookhhandlung*
butcher shop	**die Metzgerei** *dee metsgerie*
camera shop	**das Fotogeschäft** *dass foatogesehehft*
clothing store	**das Bekleidungsgeschäft** *dass bekliedungzgeshehft*

delicatessen	**das Feinkostgeschäft**
	dass fienkostgeshehft
department store	**das Kaufhaus** *dass kowfhowss*
drugstore [chemist]	**die Apotheke** *dee apotaykeh*
fish store [fishmonger]	**das Fischgeschäft** *dass fishgeshehft*
florist	**das Blumengeschäft**
	dass bloomengeshehft
gift shop	**der Geschenkladen**
	dehr geshenklaaden
grocery store	**das Lebensmittelgeschäft**
	dass laybensmittelgeshehft
health food store [shop]	**der Naturkostladen**
	dehr natoorkostlaaden
hardware store	**die Eisenwarenhandlung**
	dee iezenvaarenhandlung
jeweler	**der Juwelier** *dehr*
	yuveleer
market	**der Markt** *dehr markt*
pastry shop	**die Konditorei** *dee konditorrie*
produce store	**die Gemüsehandlung**
	dee gemewzehandlung
record [music] store	**das Plattengeschäft** *dass plattengeshehft*
shoe store	**das Schuhgeschäft** *dass shoogeshehft*
shopping mall [center]	**das Einkaufszentrum**
	dass ienkowfstsentrum
souvenir store	**der Andenkenladen**
	dehr andenkenlaaden
sporting goods store	**das Sportgeschäft** *dass shportgeshehft*
supermarket	**der Supermarkt** *dehr zoopermarkt*
tobacco store [tobacconist]	**das Tabakgeschäft** *dass tabakgeshehft*
toy store	**das Spielwarengeschäft**
	dass shpeelvaarengeshehft
liquor store [off-licence]	**die Wein- und Spirituosenhandlung**
	dee vien- unt shpiritoo-oazenhandlung

Services

clinic (for outpatients)	**die Poliklinik** *dee polikleenik*
dentist	**der Zahnarzt** *dehr tsaanaartst*
doctor	**der Arzt** *dehr aartst*
dry-cleaner	**die Reinigung** *dee rienigung*
hairdresser (ladies/men)	**der Friseur (Damen/Herren)** *dehr frizur (daamen-/hehren-)*
hospital	**das Krankenhaus** *dass krankenhowss*
laundromat	**der Waschsalon** *dehr vashzalong*
library	**die Bücherei** *dee bewkherie*
optician	**der Optiker** *dehr optiker*
police station	**die Polizei** *dee pollitsie*
post office	**das Postamt** *dass posstamt*
travel agency	**das Reisebüro** *dass riezebewroa*

Opening hours

When does the ... open/close?	**Wann öffnet/schließt ...?** *van urfnet/shleest*
Are you open in the evening?	**Haben Sie abends geöffnet?** *haaben zee aabents geurfnet*
Do you close for lunch?	**Haben Sie mittags geschlossen?** *haaben zee mittaags geshlossen*
Where is the ...?	**Wo ist ...?** *voa ist*
elevator	**der Fahrstuhl/Lift** *dehr faarshtool/lift*
It's on the ...	**Er/sie/es ist im ...** *ehr/zee/ess ist im*
1. floor [ground floor]	**Erdgeschoss** *ehrdgeshoss*
2. floor [first floor]	**ersten Stock** *ehrsten shtok*

IN A STORE

Kann ich Ihnen helfen? *kahn ikh eenen helfen*
(Can I help you?)
Danke. Ich sehe mich nur um. *dankeh ikh zayer mikh noor um (Thanks. I'm just browsing.)*

	Open	Close	Lunch	Closed
Stores	8/9 (8)	6:30(8:30 Thu) (6)[6:30]	12–1/2	Sat (fr. 2 p.m) exc. 1. Sat of month, Sun
Post office	8 (7:30)[9]	6 (5) (6:30)[6]	none (12–2) 12–2[1:45]	Sat p.m., Sun wkend
Banks	8:30 (9)[8:30]	4 (5:30 Thu) (3:30/4)[4:30–5:30]	1–2:30 12:30–1:30	wkend wkend

Business hours in Germany, (Austria), and [Switzerland], where different. Regulations for stores have been relaxed recently. In larger cities, many stores in airports and train stations are open on the weekends.

Service

Can you help me?	**Können Sie mir helfen?** *kurnen zee meer helfen*
I'm looking for …	**Ich suche …** *ikh zookheh*
I'm just browsing.	**Ich sehe mich nur um.** *ikh zayeh mikh noor um*
Do you have any …?	**Haben Sie …?** *haaben zee*
I'd like …	**Ich hätte gern …** *ikh hetteh gehrn*
Could you show me …?	**Können Sie mir … zeigen?** *kurnen zee meer … tsiegen*
How much is this/that?	**Was kostet dies/das?** *vass kostet deez/dass*
That's all, thanks.	**Danke, das ist alles.** *dankeh dass ist alless*
Where is the cash register?	**Wo ist die Kasse?** *voa ist dee kasser*

YOU MAY SEE	
GESCHÄFTSZEITEN	business hours
GESCHLOSSEN	closed
DURCHGEHEND GEÖFFNET	open all day
AUSGANG	exit
NOTAUSGANG	(emergency/fire) exit
ROLLTREPPE	escalator
STANDORT	you are here

ESSENTIAL

Welche ... möchten Sie?	What ... would you like?
Farbe/Form	color/shape
Qualität/Menge	quality/quantity
Welche Art möchten Sie?	What kind would you like?
An welche Preislage haben Sie gedacht?	What price range are you thinking of?

Preference

Around ... euros.	**Um die ... Euro.** *um dee ... oyroh*
It must be ...	**Es muss ... sein.** *ess muss ... zien*
large/small	**groß/klein** *groass/klien*
cheap/expensive	**preiswert/teuer** *priesvayrt/toyer*
dark/light	**dunkel/hell** *dunkel/hell*
light/heavy	**leicht/schwer** *liekht/shvayr*
oval/round/square	**oval/rund/quadratisch** *oavaal/runt/kvadraatish*
genuine/imitation	**echt/imitiert** *ekht/imiteert*
Do you have anything ...?	**Haben Sie etwas ...?** *haaben zee etvass*
larger/smaller	**Größeres/Kleineres** *grursseress/klieneress*
better quality	**Besseres** *besseress*
Can you show me ...?	**Können Sie mir ... zeigen?** *kurnen zee meer ... tsiegen*
that/this one	**das da/dieses hier** *dass daa/deezess heer*
these/those	**diese da/diese dort** *deezer daa/deezer dort*

YOU MAY HEAR

Werden Sie schon bedient?	Are you being served?
Kann ich Ihnen helfen?	Can I help you?
Wer ist der Nächste?	Who's next?
Was wünschen Sie?	What would you like?
Ist das alles?	Is that everything?
Sonst noch etwas?	Anything else?

Conditions of purchase

| Is there a warranty? | **Ist darauf Garantie?** |
| | *ist darowf garantee* |

| Are there any instructions with it? | **Ist eine Gebrauchsanweisung dabei?** |
| | *ist ieneh gebrowkhsanviezung dabie* |

Out of stock

| Can you order it for me? | **Können Sie es mir bestellen?** |
| | *kurnen zee ess meer beshtelen* |

| How long will it take? | **Wie lange dauert das?** |
| | *vee langeh dowert dass* |

| Where else might I get …? | **Wo sonst könnte ich … bekommen?** |
| | *voa zonst kurnteh ikh … bekommen* |

Decision

| I'll take it. | **Ich nehme es.** |
| | *ikh naymeh ess* |

| That's not quite what I want. | **Es ist nicht ganz das, was ich möchte.** |
| | *ess ist nikht gants dass vass ikh murkhteh* |

| No, I don't like it. | **Nein, das gefällt mir nicht.** |
| | *nien dass gefehlt meer nikht* |

| That's too expensive. | **Das ist zu teuer.** *dass ist tsoo toyer* |

YOU MAY HEAR

Es tut mir leid, wir haben keine.	I'm sorry, we don't have any.
Können Sie mir etwas anderes/ ein anderes Modell zeigen?	Can I show you something else/a different type?
Sollen wir es Ihnen bestellen?	Shall we order it for you?

IN A STORE

Guten Tag. Haben Sie Sweatshirts? *gooten taag haaben zee sweatshirts (Hi. Do you have sweatshirts?)*

Nein. Tut mir leid. *nien toot meer lite (No, I'm sorry.)*

Vielen Dank. *veelen dankh (Thank you very much.)*

Paying

VAT or sales tax (**MwSt**) is imposed on almost all goods and services. Tax can be reclaimed on larger purchases when returning home (outside the EU).

Small businesses tend not to accept credit cards and cash is much more widely used. Large stores, restaurants and hotels often accept major credit cards – look for the signs on the door.

YOU MAY SEE

KASSE	cashier/cash register
KASSE GESCHLOSSEN	cash register closed

Where do I pay?
Wo kann ich zahlen?
voa kan ikh tsaalen

How much is that? **Was kostet das?** *vass kostet dass*

Could you write it down please?
Können Sie das bitte aufschreiben?
kurnen zee dass bitteh owfshrieben

Do you accept …?
Nehmen Sie …? *naymen zee*

this credit card
diese Kreditkarte *deezeh kredeetkarteh*

traveler's checks
Reiseschecks *riezesheks*

I'll pay …
Ich zahle … *ikh tsaaleh*

in cash
bar *baar*

Could I have a receipt please?
Kann ich bitte eine Quittung haben?
kan ikh bitteh ieneh kvittung haaben

I think you've given me the wrong change.
Ich glaube, Sie haben mir falsch heraus-gegeben. *ikh glowbeh zee haaben meer falsh hayrowsgegayben*

May I have a shopping bag?
Kann ich eine Tragetasche haben?
kan ikh ieneh traagetasheh haaben

YOU MAY HEAR

Wie bezahlen Sie?	How are you paying?
Diese Transaktion ist nicht akzeptiert worden.	This transaction has not been approved.
Diese Karte ist ungültig.	This card is not valid.
Darf ich Ihren Ausweis sehen?	May I have further identification?

Complaints

This doesn't work.	**Das ist nicht in Ordnung.** *dass ist nikht in ordnung*
Can you exchange this, please?	**Können Sie das bitte umtauschen?** *kurnen zee dass bitteh umtowshen*
I'd like a refund.	**Ich hätte gern mein Geld zurück.** *ikh hetteh gehrn mien gelt tsoorewk*
Here's the receipt.	**Hier ist die Quittung.** *heer ist dee kvittung*
I don't have the receipt.	**Ich habe die Quittung nicht.** *ikh haabeh dee kvittung nikht*
I'd like to see the manager.	**Ich möchte mit dem Geschäftsführer sprechen.** *ikh murkhteh mit daym geshehftsfewrer shprekhen*

A **Reinigung** is a dry-cleaner, sometimes with a rapid service (**Schnellreinigung**). If you want a self-service laundromat, look for a **Waschsalon**.

Repairs/Cleaning

This is broken. Can you repair it?	**Das ist kaputt. Können Sie es reparieren?** *dass ist kaput. kurnen zee ess repareeren*
Do you have … for this?	**Haben Sie … hierfür?** *haaben zee … heerfewr*
a battery	**eine Batterie** *ieneh battehree*
replacement parts	**Ersatzteile** *ehrzatstieleh*
I'd like this …	**Können Sie das bitte …?** *kurnen zee dass bitteh*
cleaned/pressed	**reinigen/bügeln** *rieniggen/bewgeln*
Can you … this?	**Können Sie das …?** *kurnen zee dass*
alter/mend/patch	**ändern/reparieren/flicken** *ehndern/repareeren/flikken*
When will it/they be ready?	**Wann ist es/sind sie fertig?** *van ist ess/zint zee fehrtikh*
There's … missing.	**Es fehlt …** *ess faylt*

BANK/CURRENCY EXCHANGE OFFICE

At some banks, cash can be obtained from ATMs [cash machines] with bank or credit cards. Instructions are often given in English. You can also change money at travel agencies, airports, train stations and hotels, but the rate may not be as good. **Remember your passport when you want to change money.**

In 2002 the currency in most EU countries, including Germany and Austria, changed to the euro (€), divided into 100 cents. Switzerland is not in the EU and the currency there is Swiss francs, divided into 100 **Rappen**.

Germany & Austria   *Coins:* 1, 2, 5, 10, 20, 50 c.; €1, 2
                                   Notes: €5, 10, 20, 50, 100, 200, 500

Switzerland   *Coins:* 5, 10, 20, 50 rp.; 1, 2, 5 SF.
                                   Notes: 10, 20, 50, 100, 500, 1000 SF.

Where's the nearest …?	**Wo ist die nächste …?**
	voa ist dee naikhsteh
bank	**Bank** *bank*
currency exchange	**Wechselstube** *vekselshtoobeh*

Changing money

Can I exchange foreign currency here?	**Kann ich hier Devisen wechseln?** *kan ikh heer dayveezen vekseln*
I'd like to change some dollars/pounds into euros.	**Ich möchte Dollar/Pfund in Euro wechseln.** *ikh murkhteh dollar/pfunt in oyroh vekseln*
I want to cash some traveler's checks.	**Ich möchte Reiseschecks einlösen.** *ikh murkhteh riezesheks ienlurzen*
What's the exchange rate?	**Wie ist der Wechselkurs?** *vee ist dehr vekselkoors*
How much commission do you charge?	**Welche Gebühr nehmen Sie?** *velkheh gebewr naymen zee*
Can I have some small change, please?	**Kann ich bitte Kleingeld haben?** *kan ikh bitteh kliengeld haaben*

DEVISEN	foreign currency
BANKGEBÜHREN	bank charges
ALLE TRANSAKTIONEN	all transactions
KASSEN	cashiers
WECHSELSTUBE	bureau de change
GELDAUTOMAT	ATM [cash machine]

Security

YOU MAY HEAR

Kann ich ... sehen?	Can I see …?
Ihren Pass	your passport
Ihren Ausweis	some identification
Ihre Scheckkarte	your bank card
Ihre Adresse, bitte.	What's your address?
Wo wohnen Sie?	Where are you staying?
Füllen Sie bitte dieses Formular aus.	Fill in this form, please.
Bitte unterschreiben Sie hier.	Please sign here.

ATMs [Cash machines]

Can I withdraw money on my credit card here?

Kann ich hier mit meiner Kreditkarte Geld abheben? *kan ikh heer mit miener kredeetkarteh gelt aphayben*

Where are the ATMs [cash machines]?

Wo sind die Geldautomaten? *voa zint dee geltowtomaaten*

Can I use my ... card in the ATM [cash machine]?

Nimmt der Geldautomat meine Karte? *nimt dehr geltowtomaat …mieneh … karteh*

The ATM [cash machine] has eaten my card.

Der Geldautomat hat meine Karte einbehalten. *dehr geltowtomaat hat miemeh karteh ienbehalten*

138

PHARMACY

They are easily recognized by their sign: a green cross, usually lit up. If you are looking for a pharmacy at night, on Sundays or holidays, you'll find the address of all-night pharmacies **(Apotheken-Notdienst)** in the newspaper or in pharmacy windows.

Where's the nearest (all-night) pharmacy?	**Wo ist die nächste Apotheke (mit Nachtdienst)?** *voa ist dee naikhsteh apottaykeh (mit nakhtdeenst)*
Shall I wait?	**Kann ich darauf warten?** *kahn ikh darowf varten*
I'll come back for it.	**Ich hole es später ab.** *ikh hoaleh ess shpaiter ap*
I am …	**Ich bin …** *ikh bin*
diabetic	**Diabetiker** *dee-abaytiker*
epileptic	**Epileptiker** *epileptiker*
I am on the pill.	**Ich nehme die Pille.** *ikh naymeh dee pilleh*

Dosage instructions

How much should I take?	**Wie viel soll ich einnehmen?** *vee feel zoll ikh iennaymen*
How often should I take it?	**Wie oft soll ich es einnehmen?** *vee oft zoll ikh ess iennaymen*
Is it suitable for children?	**Ist es für Kinder geeignet?** *ist ess fewr kinder geiegnet*

YOU MAY HEAR

Nehmen Sie zwei Tabletten/ Teelöffel …	Take 2 tablets/teaspoons
vor/nach dem Essen	before/after meals
mit etwas Wasser	with water
ganz	whole
morgens/abends	in the morning/at night
… Tage lang	for … days

GIFT	poison
NUR ÄUSSERLICH ANWENDEN	for external use only
NICHT EINNEHMEN	not to be taken internally

Asking advice

What would you recommend for …?	**Was empfehlen Sie gegen …?** *vass empfaylen zee gaygen*
a cold	**eine Erkältung** *ieneh ehrkehltung*
a cough	**Husten** *hoosten*
diarrhea	**Durchfall** *doorkhfal*
a hangover	**einen Kater** *ienen kaater*
hayfever	**Heuschnupfen** *hoyshnupfen*
insect bites	**Insektenstiche** *inzektenshtikheh*
a sore throat	**Halsschmerzen** *hals-shmehrtsen*
sunburn	**Sonnenbrand** *zonnenbrant*
motion [travel] sickness	**Reisekrankheit** *riezekrankhiet*
an upset stomach	**Magenverstimmung** *maagenfehrstimmung*
Can I get it without a prescription?	**Kann ich das ohne Rezept bekommen?** *kan ikh dass oaneh retsept bekommen*

Over-the-counter treatment

Can I have …?	**Ich hätte gern …** *ikh hetteh gehrn*
antiseptic cream	**eine Wundsalbe** *ieneh vuntzalbeh*
(soluble) aspirin	**(lösliches) Aspirin** *(lurzlikhess) aspireen*
bandage	**einen Verband** *ienen fehrbant*
cottonballs	**Watte** *vatteh*
insect repellent/spray	**ein Insektenschutzmittel/Insektenspray** *ien inzektenshutsmittel/inzektenshpray*
pain killers	**ein Schmerzmittel** *ien shmehrtsmittel*
vitamin tablets	**Vitamintabletten** *vittameentabletten*

Toiletries

I'd like ...	**Ich hätte gern ...** *ikh hetteh gehrn*
aftershave	**ein Rasierwasser** *ien razeervasser*
after sun lotion	**After-Sun-Creme** *"after sun" kraym*
deodorant	**ein Deodorant** *ien deh-odoarant*
lip salve	**einen Lippenbalsam** *ienen lipernbalzaam*
moisturizing cream	**Feuchtigkeitscreme** *foykhtikhkietskraym*
razor blades	**Rasierklingen** *razeerklingen*
sanitary napkins [towels]	**Damenbinden** *daamenbinden*
soap	**eine Seife** *ieneh ziefeh*
sun block	**einen Sonnenblocker** *ienen zonnenblokker*
suntan lotion	**Sonnencreme/Sonnenmilch** *zonnenkraym/zonnenmilkh*
factor ...	**Lichtschutzfaktor ...** *likhtshutsfaktor*
tampons	**Tampons** *tampongs*
tissues	**Papiertaschentücher** *papeertashentewkher*
toilet paper	**Toilettenpapier** *twalettenpapeer*
toothpaste	**Zahnpasta** *tsaanpasta*

For the baby

baby food	**Babynahrung** *baybinaarung*
baby wipes	**Öltücher** *urltewkher*
diapers [nappies]	**Windeln** *vindeln*
sterilizing solution	**Sterilisierlösung** *shterilizeerlurzung*

Haircare

comb	**Kamm** *kam*
conditioner	**Spülung** *shpewlung*
hair brush	**Haarbürste** *haarbewrsteh*
hair mousse	**Schaumfestiger** *showmfestiger*
hair spray	**Haarspray** *haarshpray*
shampoo	**Haarwaschmittel** *haarvashmittel*

CLOTHING

Traditional national costume is still worn for special events. If you want to buy a traditional costume as a gift, look for **Lederhosen** (knee-length leather trousers) for boys, and **Dirndl** (traditional dress) for girls.

General

I'd like …	**Ich hätte gern …** *ikh hetteh gehrn*
Do you have any …?	**Haben Sie …?** *haaben zee*

Color

I'm looking for something in …	**Ich suche etwas in …** *kh zookheh etvass in*
beige	**beige** *bayzh*
black	**schwarz** *shvarts*
blue	**blau** *blow*
brown	**braun** *brown*
green	**grün** *grewn*
gray	**grau** *grow*
orange	**orange** *orrange*
pink	**rosa** *roaza*
purple	**lila** *leela*
red	**rot** *roat*
white	**weiß** *viess*
yellow	**gelb** *gelp*
light / dark	**hell** *hell* / **dunkel** *dunkel*
Do you have the same in …?	**Haben Sie das Gleiche in …?** *haaben zee dass gliekheh in*

Clothes and accessories

I'd like (a)…	**Ich hätte gern …** *ikh hetteh gehrn*
belt	**einen Gürtel** *ienen gewrtel*
bikini	**einen Bikini** *ienen bikeeni*
blouse	**eine Bluse** *ieneh bloozeh*
bra	**einen BH** *ienen bayhaa*
coat	**einen Mantel** *ienen mantel*
dress	**ein Kleid** *ien kliet*
handbag	**eine Handtasche** *ieneh hanttasheh*
hat	**einen Hut** *ienen hoot*
jacket	**eine Jacke** *ieneh yakeh*
jacket (of suit)	**ein Jackett** *ien zhakett*
jeans	**Jeans** *jeans*
leggings	**Leggings** *leggings*
pants	**eine Hose** *ieneh hoazeh*
pantyhose	**eine Strumpfhose** *ieneh shtrumpfhoazeh*
pullover	**einen Pullover** *ienen pulloaver*
raincoat	**einen Regenmantel** *ienen raygenmantel*
scarf	**ein Halstuch** *ien halstookh*
shirt	**ein Hemd** *ien hemt*
shorts	**Shorts** *"shorts"*
shorts/briefs	**eine Unterhose** *ieneh unterhoazeh*
skirt	**einen Rock** *ienen rok*
socks	**Socken** *zokken*
stockings	**Strümpfe** *shtrewmpfeh*
suit	**einen Anzug** *ienen antsoog*
sunglasses	**eine Sonnenbrille** *ieneh zonnenbrilleh*
sweatshirt	**ein Sweatshirt** *ien sweatshirt*
swimming trunks	**eine Badehose** *ieneh baadehoazeh*
swimsuit	**einen Badeanzug** *ienen baade-antsoog*
tie	**eine Krawatte** *ieneh kravatteh*
tights	**eine Strumpfhose** *ieneh shtrumpfhoazeh*
underpants	**eine Unterhose** *ieneh unterhoazeh*

Shoes

I'd like a pair of …	**Ich möchte ein Paar …** *ikh murkhteh ien paar*
boots	**Stiefel** *shteefel*
sandals	**Sandalen** *zandaalen*
shoes	**Schuhe** *shooeh*
slippers	**Hausschuhe** *hows-shooeh*
sneakers	**Turnschuhe** *toornshooeh*

Walking/hiking gear

knapsack/backpack	**einen Rucksack** *ienen rukzak*
walking boots	**Wanderschuhe** *vandershooeh*
waterproof jacket	**eine Regenjacke** *ieneh raygenyakkeh*
windbreaker	**einen Anorak** *ienen annorak*

Fabric

I want something in …	**Ich möchte etwas in …** *ikh murkhteh etvass in*
cotton	**Baumwolle** *bowmvolleh*
denim	**Jeansstoff** *dzeens-shtof*
lace	**Spitze** *shpitseh*
leather	**Leder** *layder*
linen	**Leinen** *lienen*
wool	**Wolle** *volleh*
Is this …?	**Ist das …?** *ist dass*
pure cotton	**reine Baumwolle** *rieneh bowmvolleh*
synthetic	**Synthetik** *zewntaytik*
Is it hand washable/ machine washable?	**Kann man es von Hand/in der Maschine waschen?** *kan man ess fon hant/in dehr masheeneh vashen*

YOU MAY SEE

VON HAND WASCHEN	handwash only
NICHT BÜGELN	do not iron

Does it fit?

Can I try this on?	**Kann ich es anprobieren?** *kan ikh ess anprobbeeren*
Where's the fitting room?	**Wo ist die Anprobekabine?** *voa ist dee anproabekabeeneh*
Do you have this in size …?	**Haben Sie das in Größe …?** *haaben zee dass in grursseh*
I don't know German sizes.	**Ich kenne die deutschen Größen nicht.** *ikh kenneh dee doychen grurssen nikht*
I'll take it.	**Ich nehme es.** *ikh naymeh ess*
It doesn't fit.	**Es passt nicht.** *ess past nikht*
It's too…	**Es ist zu …** *ess ist tsoo*
short/long	**kurz/lang** *kurts/lang*
tight/loose	**eng/weit** *eng/viet*

Sizes

	Dresses/Suits						Women's shoes			
American ⎱	8	10	12	14	16	18	6	7	8	9
British ⎰	10	12	14	16	18	20	4½	5½	6½	7½
Continental	38	40	42	44	46	48	37	38	40	41

	Shirts				Men's shoes								
American ⎱ **British**	15	16	17	18	6	7	8	8½	9	9½	10	11	
Continental	38	41	43	45	38	39	41	42	43	43	44	44	

YOU MAY SEE	
EXTRA GROSS	extra large (XL)
GROSS	large (L)
MITTEL	medium (M)
KLEIN	small (S)
KINDERGRÖSSE	children's size

Tipping: Germany and Austria: 10–15%; Switzerland: included

I'd like to make an appointment for tomorrow.	**Ich hätte gern für morgen einen Termin.** *ikh hetteh gehrn fewr morgen ienen tehrmeen*
I'd like a ...	**Ich möchte ...** *ikh murkhteh*
facial	**eine Gesichtsbehandlung** *ieneh gezikhtsbehandlung*
manicure	**eine Maniküre** *ieneh manikewreh*
massage	**eine Massage** *ieneh masaazheh*
waxing	**eine Wachsbehandlung** *ieneh vaksbehandlung*

Hairdresser

I'd like a ...	**Bitte ... Sie mir die Haare.** *bitteh ... zee meer dee haareh*
cut and blow-dry	**schneiden und fönen** *shnieden unt furnen*
shampoo and set	**waschen und legen** *vashen unt laygen*
I'd like a trim.	**Nur nachschneiden, bitte.** *noor naakhshnieden bitteh*
I'd like my hair colored/tinted.	**Bitte färben/tönen Sie mein Haar.** *bitteh fehrben/turnen zee mien haar*
I'd like my hair with bangs[a fringe].	**Bitte schneiden Sie mir einen Pony.** *bitteh shnieden zee meer ienen ponni*
I'd like my hair highlighted/permed.	**Bitte machen Sie mir Strähnchen/eine Dauerwelle.** *bitteh makhen zee meer shtrainkhen/ieneh dowervelleh*
A little more off the ...	**Bitte ... etwas kürzer.** *bitteh ... etvass kewrtser*
back/front	**hinten/vorne** *hinten/forneh*
neck/sides	**im Nacken/an den Seiten** *im nakken/an dayn zieten*
top	**oben** *oaben*
That's fine, thanks.	**Das ist gut so, danke.** *dass ist goot zoa dankheh*

HOUSEHOLD ARTICLES

I'd like (a/n)…	**Ich hätte gern …** *ikh hetteh gehrn*
adapter	**einen Adapter** *ienen adapter*
aluminum foil	**Alufolie** *aaloofoalieh*
bottle-opener	**einen Flaschenöffner** *ienen flashenurfner*
can [tin] opener	**einen Büchsenöffner** *ienen bewksenurfner*
clothes pins [pegs]	**Wäscheklammern** *vehsheklammern*
corkscrew	**einen Korkenzieher** *ienen korkentsee-er*
lightbulb	**eine Glühbirne** *ieneh glewbeerneh*
matches	**Streichhölzer** *shtriekh-hultser*
paper napkins	**Papierservietten** *papeerzehrvietten*
plastic wrap [cling film]	**Klarsichtfolie** *klaarzikhtfoalier*
plug (electrical)	**einen Stecker** *ienen shtekker*
scissors	**eine Schere** *ieneh shayreh*
screwdriver	**einen Schraubenzieher** *ienen shrowbentsee-er*

Cleaning products

bleach	**Bleichmittel** *bliekhmittel*
dish cloth [tea towel]	**Spüllappen** *shpewl-lappen*
dishwashing detergent	**Spülmittel** *shpewlmittel*
garbage [refuse] bags	**Müllbeutel** *mewllboytel*
detergent [washing powder]	**Waschpulver** *vashpulfer*
sponge	**Schwamm** *shvam*

China/Cutlery

cups	**Tassen** *tassen*
forks	**Gabeln** *gaabeln*
glasses	**Gläser** *glaizer*
knives	**Messer** *messer*
mugs	**Becher** *bekher*
plates	**Teller** *teller*
spoons	**Löffel** *lurfel*
teaspoons	**Teelöffel** *taylurfel*

JEWELER

Could I see …?	**Könnte ich … sehen?** *kurnteh ikh … zayen*
this/that	**dies/das** *deez/dass*
It's in the window.	**Es ist im Schaufenster.** *ess ist im shaoofenster*
I'd like (a/an) …	**Ich hätte gern …** *ikh hetteh gehrn*
alarm clock	**einen Wecker** *ienen vekker*
battery	**eine Batterie** *ieneh battehree*
bracelet	**ein Armband** *ien armbant*
brooch	**eine Brosche** *ieneh brosheh*
chain	**eine Kette** *ieneh ketteh*
clock	**eine Uhr** *ieneh oor*
earrings	**Ohrringe** *oar-ringeh*
necklace	**eine Halskette** *ieneh halsketteh*
ring	**einen Ring** *ienen ring*
watch	**eine Uhr** *ieneh oor*

Materials

Is this real silver/gold?	**Ist das echt Silber/Gold?** *ist dass ekht zilber/golt*
Is there any certification for it?	**Gibt es eine Bescheinigung dazu?** *gipt ess ieneh beshieniggung datsoo*
Do you have anything in …?	**Haben Sie etwas in …?** *haaben zee etvass in*
copper	**Kupfer** *kupfer*
crystal (quartz)	**Kristall** *kristal*
diamond	**Diamant** *diamant*
enamel	**Email** *ayma-ee*
pearl	**Perle** *pehrleh*
pewter	**Zinn** *tsin*
platinum	**Platin** *plaateen*
stainless steel	**Edelstahl** *aydelshtaal*
Do you have anything …?	**Haben Sie etwas …?** *haaben zee etvass*
gold-plated	**vergoldet** *fehrgoldet*
silver-plated	**versilbert** *fehrzilbert*

Foreign newspapers can usually be found at railway stations or airports, or at newsstands in major cities. English books you may find in large bookstores.

Cigarettes can be bought from specialist tobacco shops, vending machines, restaurants and supermarkets.

Do you sell English books/newspapers?	**Verkaufen Sie englische Bücher/Zeitungen?** *fehrkowfen zee englisheh bewkher/tsietungen*
I'd like (a/an) …	**Ich hätte gern …** *ikh hetteh gehrn*
book	**ein Buch** *ien bookh*
candy [sweets]	**Süßigkeiten** *zewssikhkieten*
chewing gum	**Kaugummi** *kowgummi*
chocolate bar	**einen Schokoladenriegel** *ienen shokollaadenreegel*
cigarettes (pack of)	**eine Schachtel Zigaretten** *ieneh shakhtel tsigaretten*
cigars	**Zigarren** *tsigaren*
dictionary	**ein Wörterbuch** *ien vurterbookh*
German-English	**Deutsch-Englisch** *doych-english*
envelopes	**Briefumschläge** *breefumshlaigeh*
guidebook for …	**einen Reiseführer von …** *ienen riezefewrer fon*
lighter	**ein Feuerzeug** *ien foyertsoyg*
magazine	**eine Zeitschrift** *ieneh tsietshrift*
map of the town	**einen Stadtplan** *ienen shtatplaan*
road map of …	**eine Straßenkarte von …** *ieneh shtraassenkarteh fon*
matches	**Streichhölzer** *shtriekh-hultser*
newspaper	**eine Zeitung** *ieneh tsietung*
pen	**einen Kugelschreiber** *ienen koogelshrieber*
postcard	**eine Postkarte** *ieneh posstkarteh*
stamps	**Briefmarken** *breefmarken*
tobacco	**Tabak** *tabak*

PHOTOGRAPHY

I'm looking for a/an …	**Ich suche …** *ikh zookheh*
automatic camera	**eine Automatikkamera** *ieneh owtomateekameraa*
compact camera	**eine Kompaktkamera** *ieneh kompaktkameraa*
disposable camera	**eine Einwegkamera** *ieneh ienvaygkameraa*
I'd like a/an …	**Ich hätte gern …** *ikh hetteh gehrn*
battery	**eine Batterie** *ieneh battehree*
camera case	**eine Fototasche** *ieneh foatotasher*
(electronic) flash	**einen (Elektronen)blitz** *ienen (aylektroanen)blits*
filter	**einen Filter** *ienen filter*
lens	**ein Objektiv** *ien obyekteef*
lens cap	**einen Objektivdeckel** *ienen obyekteefdekel*

Film/Processing

I'd like a … for this camera.	**Ich hätte gern einen … für diesen Fotoapparat.** *ikh hetteh gehrn ienen … fewr deezen foato-apparaat*
black and white film	**Schwarzweißfilm** *shvartsviesfilm*
color film	**Farbfilm** *farpfilm*
24/36 exposures	**vierundzwanzig/sechsunddreißig Aufnahmen** *feerunttsvantsikh/ zeksuntdriessikh owfnaamen*
I'd like this film developed, please.	**Bitte entwickeln Sie diesen Film.** *bitteh entvikeln zee deezen film*
Would you enlarge this, please?	**Können Sie das bitte vergrößern?** *kurnen zee dass bitteh fehrgrurssern*
When will the photos be ready?	**Wann sind die Fotos fertig?** *van zint dee foatoss fehrtikh*
I'd like to pick up my photos. Here's the receipt.	**Ich möchte meine Fotos abholen. Hier ist der Schein.** *ikh murkhteh mieneh foatoss aphoalen. heer ist dehr shien*

POLICE

Crime, theft, accidents or lost property should be reported to the nearest police department (**Polizei**).

To get the police in an emergency dial, ☎ 110 in Germany, ☎ 133 in Austria, ☎ 117 in Switzerland.

Where's the nearest police station?	**Wo ist die nächste Polizeiwache?** *voa ist dee naikhsteh pollitsievakher*
Does anyone here speak English?	**Spricht hier jemand Englisch?** *shprikht heer yaymant english*
I want to report ...	**Ich möchte ... melden.** *ikh murkhteh ... melden*
an attack	**einen Überfall** *ienen ewberfal*
a mugging/rape	**einen Straßenraub/eine Vergewaltigung** *ienen shtraassenrowp/ieneh fehrgevaltigung*
My child is missing.	**Mein Kind ist verschwunden.** *mien kint ist fehrshvunden*
Here's a photo of him/her.	**Hier ist ein Foto von ihm/ihr.** *heer ist ien foato fon eem/eer*
I need an English-speaking lawyer.	**Ich brauche einen Englisch sprechenden Anwalt.** *ikh browkheh ienen english shprekhenden anvalt*
I need to call the Consulate.	**Ich muss das Konsulat anrufen.** *ikh muss dass konsulaat ahnroofen*

YOU MAY HEAR

Können Sie ihn/sie beschreiben?	Can you describe him/her?
männlich/weiblich	male/female
blond/brünett	blonde/brunette
rothaarig/grau	redheaded/gray
kurzes/langes/schütteres Haar	short/long hair/balding
ungefähre Größe ...	approximate height ...
(ungefähres) Alter ...	aged (approximately) ...
Er/sie trug ...	He/she was wearing ...

STORES & SERVICES

I want to report a theft/break-in.	**Ich möchte einen Diebstahl/Einbruch melden.** *ikh murkhteh ienen deepshtaal/ienbrukh melden*
I've been robbed/mugged.	**Ich bin bestohlen / überfallen worden.** *ikh bin beshtoalen /ewberfallen vorden*
I've lost my ...	**Ich habe ... verloren.** *ikh haabeh ... fehrloaren*
Someone stole my ...	**Jemand hat ... gestohlen** *yemant hat ... geshtoalen*
camera	**meine Kamera** *mieneh kameraa*
(rental) car	**meinen (Miet)wagen** *mienen (meet)vaagen*
credit cards	**meine Kreditkarten** *mieneh kredeetkarten*
handbag	**meine Handtasche** *mieneh hant-tasheh*
money	**mein Geld** *mien gelt*
passport	**meinen Reisepass** *mienen riezepass*
ticket	**meine Fahrkarte** *mieneh faarkarteh*
wallet	**meinen Geldbeutel** *mienen geltboytel*
I need a police report for my insurance claim.	**Ich brauche eine polizeiliche Bescheinigung für meine Versicherung.** *ikh browkheh ieneh pollitsielikheh beshienigung fewr mieneh fehrzikherung*

YOU MAY HEAR

Wann ist es passiert?	When did it happen?
Wo wohnen Sie?	Where are you staying?
Wo ist es gestohlen worden?	Where was it taken from?
Wo waren Sie zu der Zeit?	Where were you at the time?
Wir besorgen Ihnen einen Dolmetscher.	We're getting an interpreter for you.
Bitte füllen Sie dieses Formular aus.	Please fill out this form.

POST OFFICE

Swiss post offices are recognized by the **PTT** sign and in Austria and Germany they are marked **Post**.

Mailboxes are yellow. They may have separate slots for postcards **(Postkarten),** letters **(Briefe)** and abroad **(Ausland)** or, in Switzerland **A** (1. class) or **B** (2. class). Stamps can be bought from vending machines, from some tobacconists, as well as from the post office.

General queries

Where is the nearest post office?	**Wo ist das nächste Postamt?** *voa ist dass naikhsteh posstamt*
What time does the post office open/close?	**Wann öffnet/schließt das Postamt?** *van urfnet/shleest dass posstamt*
Does it close for lunch?	**Ist es mittags geschlossen?** *ist ess mittaags geshlossen*
Where's the mailbox?	**Wo ist der Briefkasten?** *voa ist dehr breefkasten*

Buying stamps

A stamp for this postcard/letter, please.	**Eine Briefmarke für diese Postkarte/ diesen Brief, bitte.** *ieneh breefmarkeh fewr deezeh posstkarteh/deezen breef bitteh*
A …-cent stamp.	**Eine Briefmarke zu … Cent.** *ieneh breefmarkeh tsoo … tsent*
What's the postage for a postcard/letter to …?	**Was kostet eine Postkarte/ein Brief nach …?** *vass kostet ieneh posstkarteh/ ien breef naakh*

IN A POST OFFICE

Briefmarken für diese Postkarten, bitte. *breefmarken fewr deezehr posstkarteh bitteh* (*Stamps for these postcards, please.*)
Hier bitte. *heer bitteh* (*Here you are.*)
Vielen Dank. *veelen dankh* (*Thank you very much.*)

Sending packages

I want to send this package by …	**Ich möchte dieses Paket per … schicken.** *ikh murkhteh deezess pakayt pehr … shikken*
airmail	**Luftpost** *luftposst*
express	**Express** *ekspress*
registered mail	**Einschreiben** *ienshrieben*
It contains …	**Es enthält …** *ess enthehlt*

Telecommunications

I'd like a phonecard, please.	**Ich hätte gern eine Telefonkarte.** *ikh hetteh gehrn ieneh taylayfoankarteh*
10/20/50 units	**zehn/zwanzig/fünfzig Einheiten** *tsayn/tsvantsikh/fewnftsikh ienhieten*
Do you have a photocopier/fax machine here?	**Haben Sie hier ein Fotokopiergerät/ Telefax?** *haaben zee heer ien oatokopeergerait/taylayfaks*
I'd like to send a message…	**Ich möchte gern eine Nachricht … schicken.** *ikh murkhteh gehrn ieneh nakhrikht …shikken*
by E-mail/fax	**per E-mail/Fax** *pehr e-mail post/fax*
What's your E-mail address?	**Wie ist Ihre E-mail Adresse?** *vee ist eereh e-mail postadresseh*
Can I access the Internet here?	**Kann ich auf das Internet zugreifen?** *kan ikh awf dass internet tsoogriefen*
What are the charges per hour?	**Wie viel kostet es pro Stunde?** *vee feel kostet es pro shtundeh*
How do I log on?	**Wie logge ich ein?** *vee loggeh ikh ien*

SOUVENIRS

Here are some suggestions for souvenirs.

Germany:	beer mugs **(Bierkrüge)**
	wooden toys **(Holzspielwaren)**
	cuckoo clocks **(Kuckucksuhren)**
	furs **(Pelze)**
Austria:	petit-point embroidery and linen
	goods **(Stickerei)**
	jewelry **(Schmuck)**
	chocolate marzipan balls **(Mozartkugeln)**
	pottery **(Töpferei)**
Switzerland:	watches **(Armbanduhren)**
	cuckoo clocks **(Kuckucksuhren)**
	cheese **(Käse)**
	chocolate **(Schokolade)**
	Swiss Army knives **(Taschenmesser)**
	wooden products **(Holzartikel)**

Gifts

I'd like a …	**Ich hätte gern …** *ikh hetteh gehrn …*
bottle of wine	**eine Flasche Wein** *ieneh flasheh vien*
box of chocolates	**eine Schachtel Pralinen** *ieneh shakhtel praleenen*
calendar	**einen Kalender** *ienen kalender*
key ring	**einen Schlüsselanhänger** *ienen shlewsselanhehnger*
postcard	**eine Postkarte** *ieneh posstkarteh*
souvenir guide	**einen Andenkenbildband** *ienen andenkenbiltbant*
T-shirt	**ein T-Shirt** *ien t-shirt*
kitchen towel	**ein Geschirrtuch** *ien geshirtookh*

Music

I'd like a ...	**Ich hätte gern ...** *ikh hetteh gehrn*
cassette	**eine Kassette** *ieneh kassetteh*
compact disc	**eine CD** *ieneh tsayday*
videocassette	**eine Videokassette** *ieneh veedayoakassetteh*
Who are the popular native singers/bands?	**Welche einheimischen Sänger/Gruppen sind beliebt?** *velkheh ienhiemishen zehnger/gruppen zint beleebt*

Toys and games

I'd like a toy/game ...	**Ich hätte gern ein Spielzeug/Spiel ...** *ikh hetteh gehrn ien shpeeltsoyg/shpeel*
for a boy	**für einen Jungen** *fewr ienen yungen*
for a 5-year-old girl	**für ein fünfjähriges Mädchen** *fewr ien fewnfjairigess maitkhen*
pail and shovel [bucket and spade]	**Eimer und Schaufel** *iemer unt showfel*
chess set	**Schachspiel** *shakhshpeel*
doll	**Puppe** *puppeh*
electronic game	**Elektronikspiel** *aylektroaneekshpeel*
teddy bear	**Teddybär** *teddibair*

Antiques

How old is this?	**Wie alt ist das?** *vee alt ist dass*
Do you have anything from the ... era?	**Haben Sie etwas aus der ... Zeit?** *haaben zee etvass owss dehr ... tsiet*
Can you send it to me?	**Können Sie es mir schicken?** *kurnen zee ess meer shikken*
Will I have problems with customs?	**Bekomme ich Schwierigkeiten mit dem Zoll?** *bekommer ikh shveerikhkieten mit daym tsol*
Is there a certificate of authenticity?	**Ist eine Echtheitsurkunde vorhanden?** *ist ieneh ekhthietsoorkundeh forhanden*

SUPERMARKET/FOODSTORE

Supermarket chains: **Tengelmann, HL, Minimal, Lidl, Penny, Aldi;** Large supermarkets with the widest selection of food items and international specialties: **Toom, Wertkauf, Real.**

At the supermarket

Excuse me. Where can I find …?	**Entschuldigen Sie. Wo finde ich …?** *entshuhldigen zee. voa findeh ikh*
Do I pay for this here or at the checkout?	**Muss ich das hier oder an der Kasse bezahlen?** *muss ikh dass heer oader an dehr kasseh betsaalen*
Where are the carts [trolleys]/baskets?	**Wo sind die Einkaufswagen/ Einkaufskörbe?** *voa zint dee ienkowfsvaagen/ienkowfskurbeh*
Is there a … here?	**Gibt es hier …?** *gipt ess heer*
bakery	**eine Bäckerei** *ieneh behkerie*
cheese counter	**eine Käsetheke** *ieneh kaizertayker*
fish counter	**eine Fischtheke** *ieneh fishtayker*

YOU MAY SEE

BROT UND KUCHEN	bread and cakes
FRISCHES GEMÜSE	fresh produce
FRISCHFISCH	fresh fish
FRISCHFLEISCH	fresh meat
GEFLÜGEL	poultry
HAUSHALTSWAREN	household goods
KONSERVEN	canned goods
MILCHPRODUKTE	dairy products
PUTZMITTEL	cleaning products
SONDERANGEBOT	special offer / on sale
TIEFKÜHLKOST	frozen foods
TIERFUTTER	pet food
WEIN UND SPIRITUOSEN	wines and spirits

AT THE GROCERY STORE

Do you have any …?	**Haben Sie …?** *haaben zee*
I'd like some of that/those.	**Ich hätte gern etwas davon.** *ikh hetteh gehrn etvass dafon*
I'd like (a)…	**Ich hätte gern …** *ikh hetteh gehrn*
two slices of ham	**zwei Scheiben Schinken** *tvie shayben sheenken*
half-kilo of tomatoes	**ein halbes Kilo Tomaten** *ien halbess keelo tomaaten*
100 grams of cheese	**hundert Gramm Käse** *hundert gram kaizeh*
liter of milk	**einen Liter Milch** *ienen leeter milkh*
half-dozen eggs	**ein halbes Dutzend Eier** *ien halbess dutsent ie-er*
piece of cake	**ein Stück Kuchen** *ien shtewk kookhen*
bottle of wine	**eine Flasche Wein** *ieneh flasheh vien*
can of Coke	**eine Dose Cola** *ieneh doazeh kohla*
carton of milk	**eine Tüte Milch** *ieneh tewteh milkh*
jar of jam	**ein Glas Marmelade** *ien glaass marmelaadeh*
packet of chips [crisps]	**eine Packung Chips** *ieneh pakkung chips*
jar [tube] of mustard	**eine Tube Senf** *ieneh toobeh zenf*
That's all, thanks.	**Danke, das ist alles.** *dankheh dass ist alless*

IN A SUPERMARKET

Wo finde ich Zucker, bitte? *voa findeh ikh tsukker bitteh*
(Where do I find sugar, please?)
Dort drüben, Gang 4. *doort trewben gahng veer (Over there, aisle 4.)*
Vielen Dank. *veelen dankh (Thank you very much.)*

Provisions/picnic

apples	**Äpfel** *epfel*
beer	**Bier** *beer*
butter	**Butter** *butter*
candy [sweets]	**Süßigkeiten** *zewssikhkieten*
cheese	**Käse** *kaizeh*
chips	**Chips** *chips*
cookies [biscuits]	**Kekse** *kekseh*
eggs	**Eier** *ie-er*
grapes	**Weintrauben** *vientrowben*
ice cream	**Eis** *iess*
instant coffee	**Pulverkaffee** *pulferkafay*
jam	**Marmelade** *marmelaadeh*
loaf of bread	**Brot** *broat*
margarine	**Margarine** *margareeneh*
milk	**Milch** *milkh*
mustard	**Senf** *zenf*
oranges	**Orangen** *orrangzhen*
rolls (bread)	**Brötchen** *brurtkhen*
sausages	**Würstchen** *vewrstkhen*
soft drink	**Erfrischungsgetränk** *ehrfrishungzgetrehnk*
sugar	**Zucker** *tsukker*
tea bags	**Teebeutel** *tayboytel*
wine	**Wein** *vien*
yogurt	**Jogurt** *yoagoort*

The following conversion charts contain the most commonly used measures.

1 Gramm (g)	= 1000 milligrams	= 0.035 oz.
1 Pfund (Pfd)	= 500 grams	= 1.1 lb
1 Kilogramm (kg)	= 1000 grams	= 2.2 lb
1 Liter (l)	= 1000 milliliters	= 1.06 U.S / 0.88 Brit. quarts
		= 2.11 /1.8 US /Brit. pints
		= 34 /35 US /Brit. fluid oz.
		= 0.26 /0.22 US /Brit. gallons
1 Zentimeter (cm)	= 10 millimeters	= 0.4 inch
1 Meter (m)	= 100 centimeters	= 39.37 inches/3.28 ft.
1 Kilometer (km)	= 1000 meters	= 0.62 mile
1 Quadratmeter (qm)	= 10.8 square feet	
1 Hektar (qm)	= 2.5 acres	
1 Quadratkilometer (qkm)	= 247 acres	

Not sure whether to put on a bathing suit or a winter coat? Here is a comparison of Fahrenheit and and Celsius/Centigrade degrees.

-40° C – -40° F	5° C – 41°F	**Oven Temperatures**	
-30°C – -22° F	10°C – 50°F	100° C – 212° F	
-20°C – -4° F	15°C – 59°F	121° C – 250° F	
-10°C – 14° F	20°C – 68°F	149° C – 300° F	
-5° C – 23° F	25°C – 77°F	177° C – 350° F	
-1° C – 30° F	30°C – 86°F	204° C – 400° F	
0° C – 32° F	35°C – 95°F	260° C – 500° F	

When you know	Multiply by	To find
ounces	28.3	grams
pounds	0.45	kilograms
inches	2.54	centimeters
feet	0.3	meters
miles	1.61	kilometers
square inches	6.45	sq. centimeters
square feet	0.09	sq. meters
square miles	2.59	sq. kilometers
pints (US/Brit)	0.47 / 0.56	liters
gallons (US/Brit)	3.8 / 4.5	liters
Fahrenheit	5/9, after subtracting 32	Centigrade
Centigrade	9/5, then add 32	Fahrenheit

HEALTH

Before you leave, make sure your health insurance policy covers any illness or accident while on vacation.

In Germany, EU citizens with a form E11 are eligible for free medical treatment, However, it is still advisable to take out travel insurance. Switzerland is not part of the EU and health care is very expensive there — so insurance is strongly recommended as you'll be expected to pay for any medical treatment you receive.

German doctors tend to be titled according to their specialties. For a GP you should look for a **praktischer Arzt.**

Staff at a pharmacy/chemist can recommend a nurse if you need injections or other care.

In an emergency call the Red Cross (**Rotes Kreuz**) the medical emergency service (**Ärztlicher Notfalldienst),** which will give you a list of doctors (see the telephone directory for the number).

Ambulance: Germany ☎ 115, Austria ☎ 144, Switzerland ☎ 114 (most areas).

DOCTOR (GENERAL)

Where can I find a doctor/dentist?	**Wo finde ich einen Arzt/Zahnarzt?** *voa findeh ikh ienen aartst/ tsaanaartst*
Where is there a doctor who speaks English?	**Wo gibt es einen Arzt, der Englisch spricht?** *voa gipt ess ienen aartst dehr english shprikht*
Are you a doctor?	**Sind Sie Arzt?** *zint zee aartst*
Where's the doctor's office?	**Wo ist die Arztpraxis?** *voa ist dee aartstpraksiss*
What are the office hours?	**Wann ist Sprechstunde?** *van ist shprekhshtundeh*
Could the doctor come to see me here?	**Könnte der Arzt mich hier besuchen?** *kurnteh dehr aartst mikh heer bezookhen*
Can I make an appointment for ...?	**Kann ich ... einen Termin bekommen?** *kan ikh ... ienen tehrmeen bekommen*
today/tomorrow	**heute/morgen** *hoyteh/morgen*

Accident and injury

My ... is injured.	... ist verletzt. *ist fehrletst*
husband/ wife /friend	mein Mann/meine Frau/mein Freund *mien man/mieneh frow/mien froynd*
son/daughter	mein Sohn/meine Tochter *mien zoan/mieneh tokhter*

He/She is ...	Er/Sie ... *ehr/zee*
unconscious	ist bewusstlos *ist bevustloass*
bleeding (heavily)	blutet (schwer) *blootet (shvayr)*
(seriously) injured	ist (schwer) verletzt *ist (shvayr) fehrletst*

I've got a/an...	Ich habe ... *ikh haabeh*
cut	eine Schnittwunde *ieneh shnitvundeh*
insect bite	einen Insektenstich *ienen inzektenshtikh*
rash	einen Ausschlag *ienen ows-shlaag*
sprained muscle	eine Muskelzerrung *ieneh muskeltserung*
swelling	eine Schwellung *ieneh shvellung*

Short-term symptoms

I've been feeling sick [ill] for ... days.	Ich fühle mich seit ... Tagen nicht wohl. *ikh fewleh mikh ziet ... taagen nikht voal*
I feel faint.	Mir ist schwindelig. *meer ist shvinderlikh*
I feel feverish/shivery.	Ich habe Fieber/Schüttelfrost. *ikh haabeh feeber/shewttelfrost*
I've been vomiting.	Ich habe mich übergeben. *ikh haabeh mikh ewbergayben*
I've got diarrhea.	Ich habe Durchfall. *ikh haabeh doorkhfal*
It hurts here.	Es tut hier weh. *ess toot heer vay*
I have (a/an) ...	Ich habe ... *ikh haabeh*
cold	eine Erkältung *ieneh ehrkehltung*
cramps	Krämpfe *krehmpfeh*
headache	Kopfschmerzen *kopfshmehrtsen*
sore throat	Halsschmerzen *hals-shmehrtsen*
stomachache	Magenschmerzen *maagenshmehrtsen*

Health conditions

I am …	**Ich bin …** *ikh bin*
diabetic	**Diabetiker** *deeabaytiker*
epileptic	**Epileptiker** *epileptiker*
handicapped	**behindert** *behindert*
pregnant	**schwanger** *shvanger*

I am arthritic/asthmatic. **Ich habe Arthritis/Asthma.**
ikh haabeh aartreetiss/astma

I have a heart condition/ **Ich habe ein Herzleiden/zu hohen**
high blood pressure. **Blutdruck.** *ikh haabeh ien hehrtslieden/
tsoo hoaen blootdruk*

I had a heart attack **Ich hatte vor … Jahren einen**
… years ago. **Herzanfall.** *ikh hatteh foar … yaaren
ienen hehrtsanfal*

Parts of the body

appendix	**Blinddarm** (m) *blintdarm*		knee	**Knie** (n) *knee*
arm	**Arm** (m) *arm*		leg	**Bein** (n) *bien*
back	**Rücken** (m) *rewken*		lip	**Lippe** (f) *lippeh*
bladder	**Blase** (f) *blaazeh*		liver	**Leber** (f) *layber*
bone	**Knochen** (m) *knokhen*		mouth	**Mund** (m) *munt*
breast	**Brust** (f) *brust*		muscle	**Muskel** (m) *muskel*
ear	**Ohr** (n) *oar*		neck	**Hals** (m) *hals*
eye	**Auge** (n) *owgeh*		nerve	**Nerv** (m) *nehrf*
face	**Gesicht** (n) *gezikht*		nose	**Nase** (f) *naazeh*
finger	**Finger** (m) *finger*		rib	**Rippe** (f) *rippeh*
foot	**Fuß** (m) *fooss*		shoulder	**Schulter** (f) *shulter*
gland	**Drüse** (f) *drewzeh*		skin	**Haut** (f) *howt*
hand	**Hand** (f) *hunt*		stomach	**Magen** (m) *maagen*
head	**Kopf** (m) *kopf*		throat	**Hals** (m) *hals*
heart	**Herz** *hehrts*		thumb	**Daumen** (m) *dowmen*
jaw	**Kiefer** (m) *keefer*		toe	**Zehe** (f) *tsayeh*
joint	**Gelenk** (n) *gelenk*		tongue	**Zunge** (f) *tsungeh*
kidney	**Niere** (f) *neereh*		tonsils	**Mandeln** *mandeln*

Doctor's Inquiries

Wie lange fühlen Sie sich schon so?	How long have you been feeling like this?
Haben Sie das zum ersten Mal?	Is this the first time you've had this?
Nehmen Sie noch andere Medikamente?	Are you taking any other medications?
Sind Sie gegen irgendetwas allergisch?	Are you allergic to anything?
Leiden Sie an Appetitlosigkeit?	Have you lost your appetite?

Examination

Bitte streifen Sie den Ärmel hoch.	Roll up your sleeve, please.
Bitte machen Sie den Oberkörper frei.	Please undress to the waist.
Bitte legen Sie sich hin.	Please lie down.
Machen Sie den Mund auf.	Open your mouth.
Atmen Sie tief durch.	Breathe deeply.
Husten Sie, bitte.	Cough, please.
Wo tut es weh?	Where does it hurt?
Tut es hier weh?	Does it hurt here?

Diagnosis

Sie müssen geröntgt werden.	I want you to have an X-ray.
Ich brauche eine Blutprobe/ Stuhlprobe/Urinprobe von Ihnen.	I want a specimen of your blood/stool/urine.
Ich überweise Sie an einen Facharzt.	I want you to see a specialist.
Ich überweise Sie ins Krankenhaus.	I want you to go to the hospital.
gebrochen/verstaucht	broken/sprained
Sie haben … eine Blinddarmentzündung	You've got (a/an) … appendicitis

eine Blasenentzündung	cystitis
Sie haben ...	You've got (a) ...
eine Grippe	flu
eine Lebensmittelvergiftung	food poisoning
eine Fraktur	fracture
eine Magenschleimhautentzündung	gastroenteritis
einen Bruch	hernia
eine ... Entzündung	inflammation of ...
Masern	measles
eine Lungenentzündung	pneumonia
Ischias	sciatica
eine Mandelentzündung	tonsilitis
einen Tumor	tumor
eine Geschlechtskrankheit	venereal disease
Es ist entzündet.	It's infected.
Es ist ansteckend.	It's contagious.

Treatment

Ich gebe Ihnen ...	I'll give you ...
ein Antiseptikum	an antiseptic
ein Schmerzmittel	a pain killer
Ich verschreibe Ihnen ...	I'm going to prescribe ...
Antibiotika	a course of antibiotics
Zäpfchen	some suppositories
Sind Sie gegen bestimmte Medikamente allergisch?	Are you allergic to any medication?
Nehmen Sie 2 Tabletten/Teelöffel ...	Take 2 tablets/teaspoons ...
alle vier Stunden	every 4 hours
vor den Mahlzeiten	before meals
nach den Mahlzeiten	after meals
Kommen Sie in ... Tagen wieder.	I'd like you to come back in ... days.
Gehen Sie zum Arzt, wenn Sie wieder zu Hause sind.	Consult a doctor when you get home.

GYNECOLOGIST

I have ...	**Ich habe ...** *ikh haabeh*
abdominal pains	**Unterleibsschmerzen** *unterliebs shmehrtsen*
period pains	**Menstruationsbeschwerden** *menstruatsioansbeshvayrden*
a vaginal infection	**eine Scheidenentzündung** *ieneh shiedenentsewndung*
I haven't had my period for ... months.	**Ich habe seit ... Monaten meine Periode nicht mehr gehabt.** *ikh haabeh ziet ... moanaten mieneh perioadeh nikht mayr gehapt*
I'm on the pill.	**Ich nehme die Pille.** *ikh naymeh dee pilleh*

HOSPITAL

Notify my family.	**Benachrichtigen Sie meine Familie.** *benaakhrikhtiggen zee mieneh fameelieh*
What are the visiting hours?	**Wann ist Besuchszeit?** *van ist bezookhs-tsiet*
I'm in pain.	**Ich habe Schmerzen.** *ikh haabeh shmehrtsen*
I can't eat/sleep.	**Ich kann nicht essen/schlafen.** *ikh kan nikht essen/shlaafen*
When will the doctor come?	**Wann kommt der Arzt?** *van komt dehr aartst*
Which ward is ... in?	**Auf welcher Station liegt ...?** *owf velkher shtatsioan leegt*

OPTICIAN

I'm nearsighted/farsighted.	**Ich bin kurzsichtig/weitsichtig.** *ikh bin kurtszikhtikh/vietzikhtikh*
I've lost ...	**Ich habe ... verloren.** *ikh haabeh ... fehrloaren*
one of my contact lenses	**eine meiner Kontaktlinsen** *ieneh mieneh kontaktlinzen*
my glasses	**meine Brille** *mieneh brilleh*
Could you give me a replacement?	**Können Sie es ersetzen?** *kurnen zee ess ehrzetsen*

DENTIST

If you see a dentist, you might have to pay the bill on the spot; save all receipts for reimbursement. EU nationals should obtain the E111 form before leaving home.

I have a toothache.	**Ich habe Zahnschmerzen.** *ikh haabeh tsaanshmehrtsen*
I've broken a tooth/crown.	**Mir ist ein Zahn/eine Krone abgebrochen.** *meer ist ien tsaan/ieneh kroaneh apgebrokhen*
I've lost a filling.	**Ich habe eine Füllung verloren.** *ikh haabeh ieneh fewllung fehrloaren*
Can you repair this denture?	**Können Sie dieses Gebiss reparieren?** *kurnen zee deezess gebiss repareeren*
I don't want it extracted.	**Ich möchte ihn nicht ziehen lassen.** *ikh murkhteh een nikht tsee-en lassen*

YOU MAY HEAR

Ich gebe Ihnen eine Spritze/eine örtliche Betäubung.	I'm going to give you an injection/a local anesthetic.
Sie brauchen eine Füllung/Krone.	You need a filling/cap [crown].
Ich muss ihn ziehen.	I'll have to take it out.
Ich kann es nur provisorisch behandeln.	I can only fix it temporarily.
Sind Sie krankenversichert?	Do you have health insurance?
Kommen Sie in ... Tagen wieder.	Come back in ... days.

PAYMENT/INSURANCE

Can I have a receipt for my health insurance?	**Kann ich eine Quittung für meine Krankenkasse haben?** *kan ikh ieneh kvittung fewr mieneh krankenkasseh haaben*
Would you fill out this health insurance form, please?	**Würden Sie bitte dieses Krankenkassenformular ausfüllen?** *vewrden zee bitteh deezess krankenkassen-formulaar owsfewlen*
Do you have Form E111?	**Haben Sie das Formular E-Hundertelf?** *haaben zee dass formullaar ay-hundertelf*

DICTIONARY
ENGLISH-GERMAN

A

a few einige
a little ein wenig
a lot viel
A.P. Vollpension f
abdominal pains
Unterleibsschmerzen pl
able to be können
about *(approximately)* etwa
above *(place)* über
abroad im Ausland
abscess Abszess m
accept, to akzeptieren
access *(n)* Zugang m; Zutritt m
accessories Zubehör nt *sing*
accident Unfall m
accidentally versehentlich
accompany, to begleiten
accountant Buchhalter(in) m/f
ace *(cards)* As nt
across über
acrylic Acryl nt
activities Aktivitäten fpl
actor/actress Schauspieler/-in
adapter Adapter m
address Adresse f
adjoining nebeneinander liegend
~ room Nebenzimmer nt
admission charge Eintritt m
adult Erwachsene m/f
advance: in advance im voraus
after *(place)* nach ; *(time)*
afternoon, in the nachmittags
after shave Rasierwasser nt
aftersun lotion After-Sun-Creme f
age: what age? wie alt?
aged: ... Alter: ... nt
ago: 10 minutes ago vor 10 Minuten
agree: I agree ich bin einverstanden
air Luft f; **~ bag** Airbag m
~ conditioning Klimaanlage f ;
~ mattress Luftmatratze f ;
~ pump Luftpumpe f

airline Fluggesellschaft f
airmail Luftpost f
airplane Flugzeug nt
airport Flughafen m
aisle Gang m
alcoholic *(drink)* alkoholisch
all alle, alles
allergic, to be allergisch sein
allergy Allergie f
allowance erlaubte Menge f
allowed: is it allowed? ist es erlaubt?
almost fast
alone allein
already schon
also auch
alter, to ändern
always immer
am: I am ich bin
ambassador Botschafter(in) m/f
ambulance Krankenwagen m
American *(adj)* amerikanisch; *(n)*
Amerikaner(in) m/f;
amount Betrag m
amusement arcade Spielhalle f
anchor, to vor Anker gehen
and und
anesthetic Betäubungsmittel nt
angling Angeln nt
animal Tier nt
another noch ein;
~ time ein andermal
antacid Antazidum nt
antenna *(car/tv)* Antenne f
antibiotics Antibiotika pl
antifreeze Frostschutzmittel nt
antiques Antiquitäten pl ;
~ store Antiquitätengeschäft nt
antiseptic Antiseptikum nt
any: anymore noch mehr
anything else? sonst noch etwas?
apartment Wohnung f
apologize: I apologize es tut mir leid
apple Apfel m
appointment Termin m
approximately ungefähr
April April m
archery Bogenschießen nt
architect Architekt(in) m/f

architecture Architektur f
are you ...? sind Sie ...?
area Gegend f **~ code** Vorwahl f
arm Arm m
around *(place)* um ... herum, *(time, gegen, town)* durch
arrange: can you arrange it? können Sie dafür sorgen?
arrest, to be under festgenommen werden
arrive, to ankommen
art Kunst f
art gallery Kunstgalerie f
artery Arterie f
arthritic, to be Arthritis haben
artificial sweetener Süßstoff m
artist Künstler(in) m/f
as soon as possible so bald wie möglich
ashore, to go an Land gehen
ashtray Aschenbecher m
ask, to fragen
asleep, to be schlafen
aspirin Aspirin nt
asthmatic, to be Asthma haben
at *(place)* an; *(time)* um
at least mindestens
attack Überfall m ; *(medic.)* Anfall m
attendant *(museum)* Aufseher(in) m/f
attractive attraktiv
August August m
aunt Tante f
Australia Australien nt
Australian *(n)* Australier(in) m/f
Austria Österreich nt
Austrian *(n)* Österreicher(in) m/f
automated teller Geldautomat m
automatic *(car)* Automatikwagen m
automobile *(car)* Auto nt
autumn Herbst m
avalanche Lawine f
away weg
awful scheußlich

B

baby Baby nt ; **~ bag** Babytragetasche f
~ bottle Fläschchen nt; **~ food** Babynahrung f ; **~ seat** Babysitz m; **~sitter** Babysitter m;
back Rücken m
backache Rückenschmerzen pl
backpack Rucksack m
backpacking Rucksackwandern nt
bad schlecht
baggage Gepäck nt ; **~ allowance** Freigepäck nt; **~ check** Gepäck-aufbewahrung f ; **~ claim** Gepäckausgabe f
~ locker Schließfach nt
baked gebacken
bakery Bäckerei f
balcony Balkon m ; *(theater)* oberster Rang m
ball Ball m
ballet Ballett nt
banana Banane f
band *(musical group)* Band/Gruppe f
bandage Verband m
bank Bank f ; **~ account** Bankkonto nt; **~ card** Scheckkarte f ; **~ loan** Darlehen nt
bar Bar f ; *(hotel)* Bar f
barber Friseur m
basin Becken nt
basket: shopping basket Einkaufskorb m
basketball Basketball m
bath: to take a bath baden; **~ room** Toilette f ; Badezimmer nt **~ towel** Badetuch nt
battery Batterie f
battle site Schlachtfeld nt
be, to sein
beach Strand m
beard Bart m
beautiful schön
because weil; **~ of** wegen
bed Bett nt ; **~ and breakfast** Übernachtung f mit Frühstück; **I'm going to ~** ich gehe ins Bett; **~ room** Schlafzimmer nt
bedding Bettzeug nt
bee Biene f
beer Bier nt
before *(time)* vor

begin, to (*also* ➤ **to start**) beginnen, anfangen

beginner Anfänger m

beginning Anfang m

beige beige

Belgian (*adj*) belgisch; (*n*) Belgier(in) m/f

Belgium Belgien nt

below 15°C unter 15 Grad

belt Gürtel m

beneath unter

berth Liegewagenplatz m ; Schlafplatz m

best beste (-r; -es)

better besser

between zwischen

bicycle Fahrrad nt ; **~ helmet** Fahrradhelm m; **~ path** Radweg m

bicycle rental Fahrradvermietung f

big groß

bikini Bikini m

bill Rechnung f ; **put it on the ~** setzen Sie es auf die Rechnung

binoculars Fernglas nt sing

bird Vogel m

birthday Geburtstag m

bishop (*chess*) Läufer m

bite (*insect*) Stich m

bitter bitter

black schwarz ; **~ and white film** (*camera*) Schwarzweißfilm m

blanket Decke f

bleeding, to be bluten

bless you! Gesundheit!

blind (*n*) Rollo nt

blister Blase f

blocked, to be verstopft sein; **the road is ~** die Straße ist blockiert

blood Blut nt ; **~ group** Blutgruppe f; **~ pressure** Blutdruck m

blouse Bluse f

blue blau

blusher (*rouge*) Rouge nt

board, on (*bus*) im Bus

boarding card Bordkarte f

boat Schiff nt ; (*small*) Boot nt; **~ trip** Schiffsfahrt f

body Körper m

boil Furunkel m

boiled gekocht

boiler Boiler m

bone Knochen m

book Buch nt ; **~ store** Buchhandlung f

book, to reservieren; reservieren lassen ; buchen ; **I'd like to book ...** ich möchte ... reservieren (lassen)

booking Reservierung f ; (*restaurant*) Tischbestellung f

boots Stiefel mpl ; (*for sport*) Schuhe mpl

border (*country*) Grenze f

boring langweilig

born: I was born in ... ich bin (*year*) in (*place*) geboren

borrow: may I borrow your ...? darf ich Ihren/Ihre/Ihr ... leihen?

botanical garden Botanischer Garten m

bottle Flasche f ; **~ opener** Flaschenöffner m

bow (*ship*) Bug m

box of chocolates Schachtel Pralinen f

box office Kasse f

boxing Boxen nt

boy Junge m ; **~ friend** Freund m

bra BH m

brass Messing nt

bread Brot nt

break down, to kaputtgehen

break, to zerbrechen ; (*journey*) unterbrechen

breakage Bruch m

breakdown Panne f ; **to have a ~** eine Panne haben

breakfast Frühstück nt

break-in Einbruch m

breast Brust f

breathe, to atmen

bridge Brücke f ; (*cards*) Bridge nt

briefcase Aktenkoffer m

briefs Unterhose f

brilliant großartig

bring, to bringen

Britain Großbritannien nt

British (*adj*) britisch

Briton Brite m Britin f

brochure Broschüre f;

broken (*bone*) gebrochen sein

bronchitis Bronchitis f

bronze *(adj)* Bronze-
brother Bruder m
brown braun
browse, to sich umsehen
bruise Quetschung f
brush Bürste f
bubble bath Schaumbad nt
bucket Eimer m
build, to bauen
building Gebäude nt
built erbaut
bureau de change Wechselstube f
burglary Einbruch m
burn Verbrennung f
burn: it's burnt es ist verbrannt
bus Bus m ; **~ route** Buslinie f ;
~ station Busbahnhof m ; **~ stop**
Bushaltestelle f
business Geschäft nt;
~ class Businessklasse f ; **~ man**
Geschäftsmann m; **~ trip**
Geschäftsreise f; **~ woman**
Geschäftsfrau f; **on ~** geschäftlich
busy: I'm busy ich habe keine Zeit
but aber
butane gas Butangas nt
butcher shop Fleischerei f Metzgerei f/
Schlachterei f
butter Butter f
button Knopf m
buy, to kaufen
by *(time)* bis; vor
by car mit dem Auto
by credit card mit Kreditkarte
bye! auf Wiedersehen!
bypass Umgehungsstraße f

C

cabaret Varieté nt
cabin Kabine f
cable car Seilbahn f
cable TV Kabelfernsehen nt
café Café nt
cake Kuchen m
calculator Taschenrechner m
calendar Kalender m
call, to rufen ; *(phone)* anrufen ;
to ~ collect ein R-Gespräch führen; **call**

the police! rufen Sie die Polizei! ; **I'll
call back** ich rufe zurück
camel hair Kamelhaar nt
camera Fotoapparat m ; Kamera f
~ case Fototasche f ; **~ shop**
Fotogeschäft nt
campbed Campingliege f
camping equipment
Campingausrüstung f; **~ stove**
Campingkocher m
campsite Campingplatz m
can *(tin)* Dose f ; **~ opener**
Büchsenöffner m
can I have …? kann ich … haben?
can I? kann ich?
can you help me? können Sie mir
helfen?
Canada Kanada nt
Canadian *(n)* Kanadier(in) m/f
canal Kanal m
cancel, to stornieren/absagen
cancer *(disease)* Krebs m
candle Kerze f
candy Süßigkeiten fpl
canoe Kanu nt
canoeing Kanufahren nt
cap Mütze f
capital city Hauptstadt f
captain *(boat)* Kapitän m
car Auto nt **~ alarm** Auto-
Alarmanlage f; **~ ferry** Autofähre f;
~ rental Autovermietung f , **~ park**
Parkplatz m ; **~ repairs** Reparaturen ;
~ wash Autowaschanlage f; **by ~** mit
dem Auto; **rental ~** Mietwagen m
carafe Karaffe f
caravan Wohnwagen m
cardphone Kartentelefon nt
cards Karten fpl
careful: be careful! Vorsicht!
carousel Karussell m
carpet *(fitted)* Teppichboden m; *(rug)*
Teppich m
carrier bag Tragetasche f
carton Karton m Stange (Zigaretten) f
cartoon Cartoon m
carwash Autowaschanlage f
cash Bargeld nt; **~ card** (Geld)
automatenkarte f; **~ desk** Kasse f; **~**

machine Geldautomat m ; **to pay by ~** bar zahlen

cash, to einlösen

casino Spielkasino nt

cassette Kassette f

castle Schloss nt

cat Katze f

catch, to fangen

cathedral Dom m

cave Höhle f

CD CD f; **~-player** CD-Spieler m

cell phone Handy nt

cemetery Friedhof m

central heating Zentralheizung f

cent Cent m

center of town Stadtzentrum nt

ceramics Keramik f

certificate Urkunde f ; Zeugnis nt

certification Bescheinigung f

chair Stuhl m; **~ lift** Sessellift m

change *(coins)* Kleingeld nt

change *(n) (money)* Wechselgeld nt;
keep the change der Rest ist für Sie

change, to *(buses)* umsteigen ; *(trains)*
; *(clothes)* sich umziehen; *(money)* umtauschen; *(reservation)* ändern ; *(baby)*
wickeln; **where can I change the
baby?** wo kann ich das Baby wickeln?;
to ~ lanes die Spur wechseln

channel *(sea)* Kanal m

charcoal Holzkohle f

charge Gebühr f ; **what's the charge?**
wie viel kostet es?

charter flight Charterflug m

cheap billig ; preiswert

check Rechnung f

check in, to einchecken

check out, to *(hotel)* abreisen

check: please check … bitte überprüfen Sie …

checkered *(patterned)* kariert

checkers *(draughts)* Damespiel nt

check-in desk Abfertigungsschalter m

checkout Kasse f

cheers! zum Wohl!

cheese Käse m

chemical toilet Chemietoilette f

chess Schach nt ; **~ set** Schachspiel nt

chest Brustkorb m

chewing gum Kaugummi m

child Kind nt ;
~ care Kinderbetreuung f ;
~ seat *(car)* Kindersitz m; *(high
chair)* Kinderstuhl m

children Kinder ntpl

children's entertainer Unterhalter m
für Kinder

children's meals Mahlzeiten fpl für
Kinder

china Geschirr nt

Chinese *(adj)* chinesisch

chips Chips pl, Pommes Frites pl

chocolate Schokolade f;
~ bar Schokoladenriegel m ;
hot ~ heiße Schokolade f ;
box of ~s Schachtel f Pralinen

chop *(meat)* Kotelett nt

Christian *(adj)* christlich

Christmas Weihnachten nt

church Kirche f ;

cigar Zigarre f ;
~ shop Tabakgeschäft nt

cigarette Zigarette f ;
~ machine Zigarettenautomat m;
pack of ~ Schachtel f Zigaretten

cinema Kino nt

city wall Stadtmauer f

clamped, to be mit einer Parkkralle
festgesetzt werden

clean *(adj)* sauber ; **to ~** reinigen

cleaner Putzfrau f

cleaning Reinigung f

cleaning products Putzmittel ntpl

cleansing lotion Reinigungsmilch f ;

cleansing solution
Reinigungsflüssigkeit f

cliff Klippe f

close *(near)* nah

close, to schließen

closed *(shop)* geschlossen

clothes Kleidungsstücke ntpl ;
~ line Wäscheleine f;
~ pegs Wäscheklammern fpl ;
~ store Bekleidungsgeschäft nt

cloudy, to be bewölkt sein

clubs *(golf)* Schläger mpl

coach Überlandbus m Bus m ; *(train
compartment)* Wagen m ;

~ **bay/stop** Bushaltestelle f ;
~ **station** Busbahnhof m
coast Küste f
coat Mantel m
coatcheck Garderobe f
coat hanger Kleiderbügel m
cockroach Kakerlake f
code *(area/dialling)* Vorwahl f
coffee Kaffee m
coil *(contraceptive)* Spirale f
coin Münze f
cola Cola f
cold *(adj)* kalt ; *(n)* Erkältung f ;
~ **meats** Aufschnitt m
collapse: he's collapsed er ist zusammengebrochen
collect, to abholen, einsammeln
college: to be at college studieren
color Farbe f ; ~ **film** Farbfilm m
comb Kamm m
come back, to wiederkommen
comedy Komödie f
commission Gebühr f
communion Kommunion f
compact camera Kompaktkamera f
compact disc/disk CD f
company *(business)* Firma f; *(companionship)* Gesellschaft f
compartment *(train)* Abteil nt
compass Kompass m
complaint Beschwerde f
computer Computer m
concert Konzert nt ;
~ **hall** Konzerthalle f
concussion, to have eine Gehirnerschütterung haben
conditioner Spülung f
condoms Kondome ntpl
conductor *(music)* Dirigent(in) m/f
conference Konferenz f
confirm, to *(reservation)* bestätigen
congratulations! herzlichen Glückwunsch!
connection *(transport)* Anschluss m
conscious, to be bei Bewusstsein sein
constipated, to be Verstopfung haben
constipation Verstopfung f
Consulate Konsulat nt

consult: to consult a doctor zum Arzt gehen
contact lens Kontaktlinse f
contact, to erreichen
contact lens fluid Kontaktlinsenflüssigkeit f
contagious, to be ansteckend sein
contain, to enthalten
contemporary dance moderner Tanz m
contraceptive Verhütungsmittel nt
convenient günstig
cook Koch m Köchin f
cookbook Kochbuch nt
cook, to kochen
cooker Herd m
cookie Keks m
cooking *(cuisine)* Küche f
copper Kupfer nt
copy Kopie f
corduroy Cord m
corkscrew Korkenzieher m
corner Ecke f
correct richtig
cosmetics Kosmetika pl
cot Kinderbett nt
cottage Ferienhaus nt
cotton Baumwolle f
cotton wool/absorbent cotton Watte f
cough Husten m ; ~ **syrup** Hustensaft m; **to ~** husten
counter Theke f
country *(nation)* Land nt
country music Countrymusik f
countryside Landschaft f
couple *(pair)* Paar nt
courier *(guide)* Reiseleiter(in) m/f
course *(meal)* Gang m
cousin Cousin(e) m/f
cover *(lid)* Deckel m
cover charge Gedeckzahlung f
craft shop Kunsthandwerksgeschäft nt
cramps Krämpfe mpl
crash: I've had a crash ich hatte einen Unfall
creaks: the bed creaks das Bett knarrt
credit card Kreditkarte f ; ~ **number** Kreditkartennummer f
credit status Kreditwürdigkeit f

credit, in im Haben
cross *(crucifix)* Kreuz nt
cross, to *(road)* überqueren
crossroad Kreuzung f
crowded überfüllt
crown *(dental)* Krone f
cruise Kreuzfahrt f
crutches Krücken fpl
crystal Kristall nt
cuisine Küche f
cup Tasse f
cupboard Küchenschrank m
curlers Lockenwickler mpl
currency Währung f ;
~ exchange Wechselstube f
curtains Vorhänge/Gardinen mpl
cushion Kissen nt
customs Zoll m ;
~ declaration Zollerklärung f
cut *(wound)* Schnittwunde f
cut glass geschliffenes
Kristallglas nt
cutlery Besteck nt
cycling Rad fahren nt
cyclist Radfahrer(in) m/f
cystitis Blasenentzündung f
Czech Republic Tschechische
Republik f, Tschechien

D

daily täglich
damaged beschädigt sein
damp *(n)* Feuchtigkeit f; *(adj)* feucht
dance *(performance)* Tanz m
dancing, to go tanzen gehen
dangerous gefährlich
dark dunkel
darts, to play Pfeilwerfen spielen
data Daten pl; ~ bank Datenbank f
daughter Tochter f
dawn Tagesanbruch m
day Tag m ; ~ ticket Tageskarte f;
~ trip Tagesausflug m
dead tot; *(battery)* leer
deaf, to be taub sein
dear *(greeting)* lieber (liebe)
December Dezember m
deck *(ship)* Deck nt
deck chair Liegestuhl m

declare, to verzollen
deduct, to *(money)* abziehen
deep tief
defrost, to auftauen
degrees *(temperature)* Grad mpl
delay Verspätung f
delicate zart
delicatessen Feinkostgeschäft nt ;
Feinkostabteilung f
delicious köstlich
deliver, to liefern
denim Jeansstoff m
Denmark Dänemark nt
dental floss Zahnseide f
dentist Zahnarzt mZahnärztin f
dentures Gebiss nt sing
deodorant Deodorant nt
depart, to *(train/bus)* abfahren
department *(in store)* Abteilung f;
~ store Kaufhaus nt
departure *(train)* Abfahrt f ;
~ lounge Abflughalle f
depend: it depends on ...
es hängt von ... ab
deposit Anzahlung f ; Kaution f ; to
pay a ~ eine Kaution hinterlegen
describe, to beschreiben
design *(dress)* Entwurf m
designer Designer(in) m/f
destination Reiseziel m
details Einzelheiten fpl
detergent Waschmittel nt
develop, to *(photos)* entwickeln
diabetes Zuckerkrankheit f
diabetic, to be Diabetiker sein
diagnosis Diagnose f
diamond Diamant m
diamonds *(cards)* Karo (nt sing)
diaper changing facilities
Wickelraum m
diapers Windeln fpl
diarrhea Durchfall m ;
to have ~ Durchfall haben
dice Würfel mpl
dictionary Wörterbuch nt
diesel Diesel m
diet: I'm on a ~ ich mache eine Diät
different, something etwas anderes
difficult schwierig

digital digital
dine, to speisen
dinghy Dinghi nt
dining car Speisewagen m
dining room Speisesaal m ;
Esszimmer nt
dinner jacket Smokingjacke f
dinner, to have zu Abend essen
direct durchgehend;
~-dial telephone Telefon nt mit
Durchwahl
direct, to den Weg zeigen
direction Richtung f ; **in the direction
of ...** in Richtung ...
directions
director *(movie)* Regisseur(in) m/f; *(of
company)* Direktor(in) m/f
Directory Enquiries Auskunft f
directory *(telephone)* Telefonbuch nt
dirty schmutzig
disabled *(n)* Behinderte pl
discotheque Diskothek f
discount: can you offer me a ~? können Sie mir Rabatt geben?; **is there a ~
for children?** gibt es eine
Kinderermäßigung?
dish *(meal)* Gericht nt
dish cloth Spüllapen m
dishwashing detergent Spülmittel nt
diskette Diskette f ; **~ drive**
Diskettenlaufwerk nt
dislocated, to be verrenkt sein
disposable camera Einwegkamera f
distilled water destilliertes Wasser nt
district Gegend f
disturb: don't disturb nicht stören
dive, to tauchen
diversion Umleitung f
diving equipment Tauchrüstung f
divorced, to be geschieden sein
do you accept ...? nehmen Sie ...?
do you have ...? haben Sie ...?
dock Dock nt
doctor Arzt m Ärztin f ,
doctor's office Arztpraxis f
dog Hund m
doll Puppe f
dollar Dollar m
door Tür f

dosage Dosierung f
double *(adj)* Doppel-; **~ bed**
Doppelbett nt ; **~ cabin** Doppelkabine
f ; **~ room** Doppelzimmer nt
down hinunter
downstairs unten
downtown Innenstadt f
dozen Dutzend nt
drain Abflussrohr nt
drama Drama nt
dress Kleid nt
drink etwas zu trinken
drinking water Trinkwasser nt
drinks alkoholische Getränke f
drip: the tap drips der Hahn tropft
drive, to fahren
driver *(bus, car, etc)* Fahrer(in) m/f
driver's license Führerschein m
drop off, to absetzen, abliefern
drowning: someone is drowning
es ertrinkt jemand
drugstore Apotheke f
drunk betrunken
dry trocken
dry-clean, to reinigen
dry-cleaner Reinigung f
dry clothes, to Wäsche trocknen
dubbed, to be synchronisiert sein
due, to be *(payment)* fällig sein
during während
dusty staubig
duty-free zollfrei **~ goods** zollfreie
Waren fpl **~ shop** Duty-Free m
~ shopping zollfreier Einkauf m
duty: to pay duty verzollen
duvet Federbett nt

each: how much are they each? wie
viel kosten sie pro Stück?
ear Ohr nt ; **~ drops** Ohrentropfen
mpl; **~ ache** Ohrenschmerzen pl
~ phones Kopfhörer pl
early früh
Easter Ostern nt
east Osten m
east of ... östlich von ...
easy einfach
eat, to essen

eaten: have you eaten? haben Sie schon gegessen?; we've already eaten wir haben schon gegessen
economical wirtschaftlich
economy class Touristenklasse f
egg Ei nt
eight acht
eighteen achtzehn
eighty achtzig
either ... or entweder ... oder
elastic (adj) elastisch
electric blanket Heizdecke f
electric fire Elektroofen m
electric shaver Rasierapparat m
electrical items Elektrogeräte ntpl
electrician Elektriker m
electricity Strom m;
~ meter Stromzähler m
electronic game Elektronikspiel nt
elevator Aufzug m ; Fahrstuhl m
eleven elf
else: something else etwas anderes
e-mail e-Mail f
embark, to (boat) sich einschiffen
embassy Botschaft f
emerald Smaragd m
emergency Notfall m ;
~ exit Notausgang m;
it's an emergency es ist ein Notfall
~ room Unfallstation f
empty leer
enamel Email nt
end, to aufhören
end: at the end am Ende
engine Motor m
engineer Ingenieur(in) m/f
England England n
English (adj) englisch ; (language) Englisch nt ; does anyone here speak English? spricht hier jemand Englisch? ; English-speaking Englisch sprechend
enjoy: are you enjoying ...? gefällt Ihnen? ; are you enjoying your meal? schmeckt Ihnen das Essen? do you enjoy ...? ... Sie gern? I enjoyed it es hat mir gefallen
enlarge, to (photos) vergrößern
enough (adj) genug

ensuite bathroom eigenes Bad nt
entertainment: Unterhaltung f
~ guide Veranstaltungskalender m
entirely ganz
entrance fee Eintritt m
entry visa Einreisevisum nt
envelope Briefumschlag m
epileptic, to be Epileptiker sein
equally gleich
equipment (sports) Ausrüstung f
error Fehler m
escalator Rolltreppe f
essential wesentlich; to make ~ repairs das Nötigste reparieren
euro Euro m
Eurocheque Euroscheck m
evening dress Abendgarderobe f
evening, in the abends
events Veranstaltungen fpl
every day täglich
every week jede Woche
examination (medical) Untersuchung f
example, for zum Beispiel
except außer
excess baggage Übergepäck nt
exchange rate Wechselkurs m
exchange, to umtauschen
excluding meals ohne Mahlzeiten
excursion Ausflug m
excuse me (apology) Entschuldigung ; (getting attention) entschuldigen Sie!
excuse me? wie bitte?
exhausted, to be erschöpft sein
exhibition Ausstellung f
exit Ausgang m ; at the ~ am Ausgang
expected, to be erwartet werden
expensive teuer
expiration date Ablaufdatum nt
expire: when does it expire? wann läuft es ab?
express (mail) Express m
extension 24 Apparat 24 m
extension cord Verlängerungskabel nt
extra (additional) zusätzlich
extract, to (tooth) ziehen
extremely äußerst
eye Auge nt
eyeliner Lidstrich m

eyeshadow Lidschatten m

F

fabric *(material)* Stoff m
face Gesicht nt
facial Gesichtsbehandlung f
facilities Einrichtungen fpl
factor *(sun-cream)* Lichtschutzfaktor m
faint: I feel faint mir ist schwindelig
fairground Festplatz m
fall *(noun)* Herbst m ; *(verb)* fallen
he's had a fall er ist gefallen
family Familie f
famous berühmt
fan *(air)* Ventilator m
fan: I'm a fan of …
ich bin ein Fan von …
far weit;
how far is it? wie weit ist es?
fare Fahrpreis m
farm Bauernhof m
fashionable, to be modern sein
fast schnell ; **~ food** Schnellgerichte
ntpl ; **~ food restaurant** Schnellimbiss
m **to be ~** *(clock)* vorgehen;
you were driving too fast Sie sind zu
schnell gefahren
fat *(noun)* Fett nt
father Vater m
faucet Wasserhahn m
fault: it's my/your fault es ist
meine/Ihre Schuld
faulty nicht in Ordnung
favorite Lieblings-
fax Telefax nt ; **~ facilities**
Telefaxdienst m ; **~ machine** Telefax nt
February Februar m
feed, to füttern
feel ill, to sich nicht wohl fühlen
female weiblich
fence Zaun m
ferry Fähre f
festival Fest nt
feverish, to feel Fieber haben
few wenige
fiancé(e) Verlobte(r) (f/m)
field Feld nt
fifteen fünfzehn
fifth fünfte

fifty fünfzig
fight *(brawl)* Schlägerei f
fill out, to ausfüllen
filling *(dental)* Füllung f ; *(in sandwich)* Belag m
film Film m
filter Filter m ; **~ paper** Filterpapier nt
find out: could you find that out?
können Sie das herausfinden?
fine *(penalty)* Bußgeld nt ; *(well)* gut
finger Finger m
fire: there's a fire! es brennt! **~ alarm**
Feuermelder m; **~ department**
Feuerwehr f **~ escape** Feuerleiter f
~ extinguisher Feuerlöscher m
~ lighters Feueranzünder m ; **~ place**
Kamin m **~ wood** Brennholz nt
first erste ; **~ class** erste Klasse f ;
~ floor Erdgeschoss nt
I was first ich war zuerst da
first-aid kit Verbandskasten m
fish Fisch m
fish counter Fischtheke f
fish store Fischgeschäft nt
fishing rod Angelrute f
fishing, to go angeln gehen
fit, to *(clothes)* passen
fitting room Umkleidekabine f
five fünf
fix: can you fix it? können Sie es
reparieren?
flag Fahne f
flannel Waschlappen m
flash Blitz m
flat Platten m ;
flavor: what flavors do you have?
welche Geschmacksrichtungen
haben Sie?
flea market Flohmarkt m
flight Flug m ; **~ attendant**
Flugbegleiter(in) **~ number**
Flugnummer f
floats *(swimming)* Schwimmflügel mpl
flood Flut f
floor *(storey)* Etage f; Stock m ; **~
mop** Mop m; **~ show** Show f
florist Blumengeschäft nt
flour Mehl nt
flower Blume f

flu Grippe f
fluent: to speak fluent German fließend Deutsch sprechen
flush: the toilet won't flush die Toilettenspülung funktioniert nicht
fly *(insect)* Fliege f
fly, to fliegen
foggy, to be neblig sein
folding table Klapptisch m
folk art Volkskunst f
folk music Volksmusik f
follow, to *(signs)* folgen ;
food Essen nt ; Lebensmittel nt
~ poisoning Lebensmittelvergiftung f
foot Fuß m
football *(soccer)* Fußball m
footpath Fußweg m
for a day für einen Tag
for a week für eine Woche
forecast Wetterbericht m
foreign ausländisch; **~ currency** Devisen pl
forest Wald m
forget, to vergessen
fork Gabel f ; *(in the road)* Gabelung f
form Formular nt
formal dress Abendgarderobe f
forms Formulare ntpl
fortunately glücklicherweise
forty vierzig
forward: please forward my mail to ... bitte senden Sie meine Post nach ...
foundation *(make-up)* Grundierung f
fountain Brunnen m
four vier
four-door car viertüriges Auto
four-wheel drive Allradantrieb m
fourteen vierzehn
fourth vierte
foyer *(hotel/theater)* Foyer nt
fracture Fraktur f
frame *(glasses)* Gestell nt
France Frankreich nt
free *(of charge)* kostenlos; *(available/vacant)* frei
freezer Gefrierschrank m
French französisch nt
French fries Pommes frites pl
frequent: how frequent? wie oft?

frequently oft
fresh frisch
Friday Freitag m
fridge Kühlschrank m
fried gebraten
friend Freund(in) m/f
friendly freundlich
fries Pommes Frites pl ;
frightened, to be Angst haben
from *(place)* von
from ... to *(time)* von ... bis
front door Vordereingang m
frosty, to be frostig sein
frozen tiefgefroren
fruit juice Fruchtsaft m
frying pan Bratpfanne f
fuel *(gasoline)* Treibstoff m
full voll
full board Vollpension f
full insurance Vollkaskoversicherung f
fun, to have Spaß haben
fun: it's great fun es macht Spaß
funny *(amusing)* lustig; *(odd)* merkwürdig
furniture Möbel pl
further: how much further to Berlin? wie weit ist es noch nach Berlin?
fuse Sicherung f ; **~ box** Sicherungskasten m ; **~ wire** Schmelzdraht m

G

gable Giebel m
gallon Gallone f
gambling Glücksspiel nt
game *(toy)* Spiel nt
garage Garage f; Autowerkstatt f
garbage bag Müllbeutel m
~ cans Mülleimer mpl
garden Garten m
gardener Gärtner(in) m/f
gardening Gartenarbeit f
gas Gas f, *(gasoline)* Benzin **I smell gas!** es riecht nach Gas! **~ bottle** Gasflasche f ; **~ permeable lenses** luftdurchlässige Kontaktlinsen fpl
gas station Tankstelle f
gasoline Benzin nt ; **~ can** Benzinkanister m

gastritis Magenschleimhautentzündung f
gate *(airport)* Flugsteig m
gay club Schwulenlokal nt
general delivery postlagernd
generous: that's very generous
das ist sehr großzügig
genuine echt
geology Geologie f
German deutsch, *(language)* Deutsch
nt ;*(person)* Deutscher m Deutsche f
Germany Deutschland nt
get, to *(find)* finden
get off, to *(transport)* aussteigen
get to, to ankommen in ; **how do I get
to …?** wie komme ich zu …? ; wie
komme ich nach …?
get help! holen Sie Hilfe!
gift Geschenk nt ;
~ shop Geschenkladen m
girl Mädchen nt
girlfriend Freundin f
give, to geben
gland Drüse f
glass Glas nt
glasses Brille f sing
gliding Segelfliegen nt
glossy finish *(photos)* Hochglanz
glove Handschuh m
go, to gehen, fahren; **to ~ back**
zurückfahren ; **to ~ for a walk**
spazieren gehen **to ~ out** *(in evening)*
ausgehen; **to ~ shopping** einkaufen
gehen ; **let's go!** gehen wir!; **where
does this bus go?** wohin fährt dieser
Bus?; **go away!** gehen Sie weg!
goggles Schutzbrille f
gold Gold nt ; **~plated** vergoldet
golf Golf nt ; **~ course** Golfplatz m
good *(adj)* gut ; **to be of ~ value**
preiswert sein **~ afternoon** guten Tag
~ -bye auf Wiedersehen **~ evening**
guten Abend **~ morning** guten
Morgen **~ night** gute Nacht
got: have you got any …? haben Sie
…?
gram Gramm nt
grandparents Großeltern pl
grape Traube f
grass Gras nt

gratuity Trinkgeld nt
gray grau
graze Schürfwunde f
Greek *(adj)* griechisch
green grün
greetings
grilled gegrillt
grocery store Lebensmittelgeschäft nt
ground *(camping)* Boden m
group Gruppe f
guide *(tour)* Führer(in) m/f ;
~ book Reiseführer m
guided tour Führung f
guitar Gitarre f
gum *(mouth)* Zahnfleisch nt *(chewing
g.*) Kaugummi m
gym session Fitnesstraining nt
gynecologist Frauenarzt m
Frauenärztin f

H

hair Haar nt ; **~ brush** Haarbürste f;
~ dryer Haartrockner m; **~ gel**
Haargel nt; **~ mousse** Schaumfestiger
m ; **~ slide** Haarspange f; **~ spray**
Haarspray nt
haircut Haarschnitt m
hairdresser Friseur m, Friseuse f
half board Halbpension f
half fare halber Fahrpreis m
half past six halb sieben
half, a Hälfte f
hammer Hammer m
hand Hand f ; **~ cream** Handcreme f;
~ luggage Handgepäck nt; **~ towel**
Handtuch nt
handbag Handtasche f
handicap *(golf)* Vorgabe f
handicapped, to be behindert sein
handicrafts Kunsthandwerk nt
handkerchief Taschentuch nt
handle Griff m
hang-gliding Drachenfliegen nt
hanger Kleiderbügel m
hangover *(n)* Kater m
happen: what happened?
was ist passiert?

happy: I'm not happy with the service ich bin mit dem Service nicht zufrieden

hard shoulder *(road)* Seitenstreifen m

hardware *(computer)* Hardware f

hardware store Eisenwarenhandlung f

hat Hut m

hatchback Hecktürmodell nt

have, to haben ;

have to, to *(must)* müssen

hayfever Heuschnupfen m

head Kopf m ;

~ache Kopfschmerzen pl

head for, to fahren nach

heading: where are you heading? wohin fahren Sie?

head waiter Oberkellner m

health food store Naturkostladen m

health insurance Krankenversicherung f

healthy gesund

hear, to hören

hearing aid Hörgerät nt

heart Herz nt ; **~ attack** Herzanfall m; **~ condition** Herzleiden nt

hearts *(cards)* Herz nt sing

heater Ofen m

heating Heizung f

heavy schwer

height Größe f ; Höhe f

helicopter Hubschrauber m

hello Guten Tag ; hallo

help Hilfe f ; **to help** helfen ; **could you help me?** können Sie mir helfen?

helper Helfer(in) m/f

hemorrhoids Hämorrhoiden pl

her sie ; *(possessive)* ihr

here hier ; *(to here)* hierher

hernia Bruch m

hers ihre(-r-s) ; **it's hers** es gehört ihr

hi! hallo!

high hoch ; **~ tide** Flut f

highlight, to *(hair)* Strähnchen machen

hike *(walk)* Wanderung f

hiking Wandern nt ; **~ gear** Wanderausrüstung f

hill Hügel m

him ihn

Hindu *(n)* Hindu m; *(adj)* hinduistisch

his seine(-r-s) ;

it's his es gehört ihm

history Geschichte f

hitchhike, to trampen, per Anhalter fahren

hitchhiking Trampen nt

HIV-positive HIV-positiv

hobby *(pastime)* Hobby nt

hockey *(field)* Hockey nt

hold on! *(telephone)* bleiben Sie am Apparat!

hold, to *(contain)* enthalten ;

hole *(in clothes)* Loch nt

holiday resort Ferienort m

Holland Holland f

home: to go home nach Hause fahren; **we're going home on ...** wir fahren am ... nach Hause

homeopathic remedy homöopathisches Mittel nt

homosexual *(adj)* homosexuell

honeymoon, to be on auf der Hochzeitsreise sein

hopefully hoffentlich

horse Pferd nt

horseback trip Reitausflug m

horseracing Pferderennen nt

hospital Krankenhaus nt

hot heiß ; **warm ; ~ dog** heißes Würstchen nt ; **~ spring** Thermalquelle f; **~ water** heißes Wasser nt ; **~ water bottle** Wärmflasche f

hotel Hotel nt ;

hour Stunde f ; **in an ~** in einer Stunde

hours *(doctor's office)* Sprechstunden fpl

house Haus nt

household Haushalt m

~ articles Haushaltsartikel mpl

housewife Hausfrau f

hovercraft Luftkissenboot nt

how are you? wie geht es Ihnen?

how? wie? **~ far?** wie weit?

~ long? wie lange? **~ many?** wie viele? **~ much?** wie viel?

~ often? wie oft? **~ old?** wie alt?

hundred hundert

Hungary Ungarn nt

hungry, to be Hunger haben
hurt: it hurts es tut weh ;
to be ~ verletzt sein
husband Mann m ,

I'd like … ich hätte gern …
I'd like to … ich möchte …
I'll have … ich nehme …
ice Eis nt ; ~ dispenser Eisspender m;
~ hockey Eishockey nt; ~ rink
Eisbahn f
ice cream Eis nt ; ~ parlor Eisdiele
nt ; ~ cone Eistüte f
icy, to be eisig sein
identification Ausweis m
ill, to be krank sein
illegal, to be nicht erlaubt sein
illness Krankheit f
imitation imitiert
immediately sofort
in (place/time) in
in-law: father ~ Schwiegervater m;
mother~ Schwiegermutter f
included: is … included?
ist … inbegriffen?
inconvenient: it's inconvenient
es ist ungünstig
indicate, to (in car) blinken
indigestion Verdauungsstörung f
indoor Hallen-; ~ pool Hallenbad nt
inexpensive preiswert
infected, to be entzündet sein
infection Entzündung f
inflammation Entzündung f
informal (dress) zwanglos
information Informationen fpl ; ~ desk
Auskunft f ; ~ office Verkehrsbüro nt
injection Spritze f
injured, to be verletzt sein
innocent unschuldig
insect Insekt nt ; ~ bite Insektenstich
m ~ repellent Insektenschutzmittel nt
~ spray Insektenspray nt
inside drinnen
inside lane Innenspur f
insist: I insist ich bestehe darauf
insomnia Schlaflosigkeit f
instant coffee Pulverkaffee m

instead of statt
instructions Gebrauchsanweisung f
instructor Lehrer(in) m/f
insulin Insulin nt
insurance Versicherung f ; ~ certificate
Versicherungsschein m ~ claim
Versicherungsanspruch m ~ company
Versicherungsgesellschaft f
interest rate Zinssatz m
interest: what are your interests?
wofür interessieren Sie sich?
interesting interessant
international international
International Student Card
Internationaler Studentenausweis m
internet Internet nt
interpreter Dolmetscher m
intersection Kreuzung f
interval Pause f
into in (… hinein)
introduce, to vorstellen
invitation Einladung f
invite, to einladen
involved, to be beteiligt sein
iodine Jod nt
Ireland Irland nt
Irish (adj) irisch
Irish (n) Ire m Irin f
iron (for clothing) Bügeleisen nt; travel
~ Reisebügeleisen nt; to iron bügeln
is there …? gibt es …?
island Insel f
it is … es ist …
Italian (adj) italienisch
Italy Italien nt
itch: it itches es juckt
itemized bill detaillierte Rechnung f

jack/knave (cards) Bube m
jacket Jacke f ; (of suit) Jackett nt
jam Marmelade f
jammed, to be klemmen
January Januar m
jar Glas nt
jaw Kiefer m
jeans Jeans pl
jellyfish Qualle f

jet lag: I have jet lag der Zeitunterschied macht mir zu schaffen
jet ski Jet-Ski m
Jew (n) Jude m Jüdin f
jewelry store Juwelier m
Jewish (adj) jüdisch
job: what's your job? was machen Sie beruflich?
jogging pants Jogginghose f
jogging, to go joggen
join: may we join you? dürfen wir uns zu Ihnen setzen?
joint (body) Gelenk nt
joint passport gemeinsamer Pass m
joke Witz m
joker (cards) Joker m
journalist Journalist(in) m/f
journey Fahrt f
judo Judo nt
jug (of water) Krug m
July Juli m
jumper cables Starthilfekabel nt
junction (exit) Ausfahrt f; (intersection) Kreuzung f
June Juni m

K

keep: keep the change der Rest ist für Sie
kettle Kessel m
key Schlüssel m ; **~ ring** Schlüsselanhänger m
key board Tastatur f
kidney Niere f
kilo(gram) Kilo nt
kilometer Kilometer m
kind (pleasant) nett
kind: what kind of ... welche Art von ...
king König m
kiss, to küssen
kitchen Küche f ;
~ paper Küchenpapier nt
kitchenette Kochnische f
knee Knie nt
knife Messer nt
knight (chess) Springer m
know: I don't know ich weiß nicht
kosher koscher

L

label Etikett nt

lace Spitze f
ladder Leiter f
ladies' room [toilet] Damentoilette f
lake See m
lamp Lampe f
land, to landen
landfill (dump) Müllabladeplatz m
landing (house) Gang m
landlord/landlady Vermieter(in) m/f
lane Spur f
language course Sprachkurs m
large groß
laser Laser m;
~ printer Laserdrucker m
last (final/previous) letzte
late spät ; (delayed) verspätet;
to be late Verspätung haben
later später
laugh, to lachen
laundromat Waschsalon m
laundry service Wäschedienst m
lawn Rasen m
lawyer Anwalt m Anwältin f
laxative Abführmittel nt
lead, to (road) führen nach
leader (of group) Leiter(in) m/f
leaflet Broschüre f
leak, to undicht sein
learn, to (language/sport) lernen
learner Anfänger(in) m/f
leather Leder m
leasing Leasing nt
leather Leder m
leave me alone! lassen Sie mich in Ruhe!
leave, to (depart) abfahren; (plane) abfliegen, (leave behind car) stehen lassen **I've left my bag in ...** ich habe meine Tasche in ... gelassen
lecturer Dozent(in) m/f
left-hand side linke Seite f
left, on the auf der linken Seite
left-handed linkshändig
left-luggage office Gepäckaufbewahrung f
left:: are there any seats left? sind noch Plätze frei?
leg Bein nt
legal matter Rechtsangelegenheit fl

legal, to be erlaubt sein
leggings Leggings pl
lemon Zitrone f
lemonade Limonade f
lend: could you lend me …?
könnten Sie mir … leihen?
length Länge f
lens *(camera)* Objektiv nt ; *(optical)*
Brillenglas nt ; **~ cap** Objektivdeckel m
lesbian club Lesbenlokal nt
less weniger
lesson Unterricht m **to take lessons**
Unterricht nehmen
let: please let me know bitte sagen
Sie mir Bescheid
letter Brief m ; **~ box** Briefkasten m;
by letter schriftlich ; **~ carrier**
Postbote m
level *(ground)* eben
library Bibliothek f ; Bücherei f
license plate
Kraftfahrzeugkennzeichen n
lie down, to sich hinlegen
lifebelt Rettungsring m
lifeboat Rettungsboot nt
lifeguard Rettungsschwimmer m
lifejacket Schwimmweste f
lift pass Liftkarte f
lift:: to give someone a lift
jemanden mitnehmen
light *(adj) (color)* hell ; *(weight)* leicht ;
(electric) Licht nt **~bulb** Glühbirne f
light, to *(fire)* anzünden
lighter Feuerzeug nt
lighthouse Leuchtturm m
lightning Blitz m
lights *(bicycle)* Beleuchtung f
like: I'd like ich hätte gern;
I'd like to buy … ich möchte gern …
kaufen ;
like this *(similar to)* ähnlich wie dies, so
line *(metro)* Linie f ; *(profession)*
Beruf m; **an outside line, please**
einen Amtsanschluss, bitte
linen Leinen nt
lip Lippe f ; **~salve** Lippenbalsam m ;
~stick Lippenstift m
liqueur Likör m

liquor store Wein und
Spirituosenhandlung f
liter Liter m
little klein; **a ~** ein wenig
live, to wohnen; **to ~ together**
zusammenleben
liver Leber f
living room Wohnzimmer nt
loaf of bread Brot nt
lobby *(theaterhotel)* Foyer nt
local hiesig;
~ anesthetic örtliche Betäubung f
lock Schloss nt ; *(canal)* Schleuse f
lock, to abschließen; **to ~ oneself out**
sich aussperren
locked, to be abgeschlossen sein ;
it's locked es ist abgeschlossen
locker Schließfach nt
lollipop Lutscher m
long lang ; *(time)* lange; **how long?**
wie lange?
long-distance call Ferngespräch nt
long-distance bus Überlandbus m
longer: how much longer? wie lange
noch?
longsighted weitsichtig
look after: please look after my case
for a minute bitte achten Sie einen
Moment auf meinen Koffer
look for, to suchen
look forward: I'm looking forward
to it ich freue mich darauf
look like, to aussehen wie
look, to have a *(check)* sich … anse-
hen; **I'm just looking** ich sehe mich nur um
loose weit ; *(clothing)* locker
lose, to verlieren ;
I've lost … ich habe … verloren
lost, to be verlorengehen ; sich
verirrt haben
lost property office Fundbüro nt
lotion Lotion f
lots viel
loud laut **it's too ~** es ist zu laut
louder lauter
love: I love German food ich mag
deutsches Essen **I love you** ich liebe dich
low-fat fettarm

lower: I'd like a lower berth
ich möchte unten schlafen
lubricant Schmiermittel nt
luck: good luck! viel Glück!
luggage Gepäck nt ; **~ allowance**
Freigepäck nt; **~ carts** Kofferkulis mpl;
~ tag Gepäckanhänger m; **~ ticket**
Gepäckaufbewahrungsschein m
lump Knoten m
lumpy *(mattress)* klumpig
lunch Mittagessen nt
Luxemburg Luxemburg nt
luxury Luxus m

M

(dear) madam gnädige Frau
made of: what is it made of? woraus
besteht es?
magazine Zeitschrift f
magnetic north nördlicher
Magnetpol m
magnificent großartig
maid Zimmer-mädchen nt
maiden name Mädchenname m
mail *(post)* Post f ; **~ box** Briefkasten
m ; **~ man** Postbote m **~ office**
Postamt m
main Haupt ; **~ course** Hauptgericht
nt; **~ rail station** Hauptbahnhof m ;
~ street Hauptstraße f
mains Stromnetz nt
make *(brand)* Marke f
make an appointment, to einen
Termin vereinbaren
makeup Make-up nt
make, to machen;
~ tea/coffee Tee/Kaffee kochen
male männlich
mallet Holzhammer m
man Mann m
manager Geschäftsführer(in) m/f
manicure Maniküre f
manual *(handbook)* Handbuch nt
many viele
map Karte f; Landkarte f
March März m
margarine Margarine f
market Markt m ; **~ day** Markttag m
married, to be verheiratet sein

mascara Wimperntusche f
mask Maske f
mass *(rel. service)* Messe f
massage Massage f
match *(game)* Spiel nt
matches Streichhölzer ntpl
material Material nt, Stoff m
matinée Nachmittagsvorstellung f
matte *(photos)* matt
matter: it doesn't matter es macht
nichts; **what's the matter?** was ist los?
mattress Matratze f
May Mai m
may I? kann/darf ich?
maybe vielleicht
me mich
meal Essen nt
mean, to bedeuten
measles Masern pl
measure, to Maß nehmen
measurement Maß nt
meat Fleisch nt
medical certificate ärztliches
Zeugnis nt
medication Medikament nt
medium *(adj)* mittel/normal ; *(steak)*
mittel
meet, to treffen ; **pleased to meet
you** sehr angenehm
meeting place Treffpunkt m
member *(of club)* Mitglied nt
men's room Herrentoilette f
mend, to reparieren
mention: don't mention it gern
geschehen ; nicht der Rede wert
menu Speisekarte f
message Nachricht f
metal Metall nt
methylated spirits Brennspiritus m
microwave oven Mikrowellenherd m
midday Mittag m
midnight Mitternacht f
migraine Migräne f
mileage Kilometergeld nt
milk Milch f ; **with ~** mit Milch
million Million f
minced meat Hackfleisch nt

mind: do you mind? stört es Sie? ;
I've changed my mind ich habe es
mir anders überlegt
mine meine(-r-s) ;
it's mine es gehört mir
mineral water Mineralwasser nt
minibar Minibar f
minibus Kleinbus m
minimum (n) Minimum nt
minister Pastor, Pfarrer m
minor road Nebenstraße f
mint (adj.) neuwertig
minute Minute f
mirror Spiegel m
miss, to verpassen; **have I missed the
bus to …?** habe ich den Bus nach …
verpaßt?
missing, to be (lacking) fehlen; (person) verschwunden sein
mistake Fehler m ; Irrtum m
misunderstanding, there's been a
es war ein Missverständnis
mittens Fausthandschuhe mpl
modern modern ;
~ art moderne Kunst f
moisturizing cream
Feuchtigkeitscreme f
monastery Kloster nt
Monday Montag m
money Geld nt
month Monat m
monthly ticket Monatskarte f
monument Denkmal nt
moor, to anlegen
mooring Anlegeplatz m
moped Moped nt
more mehr ; **I'd like some more …**
ich hätte gern noch etwas …
morning, in the morgens
morning-after pill Pille f danach
Moslem (adj.) moslemisch; (n)
Moslem m
mosquito Stechmücke f
~ bite Mückenstich m
mother Mutter f
motorbike Motorrad nt
motorboat Motorboot nt
motorcycle Motorrad nt;
~ parts Motorradteile ntpl

motorway Autobahn f
mountain Berg m ; **~ bike** Mountain-
Bike nt; **~ range** Gebirge nt
mountaineering Bergsteigen nt
mousetrap Mausefalle f
moustache Schnurrbart m
mouth Mund m
move, to (rooms) umziehen ; (car)
woanders hinstellen; **don't move him!**
bewegen Sie ihn nicht!
movie Film m ; **~ theater** Kino nt
Mr. Herr
Mrs./Ms Frau
much viel
mug Becher m
mugged, to be überfallen werden
mugging Straßenraub m
multiple journey ticket Mehrfachkarte f
multiplex cinema Multiplexkino nt
multipurpose vehicle Geländewagen m
mumps Mumps m
muscle Muskel m
museum Museum nt
music Musik f ; **~ box** Musikbox f
musician Musiker(in) m/f
Muslim (adj) moslemisch; (n) Muslim m
must: I must ich muss
mustard Senf m
my mein
myself:: I'll do it myself ich mache es
selbst

N

nail Nagel m m **~ polish** Nagellack m
~ scissors Nagelschere f sing
name Name m **my name is...** ich
heiße... **what's your name?** wie
heißen Sie?
napkin (serviette) Serviette f
narrow eng
national national
nationality Nationalität f
natural history Naturkunde f
nature reserve Naturschutzgebiet nt
nausea Übelkeit f
navigation channel Fahrrinne f
navy blue marineblau
near nah; **~ here** hier in der Nähe
nearby in der Nähe

nearest nächste
necessary nötig
neck Hals m ; *(clothes)* Ausschnitt m
need: I need to ... ich möchte ...
needle Nadel f
negative *(photo)* Negativ nt
neighbor Nachbar(in) m/f
nephew Neffe m
nerve Nerv m
nervous system Nervensystem nt
Netherlands Niederlande pl
network Netzwerk nt
never nie
never mind das macht nichts
new neu
new year Neujahr nt
New Zealand Neuseeland nt
newspaper Zeitung f
newsstand Zeitungskiosk m
next nächste ; **~ stop!** die nächste
Haltestelle! **~ to** neben
nice nett
niece Nichte f
night porter Nachtportier m
night, per ~ pro Nacht; **at ~** nachts
nightclub Nachtklub m
nightdress Nachthemd nt
nine neun
nineteen neunzehn
ninety neunzig
no nein
no one niemand
noisy laut
non-alcoholic alkoholfrei
none keine(-r-s)
non-smoking *(adj)* nichtraucher pl
noon Mittag m
normal normal
Northern Ireland Nordirland nt
north of nördlich von
nose Nase f
not that one nicht das da
not yet noch nicht
note *(money)* Schein m
nothing nichts **~ else** sonst nichts
~ for me nichts für mich **~ to declare**
nichts zu verzollen
notice board Anschlagbrett nt
notify, to benachrichtigen

November November m
now jetzt ; *(immediately)* sofort
nudist beach Nacktbadestrand m
number *(telephone)* Nummer f ; **sorry,
wrong number** falsch verbunden
number plate *(car license plate)*
Nummernschild nt
nurse Krankenschwester f
nut *(for bolt)* Schraubenmutter f
nylon Nylon nt

O

o'clock, it's ... es ist ... Uhr
observatory Observatorium nt
occasionally gelegentlich
occupation Beruf m
occupied besetzt
October Oktober m
odds *(betting)* Chancen fpl
of von
of course natürlich
off-road (multipurpose) vehicle
Geländewagen m
off-season Nebensaison f
office Büro nt
often oft
oil Öl nt
oily *(hair)* fettig
okay in Ordnung, OK
old alt
old town Altstadt f
old-fashioned altmodisch
olive oil Olivenöl nt
omelet Omelett nt
on *(day/date)* am ; *(place)* auf ;
this round's on me diese Runde gebe
ich aus
on/off switch Ein- und Ausschalter m
on board *(ship)* an Bord;
(train) im Zug
on foot zu Fuß
on the left links
on the other side auf der anderen Seite
on the right rechts
on the spot *(immediately)* sofort
once einmal ; **~ a week** einmal in der
Woche
one eins ; **~way ticket** einfaches
Ticket nt **~ like that** so ein/e/en/s

open *(door)* auf; *(shop)* geöffnet ;
open to the public der Öffentlichkeit zugänglich
open, to öffnen ; *(shop)*
opening hours Öffnungszeiten fpl
opera Oper f ; ~ house Opernhaus nt
operation Operation f
operator Vermittlung f
opposite gegenüber
optician Optiker(in) m/f
or oder
orange *(adj)* orange ; *(fruit)* Orange f
orchestra Orchester nt
order Bestellung f
order, to bestellen
organized walk/hike geführte Wanderung f
ornithology Ornithologie f
others anderes
our(s) unser, unsere(-r-s)
out:: he's out er ist nicht da
outdoor Frei- ~ pool Freibad nt
outside draußen ; im Freien
oval oval
oven Backofen m
over über; ~ there dort drüben
overcharged: I've been ~ man hat mir zuviel berechnet
overdone *(food)* zu stark gebraten
overdraft Überziehungskredit m; I am overdrawn mein Konto ist überzogen
overnight über Nacht
owe: how much do I owe you? wie viel bin ich Ihnen schuldig?
own: on my own allein
owner Besitzer(in) m/f

P

pacifier Schnuller m
pack of cards Kartenspiel nt
pack, to packen
pack Packung f ; ~ of cigarettes Zigarettenschachtel f
package Paket nt
packed lunch Lunchpaket nt
paddling pool Planschbecken nt
padlock Vorhängeschloss nt
pain, to be in Schmerzen haben
pain killer Schmerzmittel nt

paint, to malen
painted gemalt
painter Maler(in) m/f
painting Gemälde nt
pair of, a Paar nt
pajamas Schlafanzug m
palace Palast m
panorama Panorama nt
pants Hose f
panty hose Strumpfhose f
paper Papier nt; ~ napkins Papierservietten fpl
paraffin Paraffin nt
paralysis Lähmung f
parcel *(package)* Paket nt
parents Eltern pl
park Park m ; ~ ranger Parkaufseher m
park, to parken
parka Anorak m
parking Parken nt ; ~ disk Parkscheibe f; ~ lot Parkplatz m ; ~ meter Parkuhr f
partner *(boyfriend/girlfriend)* Partner(in) m/f
parts *(components)* Ersatzteile pl
party *(social)* Party f ; *(group)* Gruppe f
pass Pass m
pass, to vorbeikommen an ; to ~ through auf der Durchreise sein
passenger Passagier m
passing lane Überholspur f
passport Pass m ; Reisepass m ; ~ control Passkontrolle f
pastry shop Konditorei f
path Weg m
patient Patient(in) m/f
pay phone Münzfernsprecher m
pay, to bezahlen ; zahlen ; ~ a fine ein Bußgeld bezahlen ; ~ by credit card mit Kreditkarte bezahlen
payment Zahlung f
peak Gipfel m
pearl Perle f
peddle boat Tretboot nt
pedestrian crossing Fußgängerüberweg m
pedestrian zone Fußgängerzone f
pedicure Pediküre f
pen *(ballpoint)* Kugelschreiber m
pencil Bleistift m

penicillin Penizillin nt
penknife Taschenmesser nt
penpal Brieffreund(in) m/f
people Leute pl
pepper Pfeffer m
per: per day pro Tag ; **~ hour** pro
Stunde f ; **~ night** pro Nacht f ; **~
week** pro Woche f
performance Vorstellung f
perhaps vielleicht
period Zeit f ; *(menstrual)* Periode f **~
pains** Menstruationsbeschwerden pl
perm Dauerwelle f ; **to ~** eine
Dauerwelle machen
permit Genehmigung f
pet *(n)* Haustier nt
petrol Benzin nt
petrol station Tankstelle f
pewter Zinn nt
pharmacy Apotheke f
phone Telefon nt; **~ call** Anruf m; **to
make a ~ call** telefonieren ; **~ card**
Telefonkarte f
photo: passport-size photo Passbild
nt ; **to take a ~** ein Foto machen
photocopier Fotokopiergerät nt
photographer Fotograf m
photography Fotografie f
phrase Ausdruck m ; **~ book**
Sprachführer m
piano Klavier nt
pick someone up, to jemanden abholen ; *(children)*
pick-up truck Kleintransporter m
picnic Picknick nt; **~ area**
Picknickplatz m
piece Stück nt ; **a ~ of ...** ein Stück
... ; **~ of luggage** Gepäckstück nt
pill *(contraceptive)*: **to be on the pill**
die Pille nehmen
pillow Kopfkissen nt ; **~ case**
Kopfkissenbezug m
pilot light Zündflamme f
pink rosa
pint Pint nt
pipe Pfeife f; **~ cleaners**
Pfeifenreiniger mpl; **~ tobacco**
Pfeifentabak m

pitch *(for camping)* Platz m; **~ charge**
Platzgebühr f
pity: it's a pity es ist schade
place Ort m; *(space)* Platz m
place a bet, to wetten
plain *(not patterned)* einfarbig
plane Flugzeug nt, Maschine f
plans Pläne mpl
plant Pflanze f
plastic bag Plastiktüte f
plastic wrap Klarsichtfolie f
plate Teller m
platform Bahnsteig m
platinum Platin nt
play, to *(sport/games/music)* spielen ;
(drama) gegeben werden
playground Spielplatz m
playgroup Spielgruppe f
playing cards Spielkarten fpl
playing field Sportplatz m
playwright Autor m
pleasant freundlich
please bitte
pliers Zange f sing
plug Stecker m
plumber Klempner m
p.m. nachmittags
pneumonia Lungenentzündung f
points of interest Sehenswürdigkeiten fpl
point to, to zeigen auf
poison Gift nt
poisonous giftig
poker *(cards)* Poker m
Poland Polen nt
police Polizei f; **~ report** Polizeibericht
m **~ station** Polizeiwache f ; Polizei f
pollen count Pollenflug m
polyester Polyester nt
pond Teich m
popcorn Popcorn nt
popular beliebt
port *(harbor)* Hafen m
porter Gepäckträger m
portion Portion f
possible: as soon as possible so bald
wie möglich
possibly möglicherweise
post *(mail)* Post f; **~card** Postkarte f ;
~ office Postamt nt

poster Poster nt
potatoes Kartoffeln fpl
pottery Töpferei f
pound Pfund nt
powder puff Puderquaste f
power cut Stromausfall m
power point/outlet Steckdose f
practice: to practice speaking German Deutsch sprechen üben
pregnant, to be schwanger sein
premium *(gas)* Super nt
prescribe, to verschreiben
prescription Medizin f ; Rezept nt
present *(gift)* Geschenk nt
press, to bügeln
pretty hübsch
priest Priester m
prison Gefängnis nt
private bathroom eigenes Bad nt
probably wahrscheinlich
produce store Gemüsehandlung f
program Programm nt; **~ of events** Veranstaltungskalender m
prohibited: is it prohibited? ist es verboten?
promenade deck Promenadendeck nt
pronounce, to aussprechen
propelling pencil Drehbleistift m
properly richtig
Protestant Protestant(in) m/f
public building öffentliches Gebäude nt
public holiday Feiertag m
pullover Pullover m
pump Pumpe f
puncture *(tire)* Platten m
puppet show Puppenspiel nt
pure *(material)* rein
purple violett
purpose Zweck m
purse Geldbeutel m ; Handtasche f
put: where can I put …? wo kann ich … hintun?; **can you put me up for the night?** können Sie mich heute Nacht unterbringen?

Q

quality Qualität f
quantity Menge f
quarantine Quarantäne f

quarter, a Viertel nt **~ past/after** Viertel nach **~ to/before** Viertel vor
~-deck *(ship)* Achterdeck nt
quay Kai m
queen *(cards/chess)* Dame f
question Frage f
quick schnell
quickest: what's the quickest way to …? was ist der schnellste Weg nach …?
quickly schnell
quiet leise
quieter ruhiger

R

rabbi Rabbiner m
race *(cars/horses)* Rennen nt; **~ track** Pferderennbahn f
racing bike Rennrad nt
racket *(tennis, squash)* Schläger m
radio Radio nt
rail station Bahnhof m
railroad, railway Bahn f Eisenbahn f
rain, to regnen
raincoat Regenmantel m
rape Vergewaltigung f
rapids Stromschnellen fpl
rare *(steak)* blutig; *(unusual)* selten
rarely selten
rash Ausschlag m
rather ziemlich
razor Rasierapparat m; **~ blades** Rasierklingen fpl ; **~ socket** Steckdose f für Rasierapparate
reading *(interest)* Lesen nt **~ glasses** Lesebrille f
ready fertig ; **to be ~** fertig sein ; **are you ready?** sind Sie fertig?
real *(genuine)* echt
real estate agent Immobilienmakler m
receipt Quittung f ; Schein m
reception *(desk)* Empfang m
receptionist Empfangschef(in) m/f
reclaim, to zurückfordern
recommend, to empfehlen ; **what do you recommend?** was empfehlen Sie?
record *(lp)* Schallplatte f ; **~ store** Plattengeschäft nt
red rot ; **~ wine** Rotwein m
reduction *(in price)* Ermäßigung f

re-enter, to wieder hereinkommen

refund: I'd like a refund ich hätte gern mein Geld zurück

regards: give my regards to … grüßen Sie … von mir

region Gegend f

registered mail Einschreiben nt

registration form Anmeldeformular nt

registration number Mitgliedsnummer f ; Kraftfahrzeugkennzeichen nt

regular *(gas)* Normal nt ; *(size of drink)* mittel

regulations Vorschriften fpl

religion Religion f

remember: I don't remember ich weiß es nicht mehr

rent Miete f

rent, to mieten ; **to ~ out** vermieten; *(bedding)* verleihen ; **for rent** zu vermieten

repair, to reparieren

repairs Reparaturen fpl

repeat, to wiederholen ; **please repeat that** bitte wiederholen Sie das

replacement *(n)* Ersatz m; **~ part** Ersatzteil nt

report, to melden

representative Reiseleiter(in) m/f

required, to be verlangt werden

reservation *(hotel)* Reservierung f ; *(plane, train)* Platzkarte f ; **to have a ~** reserviert haben

reservations desk *(plane)* Abfertigungsschalter; *(theater)* Vorverkaufskasse f

reserve, to *(table)* bestellen ; *(tickets)* vorbestellen

rest, to Pause machen

restaurant Restaurant nt

restrooms Toilette f

retired, to be pensioniert sein

return, to *(give back)* zurückbringen; *(come back)* zurückfahren ; zurückkommen

return ticket Rückfahrkarte f

revolting scheußlich

rheumatism Rheumatismus m

rib Rippe f

right *(correct)* richtig ; **that's right** das ist richtig / das stimmt

right of way Vorfahrt f

right, on the auf der rechten Seite

right-hand drive rechtsgesteuert

right-handed rechtshändig

rip-off *(n)* Wucher m

river Fluss m ; **~ cruise** Flussfahrt f

road Straße f ; **~ accident** Verkehrsunfall m; **~ assistance** Pannendienst m; **~ map** Straßenkarte f ; **~ signs** Verkehrszeichen ntpl; **is this the road for …?** ist dies die Straße nach …?

roast chicken Brathähnchen nt

roasted im Backofen gebraten

robbed, to be bestohlen werden

robbery Raub m

rock climbing Felsklettern nt

rocks Felsen mpl

roller blades Roller-Blades pl

rolls Brötchen n

romantic romantisch

roof *(house/car)* Dach nt; **~rack** Dachgepäckträger m

rook *(chess)* Turm m

room Zimmer nt ; **~ service** Zimmerservice m

rope Seil nt

rouge Rouge nt

round *(adj)* rund ; *(of golf)* Runde f **it's my round** diese Runde gebe ich aus

round-trip ticket *(plane)* Rückflugticket nt ; *(train)* Rückfahrkarte f

route Weg m

rowboat Ruderboot nt

rowing Rudern nt

rucksack Rucksack m

rude, to be unhöflich sein

rugby Rugby nt

ruins Ruine f

run out: to run out of gas kein Benzin mehr haben

rush hour Hauptverkehrszeit f

S

safe Safe m ; *(not dangerous)* ungefährlich ; gefahrlos

to feel ~ sich sicher fühlen

safety Sicherheit f
safety pins Sicherheitsnadeln fpl
sag: the bed sags das Bett hängt durch
sailboard Windsurfbrett nt
sailboarding Windsurfen nt
sailboat Segelboot nt
salad Salat m
sales rep Vertreter(in) m/f
sales tax Mehrwertsteuer f
salt Salz nt
same: the same again please
bitte nochmal das Gleiche;
the same der/die/dasselbe
sand Sand m
sandals Sandalen fpl
sandwich belegtes Brot nt
sandy sandig;
~ beach Sandstrand m
sanitary napkins Damenbinden fpl
satellite TV Satellitenfernsehen nt
satin Satin m
satisfied: I'm not satisfied with this
ich bin damit nicht zufrieden
Saturday Samstag m
sauce Soße f
saucepan Kochtopf m
sauna Sauna f
sausage Wurst f ; Würstchen nt ;
~ stand Würstchenstand m
saw (tool) Säge f
say: how do you say …? wie sagt
man …? **what did he say?** was hat er
gesagt?
scarf Halstuch nt
scheduled flight Linienflug m
school Schule f
sciatica Ischias nt
scissors Schere f
Scotland Schottland nt
Scottish (adj) schottisch
Scottish (person) Schotte m /Schottin f
scouring pad Topfkratzer m
screw Schraube f
screwdriver Schraubenzieher m
scrubbing brush Scheuerbürste f
scuba-diving equipment
Tauchausrüstung f
sea Meer nt
seafront Strandpromenade f

seasick: I feel seasick ich bin
seekrank
season ticket Zeitkarte f
seasoning Würze f
seat Platz m ;
second zweite ; **~ class** zweiter
Klasse ; **~ floor** (U.S.) erster Stock;
(U.K.) zweiter Stock
secondhand gebraucht;
~ shop Gebrauchtwarenladen m
secretary Sekretär(in) m/f
security guard Wächter(in) m/f
sedative Beruhigungsmittel nt
see, to sehen; **to ~ s.o. again** jemanden wiedersehen
self-catering Selbstversorgung f
self-employed, to be selbständig sein
self-service Selbstbedienung f
sell, to verkaufen
send, to schicken
senior citizen Senior(in) m/f
seniors Rentner(in) m/f
separated, to be getrennt leben
separately getrennt
September September m
septic tank Faulbehälter m
serious ernst
served (meal) serviert
service (religious) Gottesdienst m
service charge Bedienung f;
is service included? ist die Bedienung
inbegriffen?
service station (gas/petrol) Tankstelle f
set menu Menü nt
seven sieben
seventeen siebzehn
seventy siebzig
sex (gender) Geschlecht nt; (act)
Geschlechtsverkehr m
shady schattig
shallow flach
shampoo Haarwaschmittel nt ;
~ for dry/oily hair Shampoo nt für
trockenes/fettiges Haar
shape Form f
share, to teilen
sharp scharf
shavingbrush Rasierpinsel m;
~ cream Rasiercreme f

she sie
sheet *(bed)* Bettlaken nt
shelf Regal nt
ship Schiff nt
shirt Hemd nt
shock *(electric)* Schlag m
shoe laces Schnürsenkel mpl
~ polish Schuhcreme f
~ repair Schuhreparatur f
~ store Schuhgeschäft nt
shoes Schuhe mpl
shop Geschäft nt
shop assistant Verkäufer(in) m/f
shopping: ~ area Geschäftsviertel nt ~
basket Einkaufskorb m;
~ cart Einkaufswagen m;
~ list Einkaufsliste f;
~ mall Einkaufszentrum nt ;
to go ~ einkaufen gehen
shore *(sea/lake)* Ufer nt
short kurz
shorts Shorts pl
shortsighted kurzsichtig
shoulder Schulter f
shovel Schaufel f
show, to zeigen ; can you show me?
können Sie es mir zeigen? ; *(film)*
gegeben werden ; laufen
shower Dusche f ; ~ gel Duschgel nt;
~ room Dusche f
shrunk: they've shrunk sie sind ein-
gelaufen
shut *(door)* zu
shutter Fensterladen m
shy schüchtern
sick: he feels ~ ihm ist schlecht;
I feel ~ mir ist schlecht; I'm going to
be ~ ich muss mich übergeben
sickbay *(ship)* Krankenrevier nt
side *(of road)* Seite f ~ order Beilage
f ~ street Seitenstraße f ~walk
Gehsteig m
sights Sehenswürdigkeiten fpl
sightseeing Stadtrundfahrt f to go ~
auf Besichtigungstour gehen
sign *(road)* Schild nt
signal: he didn't give a ~ er hat nicht
geblinkt
signpost Wegweiser m

silk Seide f
silver Silber nt ; ~plated versilbert
similar, to be ähnlich sein
since *(time)* seit
sing, to singen
singer Sänger(in) m/f
single: ~ cabin Einzelkabine f ; ~
room Einzelzimmer nt ; to be ~ un-
verheiratet sein
sink sinken
sister Schwester f
sit, to sitzen ; sit down, please bitte
setzen Sie sich
six sechs
six-pack of beer Sechserpack m
sixteen sechzehn
sixty sechzig
size Größe f
skates Schlittschuhe mpl
skating rink Eisbahn f
ski: ~ bindings Skibindungen fpl; ~
boots Skischuhe mpl ; ~ instructor
Skilehrer(in) m/f; ~ lift Skilift m;
~ poles Skistöcke mpl ; ~ school
Skischule f; ~ suit Skianzug m; ~
trousers Skihose f
skid: we skidded wir sind geschleudert
skiing Skifahren nt
skin Haut f
skirt Rock m
skis Skier mpl
slalom Slalom m
sledge Schlitten m;
~ run Schlittenbahn f
sleep, to schlafen
sleeping bag Schlafsack m ~ car
Schlafwagen m ~ pill Schlaftablette f
sleeve Ärmel m
slice Scheibe f
slide film Diafilm m
slip *(undergarment)* Unterrock m
slippers Hausschuhe mpl
slope *(ski)* Piste f
slot machine Spielautomat m
Slovakia Slowakei f
Slovenia Slowenien nt
slow langsam ; slow down!
langsamer, bitte!
slow, to *(clock)* nachgehen

slowly langsam

SLR camera Spiegelreflexkamera f

small klein; **~ change** Kleingeld nt

smell: there's a bad smell es riecht unangenehm

smoke, to rauchen ; **I don't smoke** ich rauche nicht

smoking *(compartment)* Raucher pl

snack bar Schnellimbiss m

snacks kleine Gerichte ntpl

sneakers Turnschuhe mpl

snorkel Schnorchel m

snow Schnee m

snow, to schneien

snowed in, to be eingeschneit sein

snowplow Schneepflug m

soaking solution *(contact lenses)* Aufbewahrungsflüssigkeit f

soap Seife f ; **~ powder** Seifenpulver nt

socket Steckdose f

socks Socken fpl

soda Erfrischungsgetränk nt

sofa Sofa *nt*; **~bed** Sofabett nt

soft drink *(soda)* Erfrischungsgetränk nt

software Software f

sold out ausverkauft

sole *(shoes)* Sohle f

some einige

someone jemand

something etwas ; **~ cheaper** etwas Billigeres

sometimes manchmal

son Sohn m

soon bald ; **as soon as possible** so bald wie möglich

sore: it's sore es ist wund;**~ throat** Halsschmerzen pl

sorry! Entschuldigung! Verzeihung!

sort Art f ; **a ~ of** eine Art

sour sauer

south of ... südlich von ...

South Africa Südafrika nt

South African Südafrikaner(in) m/f

souvenir Reiseandenken nt ; **~ guide** Andenkenbildband m **~ store** Andenkenladen m

spa Kurort f

space Platz m

spade Schaufel f

spades *(cards)* Pik nt sing

spare *(extra)* überzählig

speak, to sprechen ; **to ~ to s.o.** mit jemandem sprechen ; **do you speak English?** sprechen Sie Englisch?

special rate Sonderpreis m

specialist Facharzt m Fachärztin f

speed limit Geschwindigkeitsbegrenzung f

speed, to zu schnell fahren

spell, to buchstabieren

spend, to *(money)* ausgeben; *(time)* verbringen

spicy würzig

spin-dryer Wäscheschleuder f

spine Wirbelsäule f

sponge Schwamm m

spoon Löffel m

sport Sport m

sports club Sportverein m

sports ground Sportplatz m

sports store Sportgeschäft nt

sprained, to be verstaucht sein

spring *(season)* Frühling m ; *(water)* Quelle f

square quadratisch

squash Squash nt

stadium Stadion nt

stain Fleck m

stainless steel Edelstahl m

stairs Treppe (f sing)

stall: the engine stalls der Motor stirbt ab

stamp Briefmarke f; **~ machine** Briefmarkenautomat m

stamps Briefmarken fpl

stand in line, to Schlange stehen

start *(n)* Beginn m

start, to beginnen ; anfangen ; *(car)* anspringen

starter Vorspeise f

statement Aussage f

station Bahnhof m

station wagon Kombiwagen m

stationer's Schreibwarenhandlung f

statue Statue f

stay Aufenthalt m
stay, to (*lodge*) bleiben ; wohnen ; (*remain*) bleiben
steak house Steakhaus nt
stereo Stereoanlage f
sterilizing solution Sterilisierlösung f
stern (*ship*) Heck nt
stiff neck steifer Nacken m
still: I'm still waiting ich warte immer noch
sting Stich m
stockings Strümpfe mpl
stolen, to be gestohlen werden
stomach Magen m ; **~ ache** Magenschmerzen pl ; **~ cramps** Magenkrämpfe mpl
stool (*feces*) Stuhl m
stop (*bus, tram*) Haltestelle f
stop, to halten ; anhalten ; **to ~ at** halten in ; **please stop here** bitte halten Sie hier ; **which stop?** welche Haltestelle?
stopover Zwischenlandung f
store Geschäft nt ; **~ detective** Kaufhausdetektiv m; **~ guide** Kaufhaus-Wegweiser m **~ owner** Ladenbesitzer(in) m/f
straight ahead geradeaus
strained muscle Muskelzerrung f
strange seltsam
straw (*drinking*) Strohhalm m
strawberry (*flavor*) Erdbeere f
stream Bach m
string Schnur f
striped (*patterned*) gestreift
strong stark
student Student(in) m/f
study, to studieren
stunning hinreißend
stupid: that was stupid! das war dumm!
sturdy robust
style Stil m
styling mousse Schaumfestiger m
subtitled, to be Untertitel haben
subway U-Bahn f ; **~ station** U-Bahnstation f
suede Wildleder nt
sugar Zucker m

suggest, to vorschlagen
suit Anzug m
suitable for ... geeignet sein für ...
summer Sommer m
sun Sonne f; **~ burn** Sonnenbrand m ; **~ block** Sonnenschutzcreme f ; **~ deck** (*ship*) Sonnendeck nt; **~ glasses** Sonnenbrille f sing ; **~ stroke** Sonnenstich m
sunbathe, to sonnenbaden
Sunday Sonntag m
suntan cream Sonnencreme f
suntan lotion Sonnenmilch f
super (*gas*) Super nt
superb fantastisch
supermarket Supermarkt m
supervision Aufsicht f
supplement Zuschlag m
suppositories Zäpfchen ntpl
sure: are you ~? sind Sie sicher?
surfboard Surfbrett nt
surname Nachname m
suspicious verdächtig
swallow, to (hinunter)schlucken
sweater Pullover m
sweatshirt Sweatshirt nt
sweet (*taste*) süß
sweets Süßigkeiten fpl
swelling Schwellung f
swim, to schwimmen, baden
swimming Schwimmen nt ; **~ pool** Schwimmbad nt
swimsuit Badeanzug m
Swiss (*person*) Schweizer(in) m/f
switch Schalter m
switch on/off, to ein/ausschalten
Switzerland die Schweiz f
swollen geschwollen
symptoms Symptome ntpl
synagogue Synagoge f
synthetic fabric Synthetik nt

T

T-shirt T-Shirt nt
table (*restaurant*) Tisch m; **~ cloth** Tischdecke f; **~ tennis** Tischtennis nt
tablet Tablette f
traffic jam Stau m

take, to *(bus)* nehmen; *(carry)* tragen ; *(medicine)* nehmen ; *(time)* dauern; **I'll take it** ich nehme es; **to ~ away/out** zum Mitnehmen

taken *(occupied)* besetzt; **is this seat ~?** ist dieser Platz besetzt?

take out *(restaurant)* Imbissstube f

talcum powder Körperpuder m

talk, to sprechen

tall groß

tampons Tampons mpl

tan Bräune f

tap Wasserhahn m

tape measure Maßband nt

taste Geschmack m

taxi Taxi nt ; **~ driver** Taxifahrer m; **~ rank/stand** Taxistand m

tea Tee m ; **~ bag** Teebeutel m

teacher Lehrer(in) m/f

team Mannschaft f

teaspoon Teelöffel m

teat *(baby bottle)* Sauger m

teenager Teenager m

telephone Telefon nt ; **~ bill** Telefonrechnung f **~ booth** Telefonzelle f ; **~ calls** Anrufe mpl ; **~ directory** Telefonbuch *nt*; **~ number** Telefonnummer f ; **to ~** anrufen

television Fernseher m

tell, to sagen ; **tell me** sagen Sie mir

temperature *(water)* Temperatur f

temporarily provisorisch

temporary vorübergehend

ten zehn

tennis Tennis nt ; **~ ball** Tennisball m; **~ court** Tennisplatz m

tent Zelt nt ; **~ floor** Zeltboden *m* ; **~ pegs** Heringe mpl ; **~ pole** Zeltstange f

terminus *(for streetcar)* Straßenbahndepot nt

terrible schrecklich

tetanus Wundstarrkrampf m

thank you danke

thanks for your help vielen Dank für Ihre Hilfe

that das; **~ one** jenes ; das da

that's all das ist alles

thaw, to auftauen

theater Theater nt

theft Diebstahl m

their ihr ; **theirs** ihre(-r-s)

them sie; **for ~** für sie; **to ~** zu ihnen

then *(time)* dann

there dort ; *(to there)* dorthin

there is/are ... es gibt ...

there you go bitte schön

thermometer Thermometer nt

thermos flask Thermosflasche f

these diese

they sie

thick dick

thief Dieb m

thigh Oberschenkel m

thin dünn

think: I think ich glaube ; **I ~ about it** ich überlege es mir

third dritte ; **~-party insurance** Haftpflichtversicherung f

third, a Drittel nt

thirsty durstig

thirteen dreizehn

thirty dreißig

this one dieses ; dieses hier

those diese

thousand tausend, eintausend

three drei

throat Hals m

thrombosis Thrombose f

through durch

ticket Fahrschein m ; *(sights)* Eintrittskarte f; *(sport)* Karte f ; **~ agency** Kartenvorverkaufsstelle f **~ office** Fahrkartenschalter m **tickets** *(plane)* Flugtickets ntpl ; *(train)* Fahrkarten fpl

tie Krawatte f ; **~ pin** Krawattennadel f

tight *(clothing)* eng

tights Strumpfhose f

time Uhrzeit f ; **free ~** Zeit f zur freien Verfügung; **on ~** pünktlich **what ~?** wann? **~ of day** Tageszeit f; **five times** fünfmal

timetable Flugplan m

tinfoil Stanniolpapier nt

tint, to tönen

tip Trinkgeld nt

tire Reifen m

tired, to be müde sein

tissues Papiertaschentücher ntpl

to *(place)* nach

toaster Toaster m

tobacco Tabak m

tobacco store/cigar shop Tabakgeschäft nt

today heute

toe Zehe f

together zusammen

toilet Toilette f ; **toilets** Toiletten fpl

toilet paper Toilettenpapier nt

toiletries Toilettenartikel mpl

tomorrow morgen

tongue Zunge f

tonic water Tonicwater nt

tonight heute abend ; **for ~** für heute abend

tonsillitis Mandelentzündung f

tonsils Mandeln fpl

too *(also)* auch; *(extreme)* zu ; **~ little** zu wenig **~ much** zu viel

tooth Zahn m ; **~ache** Zahnschmerzen pl; **~brush** Zahnbürste f; **~paste** Zahnpasta f

top *(adj)* oberste(-r-s); **~ floor** oberster Stock m

torch *(Brit)* Taschenlampe f *(US)* Fackel f

torn, to be *(muscle)* gerissen sein

totaled *(car)* Totalschaden m

totally völlig

tough *(food)* zäh

tour Rundfahrt f ; **~ guide** Reiseleiter(in) m/f; **~ operator** Reiseveranstalter m

tourist Tourist(in) m/f; **~ office** Fremdenverkehrsbüro nt

tow rope Abschleppseil nt

tow, to abschleppen

toward ... in Richtung ...

towel Handtuch nt

toweling Frottee m

tower Turm m

town Stadt f ; **~ hall** Rathaus nt

toy Spielzeug nt ; **~ store** Spielwarengeschäft nt

track Weg m

tracksuit Trainingsanzug m

traffic Verkehr m; **~ jam** Stau m; **~ light** Ampel f **~ violation** Verkehrsdelikt nt

trail Wanderweg m

trailer Wohnwagen m ; **~ park** Campingplatz m für Wohnwagen

train Zug m ; *(subway)* U-Bahn f ; **~ station** Bahnhof m **~ times** Abfahrtszeiten fpl

transfer, to übertragen; *(money)* überweisen

transformer Transformator m

transit, in beim Transport

translate, to übersetzen

translation Übersetzung f

translator Übersetzer(in) m/f

travel, to fahren, reisen **~ agency** Reisebüro nt ; **~ sickness** Reisekrankheit f

traveler's check Reisescheck m

tray Tablett nt

tree Baum m

trim nachschneiden

trip Ausflug m

trouble: I'm having trouble with ... ich habe Schwierigkeiten mit...

truck Lastwagen m

true: that's not true das ist nicht wahr; **true north** geografischer Nordpol m

try on, to anprobieren

Tuesday Dienstag m

tumor Tumor m

tunnel Tunnel m

Turkish *(adj)* türkisch

turn, to drehen, *(street)* abbiegen **~ down, to** *(heat)* herunterdrehen; *(volume)* leiser stellen **~ off, to** ausmachen **~ on, to** anmachen **~ up, to** *(volume/heat)* aufdrehen

TV Fernseher m

tweezers Pinzette f

twelve zwölf

twenty zwanzig

twice zweimal

twin bed Einzelbett nt

twist: I've twisted my ankle ich habe mir den Knöchel verstaucht

two zwei ; **~ door** zweitürig

type: what type of? welche Art?

5

typical typisch

ugly hässlich
U.K. Vereinigtes Königreich nt
ulcer Geschwür nt
umbrella Regenschirm m
uncle Onkel m
unconscious, to be bewusstlos sein
under *(place)* unter
underdone *(adj)* zu roh
underpants Unterhose f
underpass Unterführung f
undershirt Unterhemd nt
understand, to verstehen ; **do you ~?**
verstehen Sie? **I don't ~** ich verstehe
nicht
understanding
undress, to *(at doctor's)* freimachen
unfortunately leider
uniform Uniform f
United States Vereinigte Staaten pl
university Universität f
unleaded gas bleifreies Benzin nt
unlimited mileage ohne Kilometer-
begrenzung f
unlock, to aufschließen
unpleasant unfreundlich; unangenehm
unscrew, to aufschrauben
until bis
up to bis zu
upmarket anspruchsvoll
upset stomach Magenverstimmung f
upstairs oben
urgent dringend
urine Urin m
us: for/with us für/mit uns
use, to benutzen
useful nützlich

vacancy freies Zimmer nt
vacant frei
vacate, to räumen
vacation Ferien pl Urlaub m;
on ~ im Urlaub
vaccinated against, to be
geimpft sein gegen
vaccination Impfung f

vaginal infection
Scheidenentzündung f
valid gültig
validate, to *(ticket)* entwerten
valley Tal nt
valuable wertvoll
value Wert m
vanilla *(flavor)* Vanille f
VAT *(sales tax)* Mehrwertsteuer f
vegetable store Gemüsehändler m
vegetables Gemüse nt sing
vegetarian *(adj)* vegetarisch ; *(n)*
Vegetarier(in) m/f; **to be ~**
Vegetarier(in) m/f sein
vehicle Fahrzeug nt; **~ registration**
document Kraftfahrzeugzulassung f
vein Vene f
velvet Samt m
vender Verkäufer m
vending machine Automat m
venereal disease
Geschlechtskrankheit f
ventilator Ventilator m
very sehr
vet(erinarian) Tierarzt m Tierärztin f
video Video nt; **~ game** Videospiel nt;
~ recorder Videorekorder m
view: with a view of the sea mit
Blick auf's Meer
village Dorf nt
vineyard Weinberg m
vintner Weinhändler m
visa Visum nt
visit Aufenthalt m
visit, to *(sights)* besichtigen; *(people)*
besuchen
visiting hours Besuchszeit f sing
vitamin tablets Vitamintabletten fpl
voice Stimme f
volleyball Volleyball m
voltage Spannung f
vomit, to sich übergeben

waist Taille f
waist pouch Gürteltasche f
wait, to warten ; **to ~ for** warten auf
wait! warten Sie!
waiter/waitress Kellner/in m/f

waiting room Wartesaal m
wake, to (self) aufwachen; (s.o. else) jemanden wecken;
wake-up call Weckruf m
Wales Wales nt
walk: to go for a walk spazieren gehen; **to ~ home** nach Hause gehen
walking/hiking Wandern nt; **~ boots** Wanderschuhe mpl; **~ gear** Wanderausrüstung f; **~ route** Wanderweg m; **~ trip** Wanderausflug m
wall Wand f
wallet Brieftasche f; Geldbeutel m
want, to wollen, wünschen
ward (hospital) Station f
warm warm
warm, to wärmen
warranty Garantie f; **is there a ~ on it?** ist darauf Garantie? **no ~** keine Garantie
wash, to waschen
washable waschbar; **is it hand ~?** kann man es mit der Hand waschen?; **is it machine ~?** kann man es in der Maschine waschen?
wash basin Waschbecken nt
washer (for faucet) Dichtung f
washing instructions Waschanleitung f sing; **~ machine** Waschmaschine f; **~ powder** Waschpulver nt
washing, to do Wäsche waschen
wasp Wespe f
watch Uhr f; **~ strap/band** Uhrarmband nt
watch TV, to fernsehen
watch repairs/watchmender's Uhrmacher m
water Wasser nt **~ bottle** Wasserflasche f; **~ heater** Heißwassergerät nt; **~fall** Wasserfall m
waterskiing Wasserskilaufen nt
waterskis Wasserskier mpl
wave Welle f
waxing Wachsbehandlung f
way: I've lost my way (on foot) ich habe mich verlaufen; **on the ~** auf dem Weg
we wir

weak schwach; **I feel weak** mir ist schwach
wear, to tragen
weather Wetter nt; **~ forecast** Wetterbericht m
web Netz nt
web site Webseite f
wedding Hochzeit f; **~ ring** Ehering m
Wednesday Mittwoch m
week Woche f
weekend Wochenende nt; **~ rate** Wochenendpauschale f; **at the ~** am Wochenende
weekly ticket Wochenkarte f
weight: my weight is ... ich wiege ...
welcome to ... willkommen in ...
well-done (steak) durchgebraten
well done! (compliment) gut gemacht!
Welsh (adj) walisisch
Welsh (person) der Waliser m/ die Waliserin f
west of ... westlich von ...
wetsuit Taucheranzug m
what kind of? welche Art von ...? was für ein(e) ...?
what time...? wann ...?
what's the time? wie spät ist es?
what? was?
wheelchair Rollstuhl m
when? wann?
where? wo? **~ are you from?** woher kommen Sie? **~ can we ...?** wo können wir ...? **~ else?** wo sonst? **~ is ...?** wo ist ...?
which? welcher/welche/welches? **~ way?** wohin?
while während
whist (cards) Whist nt
white weiß; **~ wine** Weißwein m
who? wer? **~ else?** wer noch?
whole: the whole day den ganzen Tag
whose wessen
why? warum? **~ not?** warum nicht?
wide (cloths) weit, breit
wife Frau f
wildlife Tierwelt f
window Fenster nt; (shop) Schaufenster nt

window seat Fensterplatz m
windshield/windscreen Windschutzscheibe f
windsurfer Windsurfer m
windy, to be windig sein
wine Wein m ; **~ bottle** Weinflasche f **~ list** Weinkarte f
winery Weinberg m
winter Winter m
wireless drahtlos
wishes: best wishes! alles Gute!
with mit
without ohne
witness Zeuge m, Zeugin f
women's underpants Schlüpfer m
wood *(forest)* Wald m ; *(material)* Holz nt
wool Wolle f **pure wool** reine Wolle
work, to *(job)* arbeiten ; *(function)* funktionieren ; **it doesn't work** es funktioniert nicht
worry: I'm worried ich mache mir Sorgen
worse schlechter ; **it's gotten worse** es ist schlimmer geworden
worst, the das Schlimmste
worth: is it worth seeing? lohnt es einen Besuch?
wound Wunde f
write down, to aufschreiben
write: write soon! schreiben Sie bald!
wrong *(incorrect)* falsch ; **~ number!** falsch verbunden!
wrong: what's wrong? *(car)* wo liegt der Fehler? ;
there is something ~ with ... mit ... stimmt etwas nicht

XYZ

X-ray, to have an geröntgt werden
yacht Jacht f
year Jahr nt
yellow gelb
yesterday gestern
yogurt Jogurt m
you *(sing/plur)* Sie [du]; Sie [ihr]
you are here *(on map)* Standort m
young jung
your *(sing/plur)* Ihr [dein]; Ihr [ihr]

yours Ihre(-r-s); deine(-r-s) ;
it's ~ es gehört Ihnen/dir
youth hostel Jugendherberge f
zebra crossing Zebrastreifen m
zero null
zip(per) Reißverschluss m
zoo Zoo m

DICTIONARY
GERMAN-ENGLISH

This German/English dictionary concentrates on areas where you need to decode written German: hotels, public buildings, restaurants, shops, ticket offices, transport.

A

ab 18 Jahre under 18 not allowed
Abendgarderobe formal wear
Abendgebet evensong
Abendkasse evening box office
Abendvorstellung evening show
Abfahrt departure
Abfertigung check-in counter
Abflüge departures
Abgeordnetenhaus parliament building
Abo subscription *(newspapers, season tickets)*
Absender sender
(bitte) Abstand halten (please) keep your distance
Abtei abbey
Abteilung department
Abteilungsleiter department manager
Adresse address
Aerobic aerobics
alkoholfreies Bier non-alcoholic beer
alle ... Stunden every ... hours
Allee avenue, boulevard
Altglas recycled glass
Altglascontainer recycling container for glass bottles
Altpapier recycled paper
Altstadt old town
Aluminium aluminum
ambulante Patienten outpatients
5 Ampere 5 amp
Amtszeichen abwarten wait for tone
an Bord gehen embark
an der Kasse bezahlen please pay at counter
an Sonn- und Feiertagen on Sundays and holidays
Andacht prayer service

Andachtsraum chapel
andere Orte other destinations
Anfängerpiste for beginners *(ski run)*
Angebot special offer
Angeln fishing, angling
Ankauf currency bought at
Ankunft arrivals
Anlegehafen port, harbor
Anlegeplatz dock
Anlieger frei residents only
annulliert cancelled
Anprobe fitting rooms
Anschlussflug connecting flight
Anschlussstelle junction
anschnallen fasten your seatbelt
Ansichtskarten picture postcards
Antik/Antiquitäten antiques
Antiquitätenladen antiques store
Anwohner frei access (to residents) only
Apotheke drugstore, pharmacy
April April
Aquädukt aqueduct
Art style
Ärztlicher Notfalldienst emergency medical service
Arztpraxis doctor's office
auf Tournee on tour
Aufführung performance, recital
Aufnahme admissions
Aufzug elevator/lift
Augenarzt eye doctor
Augenoptik optician's
August August
Ausfahrt freihalten keep exit/driveway clear
Ausgang exit
ausgebucht full/booked up
Auskunft information
Auskunft, international international directory enquiries
Ausreisedatum date of departure
außer Betrieb out of order
Aussichtspunkt viewpoint
Ausstellungsgebäude pavilion
Ausstellungsort place of issue
ausverkauft sold out
Ausweichparkplätze extra parking
Ausweis vorzeigen ID required
Autobahn expressway [motorway]

autobahnähnliche Straße principal highway [main road]
Autobahnpolizei expressway [motorway] police
Autofähre car ferry
Autoreparaturwerkstatt car repairs
Autovermietung car rental
Autowaschanlage car wash
Autozubehör car accessories

B

Babybekleidung baby wear
Babyraum nursery
Babywickelraum baby diaper changing room
Backartikel baking supplies
Bäckerei bakery
Backwaren baking goods
Bademoden swimwear
Bademöglichkeit swimming facilities
Bademützen bathing caps
Baden verboten no bathing
Bahn railroad/railway
Bahnhof rail/train station
Bahnübergang train-crossing
Balkon balcony
Ballett ballet
Ballspielen verboten no ball games
Bankautomat ATM
Bankgebühren bank charges
Barauszahlung cash withdrawal
Bastelbücher craft books
Batterien batteries
Bauernhof farm
Baumwolle cotton
beginnt um ... starting at ...
Behandlungsraum treatment room
belegt full up, no vacancy
Benzin gasoline
Benzin bleifrei unleaded gasoline
Benzinpumpe fuel pump
Berg mountain
Bergspitze peak
Bergsteigen mountaineering
Bergwerk mine
besetzt occupied, engaged
beste Qualität excellent quality
Bestimmungsort destination
Besucherterrasse visitors' terrace

Betreten verboten keep out
Betriebszeiten von ... bis ... opening hours from ... to ...
bezahlt paid
Bibliothek library
Bier beer
Billard billiards
Binnensee lake
Biographie biography
Biokost health foods
Bischof bishop
Bistro buffet car
Bleiben Sie auf der Piste no off-trail skiing
bleifrei unleaded
Bleistift pencil
Blick aufs Meer sea/ocean view
Blumen(laden) florist's
Bodensee Lake Constance
Bordkarte boarding pass
Börse stock exchange
botanischer Garten botanical garden
Botschaft embassy
brandneu brand new
Bremse brake
Briefe letters
Briefkasten mailbox
Briefmarken stamps
Briefumschläge envelopes
Brot bread
Brot und Kuchen bread and cakes
Brücke bridge
Brunnen well, fountain
Bücherei library
Buchhandlung bookstore
Buchungen *(ticket)* reservations
Bühne stage
Bühnenbild scenery
Bundesgrenzschutz border police
Bundesstraße secondary road
Burg castle
Bürgersteig sidewalk
Burgruine ruins of a castle
Bus bus
Bushaltestelle bus stop

C

Camping verboten no camping/ tenting
Campingausweis camping permit
Campingplatz campsite

Caravan trailer/caravan
Chemische Reinigung dry cleaner's
cholesterinfrei no cholesterol
Chor choir

D

Damenmode ladie's wear
Damentoiletten ladie's room
Damenwäsche lingerie
Damm dam
Dampfer/Dampfschiff steamboat
Dauerkarte season ticket
Deckpassage deck passage
Denkmal *(ancient)* monument, memorial
Dezember December
Diät diet (foods)
Diätküche diet meals
Dichterlesung poetry reading
Dienstag Tuesday
Diesel diesel
Diözese diocese
Dirigent conductor
Dom cathedral
Domherr canon
Donnerstag Thursday
Dorf village
Dosen cans
Drogerie drugstore
drücken push
Düne dune
Durchfahrt verboten no throughway
durchschnittliche Nährwerte nutritional information
Duschen showers
DZ (Doppelzimmer) double room

E

€ euro
echt genuine
Eier eggs
Einbahnstraße one-way street
Einfahrt freihalten keep entrance/ driveway clear
Eingang entrance
Einheiten units
Einkaufszentrum/-passage shopping mall/center
Einkaufszone shopping area

einordnen get in lane
Einreisedatum date of arrival
Einrichtungen für Kinder facilities for children
Einrichtungshaus furniture store
Einschiffung boarding point
einschließlich inclusive/including
Einsteigebereit boarding now
Einsteigen nur mit gültigem Fahrausweis board only with a valid ticket
Einstieg (boarding) gate
Eintritt frei admission free
Eintrittskarten admission tickets
Eintrittspreise admission fee
Einwanderungsbehörde immigration department
Einzahlung deposits
Einzahlung und Auszahlung deposits and withdrawals
Einzelfahrschein/Einzelticket one way/ single ticket
Einzelkabinen single berth cabins
Eis ice cream
Eislaufen ice skating
Elektrogeräte und -bedarf electrical appliances
Elektrogeschäft electronics store
Empfang reception
Ende der Umleitung end of detour
Endstation terminus
Engagement gig
Entbindungsklinik maternity ward
Entfernung in Kilometer (km) distance in kilometers
entkorken uncork
entzündlich inflammable
Erdgeschoss first floor
Erfrischungsgetränke soft drinks
Erlebnispark amusement park
erste Klasse/1. Klasse first class
erster Rang dress circle
erster Stock/Etage second floor
erster Weihnachtstag Christmas Day
Erwachsene adults
Erzbischof archbishop
Essen und Trinken food and drink
Essen verboten no food
Etage floor/story
EU-Staatsangehörige EU-Nationals

EuroCity (EC) intercity train
Explosionsgefahr danger of explosion
EZ (Einzelzimmer) single room

Fabrik factory
Fahrbahnschäden poor road surface
Fähre ferry
Fahrkarte entnehmen take ticket
Fahrkarten tickets
Fahrräder bicycles
Fahrradgeschäft bicycle shop
Fahrradhelm bicycle helmet
Fahrstuhl elevator
Fallschirmspringen parachuting
... fängt um ... an ... begins at ...
Farbfilm color film
Fahrschein entwerten validate ticket
Fasching *(southern Ger.)* carnival
Fastnacht carnival
Februar February
Federball badminton
Feinkost delicatessen
Feinschmeckerart gourmet style
Feld field
Fensterplatz window seat
Feriendorf vacation village
Fernbahn long distance train
Fernsehraum television room
Fertiggerichte ready-to-serve meals
Fest festival, party
Festhalle concert hall
Festung fortress
fettarm low fat
Fettgehalt fat content
feuerhemmende Tür fire door
Feuerlöscher fire extinguisher
Feuerwehr fire brigade
Feuerwehrwache fire station
Feuerwerk fireworks
Filmmusik movie soundtrack
Firma company
Firn icy/old snow
Fisch fish
Fischen fishing
Fischen nicht erlaubt no fishing
Fischen nur mit Schein/Erlaubnis
fishing by permit only
Fischhändler fish store
Fischspezialitäten fish

Fischstand fishstall
Fitnessstudio/-center fitness center
FKK-Strand nudist beach
Fleisch meat
Fluchtweg emergency exit
Flughafen airport
Flugnummer flight number
Flugplan flight schedule
Flugplatz airfield
Flugscheine plane tickets
Flugscheinkontrolle ticket control
Flugsteig gate
Flugzeit flight time
Flugzeug plane
Fluss river
Flussfahrt river trip
Folklore folk music
Fön hairdryer
Foto/Fotogeschäft camera shop
Fotoabteilung photo department
Fotografie photography
Fotografieren nicht erlaubt no pho-
tography
Frauen women *(restrooms)*
Frauenarzt gynecologist
Frauenparkplätze parking reserved
for women
frei for hire, vacant
Freibad outdoor pool
freier Verkauf unrestricted sale
freigegeben ab ... Jahren no chil-
dren under ...; parental guidance *(film
classification)*
Freigepäck luggage allowance
Freilandeier free range eggs
Freitag Friday
Freiwillig 30 voluntary speed limit -
30 km/h
Freizeitanlage country club
Freizeitkleidung informal wear
Fremdwährung foreign currency
Friedhof cemetery
frisch fresh
frisch gestrichen wet paint
frisches Obst fresh fruit
Frischwasser drinking water
Friseur hairdresser
Fruchtsäfte fruit juices
Frühling/Frühjahr spring
Frühstück breakfast

Frühstückszimmer breakfast room
Führung guided tour
Fundbüro lost and found
für ... Tage for ... days
für Diabetiker for diabetics
für Familien mit Kindern family section
für fettendes Haar for oily hair
für Fortgeschrittene for intermediates
für normales Haar for normal hair
für trockenes Haar for dry hair
für unsere kleinen Gäste children's portion/selection
für zwei Personen for two
Fußball soccer/football
Fußgänger pedestrians
Fußgängerbereich traffic-free zone
Fußgängerüberweg pedestrian crossing
Fußgängerzone pedestrian zone
Fußpflegerin chiropodist
Fußweg footpath

G

Gabel fork
Galerie gallery
Gänge gears
Gangplatz aisle seat
Gangschaltung gear shift
Garderobe coat check
Garten garden
Gartenbedarf und -geräte/Gartencenter garden center
Gasanschluss camping gas connection
Gasse alley
Gasthaus/-hof guest house (inn)
Gastspiel performance by visiting actors
Gebärdenspiel mime
Gebet prayer
Gebirge mountain range
Gebrauchsanweisung/-information instructions for use
Gebühren frei admission free
gebührenpflichtige Straße toll road *(Switzerland)*
Geburtsdatum date of birth
Geburtshaus von ... birthplace of ....
Geburtsname maiden name
Geburtsort place of birth
Gedichte poems
Gefahr danger
gefährlich dangerous

gefährlicher Abhang dangerous slope
Gefälle gradient
Geflügel poultry
gegen Schuppen dandruff shampoo
Gegenanzeigen contraindications
Gegenverkehr two-way traffic
Gehweg sidewalk
Gel ointment
gelandet arrived
Gelbe Seiten Yellow Pages
Geldautomat ATM
Geldüberweisung money transfer
Geldwechsel currency exchange
Gemäldegalerie art gallery
Gemeinde parish
Gemüse vegetables
Gemüse nach Wahl choice of \vegetables
Gemüsekonserven canned vegetables
geöffnet von ... bis ... open from ... to ...
Gepäckannahme baggage acceptance
Gepäckaufbewahrung baggage checkroom/storage
Gepäckausgabe baggage claim
Gepäckträger carrier
Gepäckwagen luggage cart
Gericht(sgebäude) courthouse
Gesamtkilometer der Skiabfahrten length of ski runs
Geschenkartikel gifts
Geschenkladen souvenir shop
geschlossen closed
Gewerbegebiet industrial area
Gewürze spices
Gift poison
giftig poisonous, toxic
Gipfel peak
Glas glass
Glascontainer recycling container for glass
Glatteis(gefahr) icy road
Gleis platform, railway track
glutenfrei gluten-free
Gold- und Silberwaren jeweler
Gondel gondola *(ski-lift)*
Grab grave
Grabmal/Grabstätte tomb
Grenzübergang border crossing
Grillen verboten no barbecues

Grillplatz barbecue/grill pit
großer Saal large assembly room
Grundgebühr minimum fee
Grünglas green glass
Gruppen willkommen parties welcome
Gruppenführung group tours
gültig ab Kauf valid from time of purchase
gültig ab … valid from …
gültig bis … expires …
gültig für Zonen … valid for zones …
gut gekühlt servieren serve chilled

H

Hackfleisch hamburger meat
Hafen port, harbor, docks
Halbpension half board
Hallenbad indoor pool
Halt! stop!
Halt bus/subway/tram stop
Halten verboten no stopping
Handy cell phone
Handwäsche hand wash only
Hauptbahnhof main train station
Hauptstraße main street
Haus house, home
Haus- u. Küchengeräte household appliances
Hausarzt family doctor
hausgemacht homemade
Haushaltswaren household goods, kitchen equipment
Haushaltswäsche household linen
Heiligabend Christmas Eve
heilige Messe Catholic mass
Helm helmet
Herbst fall/autumn
Herrenbekleidung/-mode menswear
Herrenfriseur barber
Herren gentlemen *(restroom)*
herzlich willkommen welcome
heute today
heute Abend this evening
hier abreißen tear here
hier abtrennen cut here
(bitte) hier anstellen [please] wait here
hier Erfrischungsgetränke refreshments available here
hier öffnen open here

hier Parkschein lösen get parking ticket here
hier Telefonkarten phone cards on sale here
(bitte) hier warten [please] wait here
hier wird Englisch gesprochen English spoken
(bitte) hier zahlen [please] pay here
hinten aussteigen exit by the rear door
historische Altstadt historical old town
historische Gebäude historical buildings
Hochspannung high voltage
Höchstgeschwindigkeit top speed
höchstgelegene Bergstation highest mountain station
hochwertig excellent
homöopathischer Arzt homeopath
Honig honey
Hörer abnehmen lift receiver
Hörsaal auditorium
Hotel garni bed & breakfast
Hotelverzeichnis list of hotels
Hubschrauber helicopter
Hügel hill
Hunde bitte an der Leine führen dogs must be kept on leash
Hunde erlaubt dogs allowed
Hunderennen greyhound racing

I

Ihr Standort you are here, your location
im Kühlschrank aufbewahren keep refrigerated
im Notfall benötigen Sie keine Münzen/Telefonkarte emergency calls are free
im Preis inbegriffen included in the price
in der Tiefkühltruhe aufbewahren keep frozen
Immobilien real estate
in Wasser auflösen dissolve in water
inbegriffen included *(bill)*
Industriegebiet industrial area
Information information desk

inklusive included
Inlandsflüge domestic flights
innerhalb von 3 Tagen verbrauchen use within 3 days
Intensivstation intensive care
InterCity (IC) intercity train
InterCityExpress (ICE) express train
internat. Verkehrsflughafen international airport
internationale Flüge international flights

J

Jacht yacht
Jachthafen marina
Januar January
Jugendherberge youth hostel
Jugendliche ab 14 Jahre teenagers 14 and over
Juli July
Juni June
Juwelier jeweler

K

Kabarett cabaret
Kabinen cabins
kalorienarm low calorie
Kammermusik chamber music
Kanal canal
Kanu canoe
Kapelle chapel
Karte aufbewahren retain ticket
Karte einschieben insert card
Karten maps, tickets
Kartentelefon card phone
Käse cheese
Kasse cash register / cashier
Kassetten cassettes
Kathedrale cathedral
Kaufhaus department store
Kegeln bowling/ninepins
kein Ausgang no exit
kein Blitzlicht no flash photography
kein Durchgang no entry
kein offenes Feuer no fires
kein Zutritt no entry
(bitte) keine Abfälle zurücklassen no dumping / don't litter
keine Anlegemöglichkeit no anchorage

keine Eurocheques no checks
keine Filmschwärzung film safe
keine Haftung at your own risk
keine Kreditkarten no credit cards
keine Pause no interval
keine Rückgabe non-returnable
keine Rückgabe des Restgeldes exact change only, no change given
kein Rabatt no discounts
Kfz-Nummer license plate number
Kfz-Schein car registration papers
Kiefernorthopäde orthodontist
Kinder children
Kinderabteilung children's department, pediatric ward
Kinderarzt pediatrician
Kinderbekleidung children's wear
Kinderkino children's movie
Kindermesse children's mass
Kinderspielplatz playground
Kino movie theater/cinema
Kinopolis multiplex cinema
Kiosk snack shop/newsstand
Kirchenruine church ruins
Kirchhof churchyard
kirchlicher Feiertag religious holiday
Klassik classical music
Klassiker classics
Klebeband sticky tape
Kleider- und Kostümverleih dress rental
kleine Mahlzeit snack
Klettern rock climbing
Klinik health clinic
Klippe cliff
Kloster monastery, abbey
Kochbücher cook books
Kochmöglichkeiten cooking facilities
Kofferkulis luggage carts
Köln Cologne
Komödie comedy
Konditorei cake store, confectioner's
Konferenzsaal/-raum conference room
Konfitüre preserves, jam
Kongresshalle convention hall
Konserven canned goods
Konservierungsmittel preservatives
Konsulat consulate
Konzert concert(o)

Konzertsaal concert hall
köstlich delicious
Krankenhaus hospital
Krankenkasse health insurance
Krankenpfleger male nurse
Krankenschwester nurse
Krankenwagen ambulance
Kreditinstitut savings bank
Kreditkartennummer credit card number
Kreuzfahrt (steam) cruise
Kreuzung crossing, intersection
Kritik review
Kuchen cakes
Kugelschreiber pen, ballpoint
kühl aufbewahren keep cool
Kundenberatung customer information
Kundendienst customer service
Kundenparkplatz customer parking
Kundentoilette restroom for customers
Kunstbände art books
Kunstfaser manmade fiber
Kunstgalerie art gallery
Kunsthandlung art store/shop
Kurort spa resort
Kurzparkzone short-term parking
Küste coast
Kutsche horse-drawn coach

L

Lagerfeuer camp fire
Lagerverkauf factory outlet
Lammfleisch lamb
Landeplatz airfield
landschaftlich schöne Strecke scenic route
Landstraße road
Langlauf(ski) cross-country skiing
Langlaufloipen cross-country ski routes
bitte läuten please ring the bell
Lawinengefahr danger of avalanches
Lazarett sickbay
Lebensmittelgeschäft grocery store
Leder leather
Leerung ... collection times
Leichtathletik track & field
Leinen linen
letzter Eingang/Einlass um .... latest entry at …

Leuchtturm lighthouse
Licht einschalten switch on lights
Lieder songs
Liederabend ballad concert
Lieferverkehr frei deliveries only
Liegestuhl deck-chair
Lift elevator
Linienverkehr frei access for public transport vehicles only
Linksabbieger – Gegenverkehr beachten watch for oncoming traffic when turning left
(bitte) links halten keep to the left
Literatur literature
Live-Musik live music
LKW (Lastkraftwagen) truck
Loge box *(theater)*
Lotterie/Lotteriespiel lottery
Lotterielos lottery ticket
Lounge (für Passagiere) (passenger) lounge
Luft air
Luftkissenfahrzeug hovercraft
Luftpumpe pump
Lustspiel comedy

M

Mädchenname maiden name
mager low fat
Mai May
Männer men *(restrooms)*
Mantel coat (garment)
Märchen fairy tales
Markt market
Markthalle covered market
Marktplatz market square
Marschgebiet marsh
März March
Maschinenwäsche machine washable
maßgeschneidert made to measure
Mauer wall
Meer sea, ocean
Meeresbucht estuary
Menü set menu
Messe fair; rom. cath. mass
Metall/Plastik metal/plastic *(recycling)*
Metzgerei butcher's
mikrowellengeeignet microwaveable
Milch milk

mindestens haltbar bis Ende ... best before end of ...
mit ... with ...
mittags geschlossen closed for lunch
Mittwoch Wednesday
Möbel furniture
Möbelgeschäft furniture store
moderner Tanz modern dance
Molkerei(produkte) dairy (products)
Monat month
Monatskarte monthly ticket
Montag Monday
Moor bog
morgen tomorrow
Motor abschalten/ausschalten turn off engine
Motor abstellen turn off motor
Mühle mill
Mundwasser mouthwash
Münzen einwerfen, Parkschein entnehmen insert money and take ticket
Münztelefon coin operated phone
Museen museums
Musik music
Musikhaus music store
Musikinstrument und -zubehör musical instrument shop
MwSt. (Mehrwertsteuer) VAT/sales tax

N

nach after
Nachbar neighbor
nachmittags p.m.
Nachmittagsvorstellung matinee
nächste Führung um ... next tour at ...
nächste Leerung ... next collection at ...
nächste Tankstelle ... km next gas station ... km
Nachtbeleuchtung lit in the evenings
Nachtdienst night service
Nachtportier night porter
Nahverkehrszug local train
Name name
Name des Ehegatten name of spouse
Nationalfeiertag national holiday
Nationalpark national park
natriumarm low in salt

Naturbücher nature books
Naturfaser natural fibers
Naturschutzgebiet nature reserve
Nebenwirkungen side effects
neu new
neu im Sortiment new product
Neujahrstag New Year's Day
nicht an die Tür lehnen do not lean against door
nicht aus dem Fenster lehnen do not lean out the window
nicht besetzt vacant
(bitte) nicht betreten [please] do not enter
nicht bügeln do not iron
nicht chemisch reinigen don't dry clean
nicht EU-Staatsangehörige non-EU citizens
nicht hinauslehnen don't lean out the window
nicht inbegriffen not included *(bill)*
nicht rennen no running
Nichtraucher non-smoking
nichts zu verzollen nothing to declare
Nichtschwimmerbecken non-swimmers
(bitte) nicht stehen no standing
(bitte) nicht stören do not disturb
(Nonnen-)Kloster convent
Normalbenzin regular leaded gas
Notarztwagen ambulance car
Notausgang emergency/fire exit
Notbremse emergency brake
Notfall emergency
Notfallaufnahme accident and emergency
Notfallstation ambulance station
nur an Sonntagen und Feiertagen Sundays and holidays only
nur Flughafenpersonal flight crew only
nur für Anwohner residents only
nur für Auslandsfluggäste international passengers only
nur für das Personal staff only
nur für Fluggäste passengers only
nur für Frauen women only
nur für Gäste mit Dauerkarten season ticket holders only

nur für Herren men only
nur für Radfahrer cyclists only
nur für Rasierapparate razors only
nur gültig mit Entwerteraufdruck only good when validated
nur Handgepäck hand luggage only
nur heute today only
nur mit gültiger Fahrkarte enter only with a valid ticket
nur mit Erlaubnis with permission only
nur mit Schein permit holders only
nur an Werktagen weekdays only
nur zur äußeren Anwendung for external use only

O

Oberdeck upper deck
Obergeschoss second floor, upper floor
Observatorium observatory
Obst und Gemüse fruit and vegetables
Obstkonserven canned fruit
öffentliches Gebäude public building
Öffnungszeiten visiting/opening hours, hours of business
ohne Konservierungsstoffe without preservatives
ohne Umsteigen direct service *(train/bus)*
ohne Zucker sugar-free
Oktober October
Öl oil
Oper opera (house)
Operationssaal operating room
Optiker optician
Orchester orchestra
Orgel organ *(musical instrument)*
Orgelkonzert organ music
Orthopäde orthopedic doctor
Ostermontag Easter Monday
Ostern Easter
Ostersonntag Easter Sunday
Ozean ocean

P

Paddelboot canoe, kayak
Paddeln canoeing
Pakete packages

Palais/Palast palace
Pannenhilfe, Telefon in case of breakdown, phone/contact
Papier paper
Papier- und Schreibwaren stationery
Parkdeck car deck
Parken bis zu 2 Std. parking limited to 2 hours
Parken nur für Gäste customer parking only
Parken verboten no parking
Parkett stalls
Parkhaus/-platz parking lot/car park
Parkplatz mit WC rest area with restrooms
Parkschein anfordern press button to get ticket
Parkschein hinter die Windschutzscheibe legen place ticket behind windshield
Parkscheinautomat ticket machine
Parkverbot no parking
Pass pass; passport
Passage arcade
Passbild passport photos
Passkontrolle passport control
Passnummer passport number
Pastor pastor
Pavillon pavilion
Pedal pedal
Personalausweis vorzeigen proof of identity required
Personenfähre passenger ferry
Personenwagen passenger car
Pfad path
Pfand deposit *(on bottle)*
Pfandflaschen returnable bottles
Pfarrer father *(relig.)*
Pferdeschlittenfahrt horse-drawn sleigh ride
pflanzlich vegetable based
pflegeleicht easy-care
Pflegemittel skincare
Picknicplatz picnic site
Piste geschlossen/gesperrt ski run closed
PKW (Personenkraftwagen) car
PKW-Stellplätze vorhanden with adequate parking
planmäßig on time

Plattfuß puncture
Platz square; seat
Polizei police
Polizeiwache police station
Polyacryl acrylic
Pop International pop music
Porzellan china
Post/Postamt post office
Postanweisung postal/money orders
Preis/Liter price per liter
Preise prices, rates
Preise inkl. MwSt. price including VAT
private Krankenversicherung private health insurance
Privatgrundstück private property
Programm program
Palmsonntag Palm Sunday
Psychiater psychiatrist
Putzmittel cleaning products

Q

Quelle spring
Querstraße cross road
Quittung receipt

R

Radarkontrolle radar control
Radfahren cycling
Radweg bicycle lane/path/ track
Rang balcony
Rasen nicht betreten keep off the grass
Rastplatz rest area, picnic area
Raststätte service area
Rathaus town hall
Rauchen verboten no smoking
Raucher(abteil) smoking compartment
Räumungsverkauf closing-down sale
rechts halten keep to the right
reduziert reductions
Reflektor reflector
Reformhaus health food store
Regenjacke waterproof jacket
Reifenpanne flat tire
Reihe row, tier
reine Baumwolle 100% cotton
reine Schurwolle pure new wool
Reinigung dry cleaner's
Reisebüro travel agent's
Reiseführer travel guide

Reisezentrum travel center
Reiseziel destination
Reisezug long distance trains
Reiten horseback riding
reizend irritating to skin, charming
Rennbahn racetrack/course
Rente pension
Reparaturwerkstatt repairs, garage
reserviert reserved
Reservierung reservations
Residenzschloss palace
Rettungsboot lifeboat
Rettungsdienst ambulance station
Rettungsring lifebelt
Rettungswagen ambulance
Rettungsweg für die Feuerwehr freihalten fire lane, keep clear
Rezeption reception
Rindfleisch beef
Ringstraße ring-road
Rollstuhlgerecht suitable for wheel chair users
Rolltreppe escalator
Romane fiction
Röntgenabteilung X-ray
Rückerstattung refund
Rückfahrkarte return ticket
Rückgaberecht money-back guarantee
(bitte) Rückgeld sofort nachzählen please check your change
Rücklicht rear lamp
Ruderboot rowboat
Rudern/Rudersport rowing
Rugby rugby
Ruhetag day off
ruhige Lage in a quiet location
(bitte) ruhig verhalten keep quiet
Ruine ruins
rund um die Uhr geöffnet 24-hour service
Rundblick panorama
Rundfahrt excursion trip

S

Sackgasse cul-de-sac
saisonbedingt in season
Salbe ointment
Salz salt
Samstag Saturday
Sandboden sand (camping site)

210

Sanitäranlage/-ausstattung washing facilities
Sattel seat
SB (Selbstbedienung) self-service
Schallplatten records
Schauspiel spectacle
Schiff ship
Schiffsverbindung ferry route
Schlachtfeld battle site
Schlafwagen sleeper, sleeping compartment
Schläger racket
schlechte Fahrbahn poor road surface
Schlepplift drag lift
Schleudergefahr danger for towed trailers
Schleuse lock
Schließfächer luggage lockers
Schlittschuhe ice skates
Schlittschuhlaufen ice-skating
Schloss lock; castle
Schlosshotel castle lodging
Schlucht canyon
Schmuck jewelry
Schneeketten sind vorgeschrieben use snow chains
Schnellgerichte ready-to serve meals
Schnellimbiss take out, fast food
Schnellstraße main road/principal highway
Schokolade chocolate
schöner Ausblick/schöne Aussicht panoramic view
Schreibpapier stationery
Schuhabteilung shoes
Schuhmacher/-reparatur shoe repair
Schulbus school bus
Schule school
Schulweg caution, school ahead
Schweinefleisch pork
Schwimmbad swimming pool
Schwimmen swimming
Schwimmen nicht erlaubt no swimming/bathing
Schwimmreif rubber ring
Schwimmweste lifejacket
See lake
Seemündung estuary
Segelboot sailboat
Segelfliegen gliding

Segeln sailing
Seide silk
Seilbahn cable car
Seitenstreifen hard-shoulder
Sekt sparkling wine
selbst wählen pick and mix
Selbstbedienung self-service
selbstgemacht homemade
Selbsttanken self-service *(gas)*
Seniorenmenü senior citizens' meals
September September
Service Point service station
Serviervorschlag serving suggestion
Sessellift chair lift
Sicherheitskontrolle security check
Silber silver
Silvester New Year's Eve
Sitzplatz für Behinderte handicapped seating
Sitzplatz Nummer seat number
Skier skis
Skilaufen skiing
Skilehrer ski teacher
Skischule (mit Aufnahme von Kleinkindern) ski school (for children)
Skistiefel ski boots
Skistöcke ski poles
Skiverleih ski rental
Soldatenfriedhof cemetery for soldiers
Solist(in) soloist
Sommer summer
Sonderangebot bargain, on sale
Sonnabend Saturday
Sonnendeck sun deck
Sonnenmilch Schutzfaktor 8 factor 8 sun lotion
Sonnenschirm sunshade
Sonntag Sunday
sonstige Straße minor road
Souvenirladen gift shop
Speisekarte menu
Speisesaal dining room
Speisewagen dining car
Spezialität des Hauses specialty of the house
Spezialitäten der Region local specialties
Spielfilme feature films
Spielkarten playing cards

Spielplatz playing field *(for children)*
Spielwarengeschäft toy store
Spirituosen alcoholic beverages
Sportbekleidung sportswear
Sportgeschäft/-bedarf sports store
Sportplatz playing field
Sportzentrum sports center
Sprechzimmer consulting room
Springbrunnen fountain
Sprungbecken diving pool
Sprungbrett diving board
Spur lane
Staatsangehörigkeit nationality
Staatstheater national theater
Stadtfestung/-mauer city wall
Stadtmitte city center, downtown
Stahl steel
Standort *(on map)* you are here
Station ward *(hospital)*
Stau traffic jam
Staudamm dam
Stausee reservoir
Steigung gradient
Sternwarte observatory
Stock floor/story/cane
storniert cancelled
strahlensicher film safe
Strand beach
Straße (gesperrt) road/street (closed)
Straßenarbeiten road works
Straßenbahn streetcar
Straußwirtschaft winery's bar and restaurant
Strickwaren knitted garments
Strom electrical power
Stromschnelle rapids
Stromzähler ablesen read the meter
Sturmwarnung storm warning
Sulzschnee slush
Sumpf swamp, bog
Super (Plus) bleifrei premium unleaded gasoline
Super verbleit premium leaded gasoline
Suppen soups
Surfbrett surfboard
Süßwaren candy/sweets; cookies
SW-Film (schwarzweiß Film) black and white film
synchronisiert dubbed

Tabak/Tabakwaren tobacconist's
Tabletten pills, tablets
Tagesgedeck set menu
Tageskarte daily ticket
Tagesmenü set menu of the day
Tagesticket daily ticket
täglich daily
Tal valley, canyon
Tankstelle filling station
Tanz dance
Tänzer dancer
Tanzmusik dance music
Tarif rate
Taste drücken push button
Tauchen scuba diving
Teich pond
Telefonbuch directory
Telefonkarten telephone cards
Telefonnummer telephone number
Telefonzelle public telephone
Telegramme telegrams
Tennisplatz tennis court
Tennishalle indoor tennis
Tennisschläger tennis racket
Terrasse terrace
Textilien textile goods
Theaterstück play
Thermalbad mineral baths
Tiefgarage underground parking
tiefgefroren frozen
Tiefkühlprodukte frozen goods
Tiefschnee deep snow
Tierarzt veterinary
Tiere cattle crossing
Tierhandlung pet shop
Tip serving suggestion
Tischtennis table tennis
Toiletten restrooms
Tor geschlossen halten keep gate shut
Toto Lotto lottery
Touristenstraße scenic/tourist route
Tragödie tragedy
Trambahn streetcar
Treffpunkt meeting point
Tretboot peddle boat
Tribüne viewing gallery
Trinkwasser drinking water

trocknergeeignet can be put in the clothes dryer
Tropfen drops
Tunnel tunnel
(bitte) Tür schließen/zuziehen [please] close the door

U

U-Bahn subway
Überführung walkway
Übergepäck excess luggage
Überholverbot no passing
Überweisungen drafts / transfers
Umgehungsstraße bypass
Umkleidekabinen changing rooms
Umleitung detour
Umriss contour
umsteigen in ... change at ...
unbefestigte Straße unpaved road
Unfallstation casualty
Universität university
Unterdeck lower deck
Unterführung underground passage
Untergeschoss basement
Unterhaltungsmusik easy-listening
Unterhaltungsliteratur light fiction
Unterschrift signature
Untertitel subtitled
unzerkaut einnehmen swallow whole
Uraufführung premiere/first night

V

Varietévorstellung variety show
vegetarisch vegetarian
Verbandskasten first-aid box
verbessert improved
verbleit leaded
Verbot für Fußgänger no thorough-fare for pedestrians
... verboten ... forbidden
verengte Fahrbahn narrow road
Vergiftung poison
Vergnügungspark amusement park
Vergrößerung enlargement service
Verkauf sold here
Verkehrspolizei traffic police
Versicherungsagentur insurance agent
Verspätung delayed
verwendbar bis: ... use by: ...

verzollen goods to declare
Viehtrieb cattle crossing
Viskose rayon
Volksmusik folk music
Vollpension full board
von ... bis ... Uhr from ... to ...
vor Licht schützen keep out of light
Vorabendmesse evening mass
Vorfahrt achten yield/give way
vormittags a.m.
Vornamen given names
vorne einsteigen enter by the front door
Vorratspackung multipack
Vorsicht caution
Vorsicht Stufen! mind the step
Vorsicht Taschendiebe! beware of pickpockets
Vorspeisen appetizers
vorübergehend geschlossen temporarily closed
Vorverkauf advance sales/bookings
Vorwahl area code

W

Wahl choice, election
wählen Sie Ihre Fahrziele/Tarifgebiet/Fahrkarte select destination/zone/ticket
wahlweise at your choice
Wald forest, wood
Wanderkarten hiking maps
Wanderweg nature trail
Warnung warning
Warteraum/-zimmer waiting room
Wartezeit: ca. .... Minuten waiting time: approx ... mins.
Wäscherei launderette (_not_ self-serve)
Wäscheservice laundry service
Waschmaschinen washing machines
Waschmittel laundry detergent
Waschsalon laundromat
Wasser water
wasserdicht waterproof
Wasserhahn water faucet
Wassermühle water mill
Wasserski waterskiing
Wasserturm water tower
WC restrooms

Wechselgeld sofort nachzählen please check your change
Wechselkurs exchange rate
Wechselstube currency exchange
wegen ... geschlossen bis ... closed until ... due to ...
Wegweiser store guide
Wegwerf- disposable ..
Weiher pond
Weihnachten Christmas
Wein wine
Weinberg vineyard
Weingut winery
Weinkelter winepress
Weinprobe wine tasting
Weißglas clear glass
Werk(sausfahrt) factory (exit)
Werkstatt repair shop, garage
werktags weekdays
Wettannahmen betting
Wettkampf contest
wichtige Telefonnummern emergency services
Wild venison/game
Willkommen welcome
Windmühle windmill
Winterschlussverkauf winter season sale
wir zeigen jeden Diebstahl an shoplifting will be prosecuted
Wochenkarte weekly ticket
Wohnmobil/-wagen RV trailer
Wohnort home address
Wohnung zu vermieten apartment for rent
Wolle wool
Wurst(waren) cold meats/sausage

Z

Zahl digit/number
zahlen pay
Zahlmeister purser
Zahlungsanweisung money order
Zahnarzt dentist
Zahnpaste toothpaste
Zahnseide dental floss
Zapfsäule gas pump
Zeitschriften magazines
Zelt tent
Zelten verboten no camping
Zeltplatz campsite
Zentrum city center (downtown)
zerbrechlich – Glas fragile – glass
ziehen pull
Zimmer frei vacancies, rooms to let
Zimmerservice room service
Zimmer mit Dusche und WC rooms with private bathroom
Zimmer mit Kabel-TV/Farbfernseher ausgestattet rooms with cable TV/color TV
Zirkus circus
Zoll customs
zollfreie Ware duty-free goods
Zone 30 speed limit 30 km/h
Zoo zoo
Zoohandlung pet shop
zu den Gleisen to the platforms
zu den Verkaufsräumen to the sales floors
zu vermieten for rent
zum Halten, bitte drücken press button to request stop
zum Mitnehmen to take out/away
Zuschauer spectators
Zuschlag supplement, surcharge
Zutaten ingredients
Zweibett-Kabine two-berth cabin
zweite Klasse/2. Klasse second class
zweiter Rang upper circle

REFERENCE

GRAMMAR

Regular verbs and their tenses

The past is often expressed by using *to have* **haben** + past participle. The future is formed with *will* **werden** + infinitive.

Infinitive: **kaufen** *to buy* **arbeiten** *to work*
Past Participle: **gekauft** *bought* **gearbeitet** *worked*

	PRESENT	PAST	FUTURE
ich *I*	kaufe	habe gekauft	werde kaufen
du *you*, informal	kaufst	hast gekauft	wirst kaufen
Sie *you*, formal	kaufen	haben gekauft	werden kaufen
er/sie/es *he/she/it*	kauft	hat gekauft	wird kaufen
wir *we*	kaufen	haben gekauft	werden kaufen
ihr *you*, pl. informal	kauft	habt gekauft	werdet kaufen
Sie *you*, pl. formal	kaufen	haben gekauft	werden kaufen
sie *they*	kaufen	haben gekauft	werden kaufen

Irregular verbs have to be memorized. Verbs that indicate movement are conjugated with *to be* **sein**, e.g. *to go* **gehen**:

	PRESENT	PAST	FUTURE
ich *I*	gehe	bin gegangen	werde gehen
du *you*, inf.	gehst	bist gegangen	wirst gehen
Sie *you*, formal	gehen	sind gegangen	werden gehen
er/sie/es *he/she/it*	geht	ist gegangen	wird gehen
wir *we*	gehen	sind gegangen	werden gehen
ihr *you*, pl. inf.	geht	seid gegangen	werdet gehen
Sie *you*, pl. formal	gehen	sind gegangen	werden gehen
sie *they*	gehen	sind gegangen	werden gehen

To express future, usually the present tense is used together with a time adverb *I'll work <u>tomorrow</u>.* **Ich arbeite <u>morgen</u>.**

Nouns and articles

All nouns in German are written with a capital letter. Their indefinite articles indicate their gender: **der** (masculine), **die** (feminine), **das** (neuter). In the plural (**die**) the genders don't matter.

Examples: SINGULAR | PLURAL

der Mann *the man* **die** Männer *the men*
die Frau *the woman* **die** Frauen *the women*
das Kind *the child* **die** Kinder *the children*

The indefinite article also indicates the gender of the noun: **ein** (masculine/neuter), **eine** (feminine). There is no article in the plural.

Examples: SINGULAR | PLURAL

ein Zug *a train* **Züge** *trains*
eine Karte *a map* **Karten** *maps*

Possessive articles also relate to the gender of the noun that follows:

NOMINATIVE	ACCUSATIVE	DATIVE
mein/e *my*	**mein/e/n/** *my*	**meinem/r** *my*
dein/e *your*, informal	**dein/e/n** *your*	**deinem/r** *your*
Ihr/e *your*, formal	**Ihr/e/n** *your*	**Ihrem/r** *your*
sein/e *his*	**sein/e/n** *his*	**seinem/r** *his*
ihr/e *her*	**ihr/e/n** *her*	**ihrem/r** *her*
sein/e *its*	**sein/e/n** *its*	**seinem/r** *its*
unser/e *our*	**unser/e/n** *our*	**unserem/r** *our*
ihr/e *your*, pl. informal	**eure/n,euer** *your*	**eurem/r** *your*
Ihr/e *your*, pl. formal	**Ihr/e/n** *your*	**Ihrem/r** *your*
ihr/e *their*	**ihr/e/n** *their*	**ihrem/r** *their*

Examples: **Wo ist meine Fahrkarte?** *Where is my ticket?*
Ihr Taxi ist hier. *Your taxi is here.*
Hier ist euer Pass. *Here is your passport.*

Word order

The conjugated verb comes after the subject and before the object. When a sentence doesn't begin with a subject, the word order changes.

Examples:

Er ist in Berlin. *He is in Berlin.*
Heute ist er in Berlin. *Today he is in Berlin.*
Wir sind in Berlin gewesen. *We were in Berlin.*

Questions are formed by reversing the order of subject and verb.

Examples: **Haben Sie Bücher?** *Do you have books?*
Wie ist das Wetter? *How is the weather?*
Seid ihr in Köln gewesen? *Have you been to Cologne?*

Negations

Negative sentences are formed by adding *not* **nicht** to that part of the sentence which is to be negated.

Examples: **Wir rauchen nicht.** *We don't smoke.*
Der Bus fährt nicht ab. *The bus doesn't leave.*
Warum schreibst du nicht? *Why don't you write?*

If a noun is used, the negation is made by adding **kein**. Its ending is defined by the noun's gender.

Examples: **Ich trinke kein Bier.** *I don't drink beer.*
Wir haben keine Einzelzimmer. *We don't have any single rooms.*
Gibt es keinen Zimmerservice? *Is there no room service?*

Imperatives (command form)

du *you* (inform. sing.)	**Geh!** *Go!*	**Sei still!** *Be quiet!*
ihr *you* (inform. plural)	**Geht!** *Go!*	**Seid still!** *Be quiet!*
Sie *you* (form. sing./pl.)	**Gehen Sie!** *Go!*	**Seien Sie still!** *Be quiet!*
wir *we*	**Gehen wir!** *Let's go!*	---

Examples: **Hört mal alle zu!** *Listen everybody!*
Seid nicht so laut! *Don't be so noisy!*

Pronouns

Pronouns serve as substitutes and relate to the gender.

NOMINATIVE	ACCUSATIVE	DATIVE
ich *I*	**mich** *me*	**mir** *me*
du *you*, informal	**dich** *you*	**dir** *you*
Sie *you*, formal	**Sie** *you*	**Ihnen** *you*
er *he*	**ihn** *him*	**ihm** *him*
sie *she*	**sie** *her*	**ihr** *her*
es *it*	**es** *it*	**ihm** *him*
wir *we*	**uns** *us*	**uns** *us*
ihr *you*, pl. informal	**euch** *you*	**euch** *you*
Sie *you*, pl. formal	**Sie** *you*	**Ihnen** *you*
sie *they*	**sie** *them*	**ihnen** *them*

Examples: **Ich sehe sie.** *I see them.*
Hören Sie mich? *Do you hear me?*

Adjectives

Adjectives describe nouns. Their endings depend on the case.

Examples: **Wir haben ein alt<u>es</u> Auto.** *We have an old car.*

Wo ist mein neu<u>er</u> Koffer? *Where is my new suitcase?*

Gut<u>e</u> Arbeit, Richard! *Good work, Richard!*

Adverbs and adverbial expressions

In German, adverbs are usually identical with adjectives. They describe verbs but, unlike adjectives, their endings don't change.

Examples: **Linda fährt sehr langsam.** *Linda drives very slowly.*

Robert ist noch nicht hier. *Robert isn't here yet.*

Sie sprechen gut Deutsch. *You speak German well.*

Some common adverbial time expressions:

zur Zeit *presently* **bald** *soon* **immer noch** *still* **nicht mehr** *not anymore*

Comparisons and superlatives

Most German adjectives add **–er** for their comparative and **–(e)st** for their superlative. The following list contains only a small selection to illustrate formation and irregularities.

ADJECTIVE	COMPARATIVE	SUPERLATIVE
klein *small, little*	**kleiner** *smaller*	**am kleinsten** *the smallest*
billig *cheap*	**billiger** *cheaper*	**am billigsten** *the cheapest*
neu *new*	**neuer** *newer*	**am neusten** *the newest*
schlecht *bad*	**schlechter** *worse*	**am schlechtesten** *the worst*
groß *big, large*	**grö<u>ß</u>er** *bigger*	**am grö<u>ß</u>ten** *the biggest*
alt *old*	**<u>ä</u>lter** *older*	**am <u>ä</u>ltesten** *the oldest*
lang *long*	**l<u>ä</u>nger** *longer*	**am l<u>ä</u>ngsten** *the longest*
kurz *short*	**k<u>ü</u>rzer** *shorter*	**am k<u>ü</u>rz<u>e</u>sten** *the shortest*
gut *good*	**<u>besser</u>** *better*	**am <u>besten</u>** *the best*
teuer *expensive*	**teu<u>r</u>er** *more expensive*	**am teuersten** *the most expensive*

Examples: **Diese Postkarten sind billig<u>er</u>.**
These postcards are cheaper.

Wo ist der best<u>e</u> Buchladen?
Where is the best bookstore?

NUMBERS

siebenundachtzig (7 and 80 = 87)

On the phone, **zwo** is often used for **zwei**.

In large numbers periods, <u>not</u> commas, are used: **3.500**

0	**null** *nul*		31	**einunddreißig**
1	**eins** *iens*			*iennuntdriessikh*
2	**zwei** *tsvie*		50	**fünfzig** *fewnftsikh*
3	**drei** *drie*		60	**sechzig** *zekhtsikh*
4	**vier** *feer*		70	**siebzig** *zeebtsikh*
5	**fünf** *fewnf*		80	**achtzig** *akhtsikh*
6	**sechs** *zeks*		90	**neunzig** *noyntsikh*
7	**sieben** *zeeben*		100	**(ein)hundert** *(ien)hundert*
8	**acht** *akht*		101	**hunderteins** *hundertiens*
9	**neun** *noyn*		200	**zweihundert** *tsviehundert*
10	**zehn** *tsayn*		1000	**(ein)tausend** *(ien)towzent*
11	**elf** *elf*		2001	**zweitausendeins**
12	**zwölf** *tsvurlf*			*tsvietowzentiens*
13	**dreizehn** *drietsayn*		the 90s	**die neunziger Jahre**
14	**vierzehn** *feertsayn*			*dee noyntsiger yahreh*
15	**fünfzehn** *fewnftsayn*		10.000	**zehntausend**
16	**sechzehn** *zekhtsayn*			*tsayntowzent*
17	**siebzehn** *zeeptsayn*		1.000.000	**eine Million**
18	**achtzehn** *akhttsayn*			*ieneh millioan*
19	**neunzehn** *noyntsayn*		first	**erste/r** *ehrste/r*
20	**zwanzig** *tsvantsikh*		second	**zweite/r** *tsviete/r*
21	**einundzwanzig**		third	**dritte/r** *dritte/r*
	iennunttsvantsikh		fourth	**vierte/r** *feerte/r*
22	**zweiundzwanzig**		fifth	**fünfte/r** *fewnfte/r*
	tsvieunttsvantsikh		once	**einmal** *ienmaal*
30	**dreißig** *driessikh*		twice	**zweimal** *tsviemaal*

3 times	**dreimal**	*driemaal*
a half	**eine Hälfte**	*ieneh hehlfteh*
1/2 hour	**eine halbe Stunde**	*ieneh halbeh shtundeh*
a quarter	**ein Viertel**	*ien feertel*
a third	**ein Drittel**	*ien drittel*
a pair	**ein Paar**	*ien paar*
a dozen	**ein Dutzend**	*ien dutsent*

Days

Monday	**Montag** *moantaag*
Tuesday	**Dienstag** *deenstaag*
Wednesday	**Mittwoch** *mitvokh*
Thursday	**Donnerstag** *donnerstaag*
Friday	**Freitag** *frightaag*
Saturday	**Samstag/Sonnabend** *zamstaag/zonnaabent*
Sunday	**Sonntag** *zontaag*

Months

January	**Januar** *yanuaar*
February	**Februar** *faybruaar*
March	**März** *mehrts*
April	**April** *april*
May	**Mai** *mie*
June	**Juni** *yooni*
July	**Juli** *yooli*
August	**August** *owgust*
September	**September** *zeptember*
October	**Oktober** *oktoaber*
November	**November** *novvember*
December	**Dezember** *daytsember*

Dates

It's …	**Es ist …** *ess ist*
Tuesday, March 1	**Dienstag, der erste März** *deenstaag dehr ehrsteh mehrts*
yesterday/today/ tomorrow	**gestern/heute/morgen** *gestern/hoyteh/morgen*
last week/month/ year	**letzte Woche/letzten Monat/letztes Jahr** *letsteh vokheh/letsten moanat/letstess yaar*
next	**nächste/n/s** *naikhsteh/n/s*
every week/month/ year	**jede Woche/jeden Monat/jedes Jahr** *yaydeh vokheh/yayden moanat/yaydess yaar*
on [at] the weekend	**am Wochenende** *am vokhenendeh*

SEASONS

spring/summer	**Frühling/Sommer** *frewling/zommer*
fall [autumn]/winter	**Herbst/Winter** *hehrpst/vinter*

GREETINGS

Happy birthday!	**Herzlichen Glückwunsch zum Geburtstag!** *hehrtslikhen glewkvunsh tsum gerboorstaag*
Merry Christmas!	**Fröhliche Weihnachten!** *frurlikheh vienakhten*
Happy New Year!	**Ein glückliches Neues Jahr!** *ien glewklikhess noyess yaar*
Congratulations!	**Herzlichen Glückwunsch!** *hehrtslikhen glewkvunsh*
Good luck!	**Viel Glück!** *feel glewk*
Have a good trip!	**Gute Reise!** *gooteh riezeh*

PUBLIC HOLIDAYS

National holidays in Germany (D), Austria (A), Switzerland (CH):

Jan. 1	**Neujahr**	New Year's Day	D	A	CH
Jan. 2					CH*
Jan. 6	**Dreikönigstag**	Epiphany		A	
May 1	**Tag der Arbeit**	Labor Day	D	A	
Aug. 1	**Nationalfeiertag**	National Holiday			CH*
Aug. 15	**Maria Himmelfahrt**	Assumption Day		A	
Oct. 3	**Tag der Deutschen Einheit**	National Unity Day	D		
Nov. 1	**Allerheiligen**	All Saints Day		A	
Dec. 8	**Maria Empfängnis**	Immaculate Conception		A	
Dec. 25	**1.Weihnachtstag**	Christmas	D	A	CH
Dec. 26	**2. Weihnachtstag**	St Stephen's Day	D	A	CH

Movable dates:

Karfreitag	Good Friday	D		CH*
Ostermontag	Easter Monday	D	A	CH*
Christi Himmelfahrt	Ascension	D	A	CH
Pfingstmontag	Whit Monday	D	A	CH*
Fronleichnam	Corpus Christi		A	

*most cantons

221

TIME

The official time system uses the 24-hour clock. However, in ordinary conversation, time is generally expressed as shown below, often with the addition of **morgens** (morning), **nachmittags** (afternoon) or **abends** (evening).

Excuse me. Can you tell me the time?	**Entschuldigen Sie. Können Sie mir sagen, wie spät es ist?** *entshuldigern zee. kurnen zee meer zaagen vee shpait ess ist*
It's …	**Es ist …** *ess ist*
five past one	**fünf nach eins** *fewnf naakh ienss*
ten past two	**zehn nach zwei** *tsayn naakh tsvie*
a quarter past three	**Viertel nach drei** *feerterl naakh drie*
twenty past four	**zwanzig nach vier** *tsvantsikh naakh feer*
twenty-five past five	**fünf vor halb sechs** *fewnf foar halp zeks*
half past six	**halb sieben** *halp zeeben*
twenty-five to seven	**fünf nach halb sieben** *fewnf naakh halp zeeben*
twenty to eight	**zwanzig vor acht** *tsvantsikh foar akht*
a quarter to nine	**Viertel vor neun** *feertel foar noyn*
ten to ten	**zehn vor zehn** *tsayn foar tsayn*
five to eleven	**fünf vor elf** *fewnf foar elf*
twelve o'clock	**zwölf Uhr** *tsvurlf oor*
noon/midnight	**Mittag/Mitternacht** *mittaag/mitternakht*

at dawn	**bei Tagesanbruch** *bigh taagersanbrukh*
in the morning	**morgens** *morgens*
during the day	**tagsüber** *taagsewber*
before lunch	**vor dem Mittagessen** *foar daym mittaagessen*
after lunch	**nach dem Mittagessen** *naakh daym mittaagessen*
in the afternoon	**nachmittags** *naakhmittaags*
in the evening	**abends** *aabernts*
at night	**nachts** *nakhts*
I'll be ready in 5 minutes.	**Ich bin in fünf Minuten fertig.** *ikh bin in fewnf minooten fehrtikh*
He'll be back in a quarter of an hour.	**Er ist in einer Viertelstunde wieder da.** *ehr ist in iener feerterlshtundeh veeder daa*
She arrived half an hour ago.	**Sie ist vor einer halben Stunde angekommen.** *zee ist foar iener halben shtundeh angerkommehn*
The train leaves at …	**Der Zug fährt um …** *dehr tsoog fairt um*
1:04 p.m.	**dreizehn Uhr vier** *drietsayn oor feer*
12:40 a.m.	**null Uhr vierzig** *nul oor feertsikh*
He came 10 minutes early/late.	**Er kam zehn Minuten zu früh/zu spät.** *ehr kaam tsayn minooten tsoo frew/tsoo shpait*
The clock is 5 seconds fast/slow.	**Die Uhr geht fünf Sekunden vor/nach.** *dee oor gayt fewnf zekundern foar/naakh*
from 9:00 to 5:00	**von neun bis siebzehn Uhr** *fon noyn biss zeeptsayn oor*
between 8:00 and 2:00	**zwischen acht und vierzehn Uhr** *tsvishen akht unt feertsayn oor*
I'll be leaving by 11 o'clock.	**Ich reise vor elf Uhr ab.** *ikh riezeh foar elf oor ap*
Will you be back before 8 p.m.?	**Kommen Sie vor zwanzig Uhr wieder?** *kommern zee foar tsvantsikh oor veeder*
We'll be here until Friday.	**Wir sind bis Freitag hier.** *veer zint biss frietaag heer*

DENMARK

SWEDEN

Ostsee

POLAND

Nordsee

THE NETHERLANDS

Rostock

Hamburg

Bremen

Elbe

Berlin

Hannover

Essen

Ruhr

Halle

Leipzig

Elbe

Düsseldorf

Göttingen

Köln

Dresden

Rhein

Bonn

DEUTSCHLAND

Frankfurt

CZECH
REPUBLIC

Nürnberg

FRANCE

Stuttgart

Linz

Salzburg

München

LIECHTENSTEIN

Berchtesgaden

Basel

Zürich

Bern

SCHWEIZ

ÖSTERREICH